Reconstruction:
Core Documents

Reconstruction: Core Documents

Selected and Introduced by

Scott Yenor

Ashbrook Press

© 2018 Ashbrook Center, Ashland University

Library of Congress Cataloging-in-Publication Data

Reconstruction: Core Documents;
Selected and Introduced by Scott Yenor

p.   cm.
Includes Index
1. United States – Politics and government.

ISBN   978-1-878802-45-3

(pbk.)

Cover Images, above the title, left to right:
John Sartain, *Andrew Johnson*, 1865. National Portrait Gallery, Smithsonian Institution, NPG.85.166. https://goo.gl/E8iaMC.

Hon. Alexander H. Stephens of Georgia, photographed between 1865 and 1880. Brady-Handy photograph collection, Library of Congress, Prints and Photographs Division, LC-DIG-cwpbh-04097. https://goo.gl/nv1xn2

Alexander Gardner, *Abraham Lincoln, President of the US*, February 5, 1865. Library of Congress Prints and Photographs Division Washington, D.C., LC-DIG-ppmsca-19215. https://goo.gl/LvEAFQ.

Hon. Thaddeus Stevens of Pennsylvania, photographed between 1860 and 1875. Brady-Handy photograph collection, Library of Congress, Prints and Photographs Division, LC-DIG-cwpbh-00460. https://goo.gl/WtA1RF

George Kendall Warren, *Frederick Douglass*, 1876. National Portrait Gallery, Smithsonian Institution, NPG.80.28. https://goo.gl/hvgNLg

Cover Image, below the title:
Matt Morgan, *Massacre of the Negroes at Colfax Court House*, 1873. Courtesy of the Historic New Orleans Collection, 1995.10.4. https://goo.gl/aorY8j

Ashbrook Center at Ashland University
401 College Avenue
Ashland, Ohio 44805
www.Ashbrook.org

Errata

page	for	read
159, document date	July 26, 1945	April 16, 1883

About the Ashbrook Center

The Ashbrook Center restores and strengthens the capacities of the American people for constitutional self-government. Ashbrook teaches students and teachers across our country what America is and what she represents in the long history of the world. Offering a variety of resources and programs, Ashbrook is the largest university-based educator in the enduring principles and practice of free government. Dedicated in 1983 by President Ronald Reagan, the Ashbrook Center is governed by its own board and responsible for raising all of the funds necessary for its many programs.

Visit us online at Ashbrook.org, TeachingAmericanHistory.org, and 50coredocs.org.

Contents

General Editor's Introduction.. i

Introduction... iii

1. President Abraham Lincoln to General Nathaniel Banks, August 5, 1863 1

2. President Abraham Lincoln, Proclamation of Amnesty and Reconstruction, December 8, 1863 3

3. Wade-Davis Bill and President Lincoln's Pocket Veto Proclamation, July 2 and 8, 1864 6

4. The 13th Amendment to the Constitution, December 18, 1865 11

5. President Lincoln's Last Public Address, April 11, 1865 13

6. President Andrew Johnson, Proclamation on Reorganizing Constitutional Government in Mississippi, June 13, 1865 18

7. Richard Henry Dana, "Grasp of War", June 21, 1865 21

8. Black Codes of Mississippi, October - December, 1865 25

9. President Andrew Johnson, First Annual Address, December 4, 1865 31

10. Carl Schurz, Report on the Condition of the South, December 19, 1865 37

11. Frederick Douglass, Reply of the Colored Delegation to the President, February 7, 1866 47

12. Alexander Stephens, Address Before the General Assembly of the State of Georgia, February 22, 1866 50

13. An Act to Protect All Persons in the United States in Their Civil Rights, and Furnish the Means of their Vindication, April 9, 1866 56

14. Congressional Debate on the 14th Amendment, February - May, 1866 59

15. Charles Sumner, "The One Man Power vs. Congress!", October 2, 1866 67

16. Thaddeus Stevens, Speech on Reconstruction, January 3, 1867 75

17. Reconstruction Acts, March 2 and 23, and July 19, 1867 80

18. President Andrew Johnson, Veto of the First Reconstruction Act, March 2, 1867 86

19. Thaddeus Stevens, "Damages to Loyal Men", March 19, 1867 91

20. Democratic and Republican Party Platforms of 1868, May 20, 1868 and July 4, 1868 96

21. Executive Documents on State of the Freedmen, November 20, 1868 101

22. The 15th Amendment, February 2, 1870 106

23. The Enforcement Acts, 1870, 1871 108

24. President Ulysses S. Grant, Proclamation on Enforcement of the 14th Amendment, May 3, 1871 115

25. Charlotte Fowler's Testimony to Sub-Committee on Reconstruction in Spartanburg, South Carolina, July 6, 1871 117

26. Senator Carl Schurz, "Plea for Amnesty", January 30, 1872 123

27. Associate Justices Samuel Miller and Stephen Field, The Slaughterhouse Cases, The United States Supreme Court, April 14, 1873 132

28. Colfax Massacre Reports, U.S. Senate and the Committee of 70, 1874 and 1875 140

29. Chief Justice Morrison Waite, *United States v. Cruikshank*, The United States Supreme Court, March 27, 1876 150

30. President Rutherford B. Hayes, Inaugural Address, March 5, 1877 155

31. Frederick Douglass, "The United States Cannot Remain Half-Slave and Half-Free", April 16, 1883 159

Appendices 167

Appendix A: Declaration of Independence 169

Appendix B: Constitution of the United States of America 174
Appendix C: Thematic Table of Contents 188
Appendix D: Study Questions 191
Appendix E: Suggestions For Further Reading 204

General Editor's Introduction

This volume continues the Ashbrook Center's collection of primary documents covering major periods, themes, and institutions in American history and government. It is the third of a planned trilogy on the conflict over slavery. (The earlier volumes, *Causes of the Civil War* and *The Civil War*, will be published as they are completed.) This volume begins with a letter Lincoln penned in the midst of the Civil War, as Union forces retook territory and the U.S. Government had to decide how to deal with freedmen and former slaveholders in the subdued rebel areas. It concludes with Frederick Douglass' reflections in 1883 on a nation still divided racially—still, as he saw it, half slave and half free. The intervening documents tell the story of the effort to reunite the country while guaranteeing the rights of the freedmen, as well as of the opposition in both South and North that doomed that effort.

As we build out the series of Ashbrook document collections, we aim to compile a comprehensive and authoritative account of America's story, told in the words of those who wrote it—America's presidents, labor leaders, farmers, philosophers, industrialists, politicians, workers, explorers, religious leaders, judges, soldiers; its slaveholders and abolitionists; its expansionists and isolationists; its reformers and stand-patters; its strict and broad constructionists; its hard-eyed realists and visionary utopians—all united in their commitment to equality and liberty, yet all also divided often by their different understandings of these most fundamental American ideas. The documents are about all this—the still unfinished American experiment with self-government.

As this volume does, each of the volumes in the series will contain key documents on its period, theme, or institution, selected by an expert and reviewed by an editorial board. Each volume will have an introduction highlighting key documents and themes. In an appendix to each volume, there will also be a thematic table of contents, showing the connections between various documents. Another appendix will provide study questions for each document, as well questions that refer to other documents in the collection, tying them together as the thematic table of contents does. Each document will be checked against an authoritative original source and have an introduction outlining its significance. We will provide notes to each document to identify people, events, movements, or ideas that may be unfamiliar to non-specialist readers and to improve understanding of the document's historical context.

In sum, our intent is that the documents and their supporting material provide reliable and unique access to the richness of the American story.

Scott Yenor, Professor of Political Science at Boise State University, selected the documents and wrote the introductions for this volume. David Tucker was the General Editor, Ellen Tucker the copyeditor. Lisa Ormiston oversaw production and Ali Brosky provided assistance with various aspects of the process, as did Ashbrook interns Kitty Sorah, Matt Reising, Sabrina Maristela, and Morgan Miller. Professor Yenor thanks the Idaho Humanities Council for a faculty grant to study Reconstruction that helped make his work on this volume possible. This publication itself was made possible through the support of a grant by the John Templeton Foundation. The opinions expressed in this publication are those of the editors and do not necessarily reflect the views of the John Templeton Foundation.

David Tucker
Senior Fellow
Ashbrook Center

Introduction

Before Union victory in the Civil War was assured, President Abraham Lincoln and his advisors were turning their attention to "reconstruction" in the South. It would be a time for reconciling the North and South, bringing the formerly rebellious Southern governments back into their proper relation with the union, and protecting the basic civil rights of freedmen, blacks, and Unionists in those Southern states. Each of these goals would be difficult in its own right. Reconstruction demanded them all, and that they all be done at the same time. It is no wonder, then, that Lincoln had been heard to say that Reconstruction posed the greatest question ever presented to practical statesmanship.

There are theoretical and practical reasons why Reconstruction proved to be too great a challenge for post-Civil War statesmen and politicians.

As a matter of theory, the American constitutional system carves out significant space for state sovereignty. The principles of the Declaration of Independence demand respect for government by consent of the governed and for the principles of human equality and the protection of natural rights.

Reconstruction revealed contradictions among these principles. State and local majorities in the defeated Southern states were uninterested in protecting the civil rights of freedmen and also uninterested in acknowledging human equality. What should be done under this circumstance? Should the national government limit the powers of state and local majorities? If so, would that be consistent with the consent of the governed? Should former rebels be considered part of the state and local majorities? If not, would that be consistent with the consent of the governed? Should the national government protect the rights of freedmen itself? Did the national government even have the capacity – constitutionally and practically – to protect freedmen in the states?

President Lincoln had to begin adopting policies about these issues while the Civil War still raged. Generally, Lincoln offered a generous amnesty to Southerners (Document 2) if they would quit the rebellion. He was unwilling to insist on very many abridgments of state sovereignty in Southern states that had been won back into the Union (Document 1). Most Republicans in Congress opposed Lincoln's charitable policy toward Southern governments (Document 3), yet Lincoln stood firm during the war with his generous amnesty and limited national oversight. He did gain passage of the 13th Amendment (Document 4), which limited state sovereignty by abolishing slavery throughout the Union. Even in his "Last Public Address" (Document 5),

Lincoln deferred quite a bit to majorities in a reconstructed Louisiana government that did not extend the vote to freed slaves and did not provide education for freed slaves. We cannot know whether Lincoln would have persisted in this policy, since he was assassinated just days after his last public address (Document 5).

President Andrew Johnson, who assumed the presidency after Lincoln's assassination, was a Tennessee Unionist. It was soon revealed that he opposed policies to protect and aid the freedmen. He allowed Southern governments to re-organize and regain their status in the Union with relative ease – demanding only that they adopt the 13th amendment, repudiate Confederate debt, and foreswear secession (Documents 6, 9, and 11). The governments that organized under Johnson's plan did much to discredit his approach. Most famously, Confederate rebels won elective office. These rebels and their sympathizers led governments that adopted "black codes," local regulations that appeared to be the re-introduction of slavery by another name (Document 8). These laws generally reflected the state of Southern public opinion as reported to Congress by Carl Schurz, a Union general who went on a fact-finding tour of the South, in December 1865 (Document 10). Union feeling and respect for black civil rights, Schurz argued, were barely noticeable in the South; Johnson's easy restoration of Southern states seemed to undermine the twin goals of recreating a healthy Union and winning genuine emancipation for blacks, Schurz argued.

Johnson's evident satisfaction with his approach (Document 9) put him on a collision course with the Republicans, who demanded that a deeper change in Southern society and governance accompany the Union victory. Republicans looked for ways to require that Southern governments protect the civil rights of freedmen and provide equal protection of the laws. With these goals in mind, "Radical" Republicans in Congress first empowered the national government to protect civil rights, when states failed to do it, in the Civil Rights Act of 1866 (Document 13); they made these changes part of the constitutional fabric through the 14th Amendment (Document 14) that same year.

Then Congress did much to throw out Johnson's restored Southern governments through the Reconstruction Acts of 1867 (Document 17). These Acts provided a more thorough process, directed by the military, for Southern states to regain their place in the Union. Self-government established through this more thoroughly supervised process, prominent Republicans hoped, would produce constitutions and working majorities in Southern states that would protect the civil rights of freedmen and loyal Union men. Loyalists would form the backbone of these governments, they hoped. Prominent Republicans learned that extending the vote to freedmen and prohibiting racial discrimination in voting had to be part of any post-Reconstruction Southern order that would protect civil rights and provide equal protection of the laws (Documents 15 and 16).

The Democratic and Republican party platforms of 1868 reveal much about the Republicans' pride in their accomplishments and the Democratic hope to undo them (Document 20).

All Southern governments had been restored to the Union under the Reconstruction Acts by the first months of Ulysses S. Grant's first term in 1869. Reconstruction appeared to be over. Yet all was not well under these reconstructed Southern governments. Reports from throughout the South suggested that loyal Union men, blacks, and freed slaves were subject to violence and threats of violence, if they participated in politics or asserted their civil rights (Document 15, 21, and 24). Few Southern whites would do much to protect blacks or Republicans. The processes under the Reconstruction Acts were insufficient to protect the right to vote from private intimidation and governmental inaction, if whites controlled local government and working majorities arose after elections fraught with intimidation and violence.

In light of this evidence, Republicans in Congress, with Grant's blessing, passed a series of bills known as Enforcement Acts, or the Ku Klux Klan Acts, in 1870 and 1871 (Documents 23 and 24). This marked an additional phase in Reconstruction. These bills made actions that hindered the right to vote or that intimidated people against exercising their civil rights, among many other things, into federal crimes. With such federal protection, it was hoped, elections in the Southern states could be fair representations of the state population. Such federal action seemed necessary to secure the consent of all the governed. Grant especially appealed to the citizens of the South to turn on the Ku Klux Klan and other private organizations that hindered their fellow citizens from voting. In some cases (Document 24), Grant even brought federal troops into Southern states to provide protection for black citizens. A low-level civil war seemed to be breaking out in various parts of the South, and military protection seemed necessary for freedmen to enjoy their civil rights and voting rights (Document 28).

It was very difficult to maintain sufficient support to keep up such forceful actions. Many in the North, including now Senator Carl Schurz, who had earlier supported vigorous national action (Document 10), begged for a broad amnesty so that former rebels could hold office (Document 26). Schurz's efforts in this respect were part of a broader effort within the Republican Party called Liberal Republicanism to end national efforts to reconstruct the South. A series of Supreme Court cases during Grant's second term offered narrow conceptions of national power under the 14th and 15th amendments. The Slaughterhouse Cases (Document 27) and *United States v. Cruikshank* (Document 29) undermined the national government's ability to protect freedmen and loyal Union men in the South.

Waning Northern support and the sheer difficulty of the task led even the Republican Party, ultimately, to limit its efforts to protect civil and voting rights in the South. With the election of Rutherford B. Hayes to the presidency in 1876, the Republicans ended military oversight in the South (Document 30). Republicans, who had fought for the Union, done much in law to protect civil rights, and done not a little to improve the lives of freedmen in the South, ended up – unwittingly, perhaps – allowing a return to white home rule in the South during Hayes's Presidency. Some observers, including the great abolitionist Frederick Douglass, even wondered whether the Union soldiers slain in the Civil War had died in vain and whether the country still existed half slave and half free (Document 31).

No task was more difficult than Reconstruction. Perhaps more radical efforts (such as land confiscation and redistribution) to punish rebels could have changed the South (Document 19). Perhaps Lincoln, had he lived, would have worked out a more acceptable accommodation protecting the freedmen while sewing up the Union. Perhaps if Lincoln had not selected Andrew Johnson to be his Vice President, a more responsible and committed reformer would have brought about a better result. No one had more political skill and upright intention than Lincoln, and no one had less of each than Johnson.

Republicans tried several times to "start over" on Reconstruction, but the South was no blank slate and starting over was not a realistic option. Perhaps only time could bring about the changes necessary to reconcile Southern home rule and protection for freedmen, as Lincoln himself seemed to suggest in his first statement on these matters (Document 1).

A Note on Usage:

To promote readability, we have in most instances modernized spelling and in some instances punctuation. Occasionally, we have inserted italicized text, enclosed in brackets, to bridge gaps in syntax occurring due to apparent errors or illegibility in the source documents, or to briefly explain long passages of text left out of our excerpts. With regard to capitalization, however, we have in most cases allowed usage to stand where it is internally consistent, even when varying from today's usage, since authors writing in the aftermath of the Civil War may signal their attitudes toward the balance between state and federal power through capitalization.

Reconstruction:
Core Documents

Document 1

President Abraham Lincoln to General Nathaniel Banks
August 5, 1863

New Orleans came into Union hands in April 1862 and much of Louisiana followed. It was among the first Confederate states to be re-occupied through Union military action. As an occupied territory, it was under military authority, including that of the Commander of the Union's Gulf Forces, General Nathaniel Banks (1816-1894) from Massachusetts, a former Speaker of the House of Representatives. He wrote President Lincoln about his efforts in Louisiana on April 17, 1863. Lincoln appreciated the political minefield that Banks faced. Unionists in Louisiana were lukewarm and unwilling to act, while secessionists wanted a restored Louisiana allowed into the Union with slavery unimpeded, or with as little change to race relations as possible. Banks experimented with mandatory contractual relations, where slaves would be under contracts to their old masters as a temporary measure, and also with efforts to graft a new state constitution onto the old. These efforts raised important issues about how a reconstructed government would be organized, whether defeated Southerners were ready to emancipate freedmen (since the Emancipation Proclamation had been issued on January 1, 1863), and what role the national government should take in the reconstruction of the state governments. Lincoln deliberated on these issues and answered Banks in August 1863 (after the victory of Vicksburg on July 4, 1863, which put the entire Mississippi in Union hands).

Source: Collected Works of Abraham Lincoln, edited by Roy Basler, Volume 6 (The Abraham Lincoln Association, 2006), 364–365. https://goo.gl/APSo23

My dear General Banks,

Being a poor correspondent is the only apology I offer for not having sooner tendered my thanks for your very successful, and very valuable military operations this year. The final stroke in opening the Mississippi never should, and I think never will, be forgotten....

... While I very well know what I would be glad for Louisiana to do, it is quite a different thing for me to assume direction of the matter. I would be glad for her to make a new Constitution recognizing the emancipation proclamation, and adopting emancipation in those parts of the state to which the proclamation does not apply. And while she is at it, I think it would not be objectionable for her to adopt some practical system by which the two races could gradually live themselves out of their old relation to each other, and both come out better prepared for the new. Education for young blacks should be included in the plan. After all, the power, or element, of "contract" may be sufficient for this probationary period; and, by its simplicity, and flexibility, may be the better.

As an anti-slavery man I have a motive to desire emancipation, which pro-slavery men do not have; but even they have strong enough reason to thus place themselves again under the shield of the Union; and to thus perpetually hedge against the recurrence of the scenes through which we are now passing. ...

For my own part I think I shall not, in any event, retract the emancipation proclamation; nor, as executive, ever return to slavery any person who is free by the terms of that proclamation, or by any of the acts of Congress.

If Louisiana shall send members to Congress, their admission to seats will depend, as you know, upon the respective Houses, and not upon the President.

If these views can be of any advantage in giving shape, and impetus, to action there, I shall be glad for you to use them prudently for that object. Of course you will confer with intelligent and trusty citizens of the State. ... Still it is perhaps better to not make the letter generally public.

Document 2

Proclamation of Amnesty and Reconstruction
President Abraham Lincoln
December 8, 1863

By the winter of 1863, the Mississippi River was in Union hands. The South's invasion of the North had been repelled at Gettysburg. Union arms were securing Arkansas, Tennessee and Texas, and the next campaign season promised the overthrow of more rebellious states. President Lincoln needed a more formal plan for reintegrating these states into the Union and for laying out the process for the former rebels to become citizens again. Many of the issues were anticipated in his letter to General Banks (Document 1). Lincoln issued a formal policy on how amnesty was to be received and how states were to reconstruct themselves as members of the Union together with his 3rd Annual Message to Congress in December 1863. In his Annual Message, Lincoln called his Proclamation "a rallying point – a plan of action" for those states ready to join the Union.

Source: Abraham Lincoln, Proclamation of Amnesty and Reconstruction, December 8, 1863. https://goo.gl/HcmgVh

---

Whereas, in and by the Constitution of the United States, it is provided that the President "shall have power to grant reprieves and pardons for offences against the United States, except in cases of impeachment;" and

Whereas a rebellion now exists whereby the loyal state governments of several states have for a long time been subverted, and many persons have committed and are now guilty of treason against the United States; and

Whereas, with reference to said rebellion and treason, laws have been enacted by Congress, declaring forfeitures and confiscation of property and liberation of slaves . . . .

Whereas, with reference to said rebellion, the President of the United States has issued several proclamations, with provisions in regard to the liberation of slaves; and

Whereas it is now desired by some persons heretofore engaged in said rebellion to resume their allegiance to the United States, and to re-inaugurate loyal state governments within and for their respective states: Therefore,

I, Abraham Lincoln, President of the United States, do proclaim... to all persons who have, directly or by implication, participated in the existing rebellion, except as hereinafter excepted, that a full pardon is hereby granted to them and each of them, with restoration of all rights of property, except as to slaves, and in property cases where rights of third parties shall have intervened, and upon the condition that every such person shall take and subscribe an oath, and thenceforward keep and maintain said oath inviolate; and which oath shall be registered for permanent preservation, and shall be of the tenor and effect following, to wit:

"I, _____ , do solemnly swear, in presence of Almighty God, that I will henceforth faithfully support, protect and defend the Constitution of the United States, and the union of the States thereunder; and that I will in like manner abide by and faithfully support all acts of Congress passed during the existing rebellion with reference to slaves so long and so far as not repealed, modified, or held void by Congress or by decision of the Supreme Court: and that I will in like manner abide by and faithfully support all proclamations of the President made during the existing rebellion having reference to slaves, so long and so far as not modified or declared void by decision of the Supreme Court. So help me God."

The persons excepted from the benefits of the foregoing provisions are all who are, or shall have been, civil or diplomatic officers or agents of the so-called Confederate Government; all who have left judicial stations under the United States to aid the rebellion; all who are, or shall have been, military or naval officers of said so-called Confederate Government above the rank of colonel in the army, or of lieutenant in the navy; all who left seats in the United States Congress to aid the rebellion; all who resigned commissions in the Army or Navy of the United States, and afterwards aided the rebellion; and all who have engaged in any way in treating colored persons, or white persons, in charge of such, otherwise than lawfully as prisoners of war, and which persons may have been found in the United States service, as soldiers, seamen, or in any other capacity.

And I do further proclaim... that whenever, in any of the States of Arkansas, Texas, Louisiana, Mississippi, Tennessee, Alabama, Georgia, Florida, South Carolina, and North Carolina, a number of persons, not less than one tenth in number of the votes cast in such State at the presidential election of the year of our Lord one thousand eight hundred and sixty, each having taken the oath aforesaid and not having since violated it . . . shall re-establish a State government which shall be republican, and in no wise contravening said oath, such shall be recognized as the true government of the State, and the State shall receive thereunder the benefits of the constitutional provision which declares that "the United States shall guarantee to every state in this union a republican form of government, and shall protect each of them against invasion; and, on application of the legislature, or the executive (when the legislature cannot be convened), against domestic violence."

And I do further proclaim . . . that any provision which may be adopted by such state government in relation to the freed people of such state, which shall recognize and declare their permanent freedom, provide for their education, and which may yet be consistent, as a temporary arrangement with their present condition as a laboring, landless, and homeless class, will not be objected to by the National Executive.

And it is suggested as not improper that, in constructing a loyal state government . . . the constitution, and the general code of laws, as before the rebellion, be maintained, subject only to the modifications made necessary by the conditions hereinbefore stated, and such others, if any, not contravening said conditions, and which may be deemed expedient by those framing the new State government.

To avoid misunderstanding. . . . it may be proper to further say that whether members sent to Congress from any state shall be admitted to seats, constitutionally rests exclusively with the respective houses, and not to any extent with the Executive. And, still further, that this proclamation is intended to present the people of the states wherein the national authority has been suspended and loyal state governments have been subverted, a mode in and by which the national authority and loyal state governments may be re-established . . . and, while the mode presented is the best the Executive can suggest, with his present impressions, it must not be understood that no other possible mode would be acceptable. . . .

Document 3

Wade-Davis Bill and President Lincoln's Pocket Veto Proclamation

U.S. Congress and President Abraham Lincoln
July 2 and 8, 1864

Many Republicans were dissatisfied with what they perceived as the excessive leniency of President Lincoln's terms for re-inaugurating federal authority in rebel states, as contained in his Proclamation of Amnesty and Reconstruction (Document 2). The quickness and ease of reconstruction that Lincoln's plan allowed for, critics worried, made it likely that little would change in the South's approach to governing or for the freed slaves. Lincoln recommended much in his policy but required only emancipation as a condition for re-admission. Louisiana had adopted emancipation in its constitutional convention, but other provisions left freedmen bereft of rights. Arkansas and Florida too had failed to do much to protect or educate freedmen. Congress also felt that it needed to assert its power to direct future postwar policy. In June, Congress had tried to create a federal bureau to protect freedmen (later the Freedman's Bureau), but it lacked the votes. A constitutional amendment to abolish slavery had also failed in June. On the last day of the Congressional session in July 1864, Congress passed the Wade-Davis Bill, named for Ohio Senator Ben Wade (1800-1878) and Maryland Representative Henry Winter Davis (1817-1865), both well-known radical Republicans. Lincoln declined to sign the measure before Congress adjourned (a so-called pocket veto; see the U.S. Constitution, Article I, Section 7). Lincoln issued a Proclamation explaining why he vetoed the Wade-Davis bill on July 8, 1864.

Source: Abraham Lincoln, "Proclamation 115 – Concerning a Bill To Guarantee to Certain States, Whose Governments Have Been Usurped or Overthrown, a Republican Form of Government." Online by Gerhard Peters and John T. Woolley, The American Presidency Project, https://goo.gl/aD9LKG. This site contains the text of both the Wade-Davis Bill and Lincoln's veto proclamation.

Wade-Davis Bill

Be it enacted... That in the States declared in rebellion against the United States, the President shall, by and with the advice and consent of the Senate, appoint for each a provisional governor... who shall be charged with the civil administration of such State until a State government therein shall be recognized as hereinafter provided.

SEC. 2.... That so soon as the military resistance to the United States shall have been suppressed in any such state... the provisional governor shall direct the marshal of the United States... to name a sufficient number of deputies, and to enroll all white male citizens of the United States resident in the State in their respective counties, and to request each one to take the oath to support the Constitution of the United States, and in his enrollment to designate those who take and those who refuse to take that oath, which rolls shall be forthwith returned to the provisional governor; and if the persons taking that oath shall amount to a majority of the persons enrolled in the State, he shall, by proclamation, invite the loyal people of the State to elect delegates to a convention charged to declare the will of the people of the State relative to the reestablishment of a State government subject to, and in conformity with, the Constitution of the United States.

SEC. 3.... That the convention shall consist of as many members as both houses of the last constitutional State legislature, apportioned by the provisional governor among the counties, parishes, or districts of the State, in proportion to the white population, returned as electors, by the marshal, in compliance with the provisions of this act. The provisional governor shall, by proclamation, declare the number of delegates to be elected by each county, parish, or election district; name a day of election not less than thirty days thereafter; designate the places of voting in each county, parish, or district, conforming as nearly as may be convenient to the places used in the State elections next preceding the rebellion; appoint one or more commissioners to hold the election at each place of voting, and provide an adequate force to keep the peace during the election.

SEC. 4.... That the delegates shall be elected by the loyal white male citizens of the United States of the age of twenty-one years, and resident at the time in the county, parish, or district in which they shall offer to vote, and enrolled as aforesaid, or absent in the military service of the United States, and who shall take and subscribe the oath of allegiance to the United States...; but no person who has held or exercised any office, civil or military, State or Confederate, under the rebel usurpation, or who has voluntarily borne arms against the United States, shall vote, or be eligible to be elected as delegate, at such election.

SEC. 5.... That... commissioners... shall hold the election in conformity with this act, and, so far as may be consistent therewith, shall proceed in the manner used in the state prior to the rebellion. The oath of allegiance shall be taken and subscribed on the poll-book by every voter... but every person known by or proved to the commissioners to have held or exercised any office, civil or military, state or confederate, under the rebel usurpation, or to have voluntarily borne arms against the United States, shall be excluded, though he offer to take the oath....

SEC. 6.... That the provisional governor shall, by proclamation, convene the delegates elected as aforesaid, at the capital of the state, on a day not more than three months after the election, giving at least thirty days' notice of such day.... He shall preside over the deliberations of the convention, and administer to each delegate... the oath of allegiance to the United States in the form above prescribed.

SEC. 7.... That the convention shall declare, on behalf of the people of the State their submission to the Constitution and laws of the United States, and shall adopt the following provisions, hereby prescribed by the United States in the execution of the constitutional duty to guarantee a republican form of government to every State, and incorporate them in the constitution of the State, that is to say:

First. No person who has held or exercised any office, civil or military, except offices merely ministerial, and military offices below the grade of colonel, state or confederate, under the usurping power, shall vote for or be a member of the legislature, or governor.

Second. Involuntary servitude is forever prohibited, and the freedom of all persons is guaranteed in said State....

SEC. 8.... That when the convention shall have adopted those provisions it shall proceed to re-establish a republican form of government and ordain a constitution containing those provisions, which, when adopted, the convention shall by ordinance provide for submitting to the people of the State, entitled to vote under this law, at an election to be held in the manner prescribed by the act for the election of delegates... at which election the said electors... shall vote directly for or against such constitution and form of State government. And the returns of said election shall be made to the provisional governor... and if a majority of the votes cast shall be for the constitution and form of government, he shall certify the same... to the President of the United States, who, after obtaining the assent of Congress, shall . . . recognize the government so established ... as the constitutional government of the State, and from the date of such recognition, and not before, Senators and Representatives, and electors for President and Vice President may be elected in such State, according to the laws of the State and of the United States.

SEC. 9. ... That if the convention shall refuse to reestablish the State government on the conditions aforesaid, the provisional governor shall declare it dissolved....

SEC. 10. ... That, until the United States shall have recognized a republican form of State government the provisional governor in each of said States shall see that this act, and the laws of the United States, and the laws of the State in force when the State government was overthrown by the rebellion, are faithfully executed within the State; but no law or usage whereby any person was heretofore held in involuntary servitude shall be recognized or enforced by any court or officer in such state, and the laws for the trial and punishment of white persons shall extend to all persons, and jurors shall have the qualifications of voters under this law for delegates to the convention....

SEC. 11. ... That until the recognition of a state government ... the provisional governor shall ... cause to be assessed, levied, and collected, for the year 1864 and every year thereafter, the taxes provided by the laws of such State to be levied during the fiscal year preceding the overthrow of the State government thereof, in the manner prescribed by the laws of the State, as nearly as may be; and the officers appointed as aforesaid are vested with all powers of levying and collecting such taxes, by distress or sale, as were vested in any officers or tribunal of the state government aforesaid for those purposes....

SEC. 12. ... That all persons held to involuntary servitude or labor in the states aforesaid are hereby emancipated and discharged therefrom, and they and their posterity shall be forever free. And if any such persons or their posterity shall be restrained of liberty ... the courts of the United States shall, on habeas corpus, discharge them.

SEC. 13. ... That if any person declared free by this act, or any law of the United States or any proclamation of the President, be restrained of liberty, with intent to be held in or reduced to involuntary servitude or labor, the person convicted before a court of competent jurisdiction of such act shall be punished by fine ... and be imprisoned not less than five nor more than twenty years.

SEC. 14. ... That every person who shall hereafter hold or exercise any office, civil or military (except offices merely ministerial, and military offices below the grade of colonel) in the rebel service, state or confederate, is hereby declared not to be a citizen of the United States.

President Lincoln's Pocket Veto Proclamation

WHEREAS at the late session Congress passed a bill to "guarantee to certain states, whose governments have been usurped or overthrown, a republican form of government," a copy of which is hereunto annexed;

And whereas the said bill was presented to the President of the United States for his approval less than one hour before the *sine die* adjournment of said session, and was not signed by him; and

Whereas the said bill contains, among other things, a plan for restoring the States in rebellion to their proper practical relation in the Union, which plan expresses the sense of Congress upon that subject, and which plan it is now thought fit to lay before the people for their consideration:

Now, therefore, I, ABRAHAM LINCOLN . . . do proclaim . . . that, while I am (as I was in December last, when by proclamation I propounded a plan for restoration) unprepared by a formal approval of this bill, to be inflexibly committed to any single plan of restoration; and, while I am also unprepared to declare that the free state constitutions and governments already adopted and installed in Arkansas and Louisiana shall be set aside and held for naught, thereby repelling and discouraging the loyal citizens who have set up the same as to further effort, or to declare a constitutional competency in Congress to abolish slavery in states, but am at the same time sincerely hoping and expecting that a constitutional amendment abolishing slavery throughout the nation may be adopted, nevertheless I am truly satisfied with the system for restoration contained in the bill as one very proper plan for the loyal people of any State choosing to adopt it, and that I am, and at all times shall be, prepared to give Executive aid and assistance to any such people, so soon as the military resistance to the United States shall have been suppressed in any such State, and the people thereof shall have sufficiently returned to their obedience to the Constitution and the laws of the United States, in which cases military governors will be appointed, with directions to proceed according to the bill. . . .

Document 4

The 13th Amendment to the Constitution
January 31, 1865 (passed by Congress)
December 18, 1865 (ratified)

President Abraham Lincoln's Emancipation Proclamation, issued on January 1, 1863, was a war measure ending slavery where the rebellion was still operative. Questions remained about whether emancipation accomplished through this war measure would last beyond the war. The Constitution, after all, left the states the power to decide whether or not to adopt slavery. This left open the possibility that defeated rebellious states could reenter the Union without giving up slavery. Republicans opposed such a result as a betrayal of the Union's war aims. Attention thus turned to amending the Constitution as a means of accomplishing emancipation. The model for the wording of the 13th Amendment was the Northwest Ordinance of 1787, which prohibited slavery from spreading into the free territories of Indiana, Michigan, Wisconsin, Illinois, and Ohio. The Senate approved what became the 13th Amendment in April 1864 by an overwhelming margin (38-6), but in June 1864 the House fell 13 votes shy of the necessary 106 votes to submit the amendment to the states. Meanwhile, border states such as West Virginia and Maryland and formerly rebellious states such as Louisiana and Arkansas adopted emancipation in their state constitutions. Emancipation was proceeding apace. Scant weeks after Lincoln and the Republicans won resounding victory in the November 1864 elections, the same Congress took its seats for its "lame duck" session. Lincoln pressed Congress to reconsider the measure in light of the election returns. "There is only a question of time as to when the proposed amendment will go to the States for their action," Lincoln argued in his 1864 Annual Message on December 6, 1864. "And as it is to so go at all events, may we not agree that the sooner the better?" Congress agreed, passing the amendment by a vote of 119-56. The amendment then went to the states for ratification. Only time would tell whether the mechanism for keeping slavery out of the territories would suffice for uprooting it where it had long existed.

Source: Transcript of 13th Amendment to the U.S. Constitution: Abolition of Slavery (1865), Our Documents: 100 Milestone Documents from the National Archives, National Archives and Records Administration. https://goo.gl/8PQnBs.

Section 1. Neither slavery nor involuntary servitude, except as a punishment for crime whereof the party shall have been duly convicted, shall exist within the United States, or any place subject to their jurisdiction.

Section 2. Congress shall have power to enforce this article by appropriate legislation.

Document 5

Last Public Address
President Abraham Lincoln
April 11, 1865

Louisiana was the central location for many of the controversies concerning Reconstruction. Among the first states brought under Union control (Document 1), it was also among the first states organized under President Lincoln's plan for amnesty and reconstruction (Document 2). Louisiana organized a constitutional convention according to Lincoln's plan in 1864 and the convention ratified a constitution that abolished slavery. Yet that convention did not go too far in other directions. It petitioned the U.S. Congress to compensate loyal planters for the loss of their slaves, it failed to disenfranchise those who had joined the rebellion, and it did not extend the franchise to freed slaves and blacks. Elections in 1864 were held under this new state constitution and Congress faced the question of whether to seat Congressmen and Senators who had been elected pursuant to it. Radicals, who had pushed a much different plan for reconstruction (Document 3), opposed seating Louisiana's delegation. The war was over when Lincoln publicly weighed in on this question. (General Robert E. Lee had surrendered two days before, April 9, 1865.) There was no longer any reason to offer lenient terms in the hopes for an early Confederate surrender. So, in response to a group gathered outside the White House, Lincoln delivered a somewhat informal address on the matter.

Source: Collected Works of Abraham Lincoln, edited by Roy Basler, Volume 8 (The Abraham Lincoln Association, 2006), 399–405. https://goo.gl/kdg3Jd

---

We meet this evening, not in sorrow, but in gladness of heart. The evacuation of Petersburg and Richmond, and the surrender of the principal insurgent army, give hope of a righteous and speedy peace whose joyous expression cannot be restrained. In the midst of this, however, He, from Whom all blessings flow, must not be forgotten. A call for a national thanksgiving is being prepared, and will be duly promulgated....

By these recent successes the re-inauguration of the national authority – reconstruction – which has had a large share of thought from the first, is pressed much more closely upon our attention. It is fraught with great difficulty. Unlike the case of a war between independent nations, there is no authorized organ for us to treat with. No one man has authority to give up the rebellion for any other man. We simply must begin with, and mold from, disorganized and discordant elements. Nor is it a small additional embarrassment that we, the loyal people, differ among ourselves as to the mode, manner, and means of reconstruction.

As a general rule, I abstain from reading the reports of attacks upon myself, wishing not to be provoked by that to which I cannot properly offer an answer. In spite of this precaution, however, it comes to my knowledge that I am much censured for some supposed agency in setting up, and seeking to sustain, the new State Government of Louisiana. In this I have done just so much as, and no more than, the public knows. In the Annual Message of Dec. 1863 and accompanying Proclamation,[1] I presented *a* plan of reconstruction (as the phrase goes) which, I promised, if adopted by any State, should be acceptable to, and sustained by, the Executive government of the nation. I distinctly stated that this was not the only plan which might possibly be acceptable; and I also distinctly protested that the Executive claimed no right to say when, or whether members should be admitted to seats in Congress from such States. This plan was, in advance, submitted to the then Cabinet, and distinctly approved by every member of it.... The new constitution of Louisiana, declaring emancipation for the whole State, practically applies the Proclamation to the part previously excepted. It does not adopt apprenticeship for freed-people; and it is silent, as it could not well be otherwise, about the admission of members to Congress.... The Message went to Congress, and I received many commendations of the plan, written and verbal; and not a single objection to it, from any professed emancipationist, came to my knowledge, until after the news reached Washington that the people of Louisiana had begun to move in accordance with it. From about July, 1862, I had corresponded with different persons, supposed to be interested, seeking a reconstruction of a State government for Louisiana. When the Message of 1863, with the plan before mentioned, reached New Orleans, Gen. Banks wrote me that he was confident the people, with his military co-operation, would reconstruct, substantially on that plan. I wrote him,[2] and some of them to try it; they tried it, and the result is known. Such only has been my agency in getting up the Louisiana government. As to sustaining it, my promise is out, as before stated. But, as bad promises are better broken than kept, I shall treat this as a bad promise, and break it, whenever I shall be

---

[1] Document 2
[2] Document 1

convinced that keeping it is adverse to the public interest. But I have not yet been so convinced.

I have been shown a letter on this subject, supposed to be an able one, in which the writer expresses regret that my mind has not seemed to be definitely fixed on the question whether the seceded States, so called, are in the Union or out of it. It would perhaps, add astonishment to his regret, were he to learn that since I have found professed Union men endeavoring to make that question, I have *purposely* forborne any public expression upon it. As appears to me that question has not been, nor yet is, a practically material one, and that any discussion of it, while it thus remains practically immaterial, could have no effect other than the mischievous one of dividing our friends. As yet, whatever it may hereafter become, that question is bad, as the basis of a controversy, and good for nothing at all – a merely pernicious abstraction.

We all agree that the seceded States, so called, are out of their proper practical relation with the Union; and that the sole object of the government, civil and military, in regard to those States is to again get them into that proper practical relation. I believe it is not only possible, but in fact, easier, to do this, without deciding, or even considering, whether these states have even been out of the Union, than with it. Finding themselves safely at home, it would be utterly immaterial whether they had ever been abroad. Let us all join in doing the acts necessary to restoring the proper practical relations between these states and the Union; and each forever after, innocently indulge his own opinion whether, in doing the acts, he brought the States from without, into the Union, or only gave them proper assistance, they never having been out of it.

The amount of constituency, so to speak, on which the new Louisiana government rests, would be more satisfactory to all, if it contained fifty, thirty, or even twenty thousand, instead of only about twelve thousand, as it does. It is also unsatisfactory to some that the elective franchise is not given to the colored man. I would myself prefer that it were now conferred on the very intelligent, and on those who serve our cause as soldiers. Still the question is not whether the Louisiana government, as it stands, is quite all that is desirable. The question is "Will it be wiser to take it as it is, and help to improve it; or to reject, and disperse it?" "Can Louisiana be brought into proper practical relation with the Union sooner by *sustaining*, or by *discarding* her new State Government?"

Some twelve thousand voters in the heretofore slave-state of Louisiana have sworn allegiance to the Union, assumed to be the rightful political power of the State, held elections, organized a State government, adopted a free-state constitution, giving the benefit of public schools equally to black and white, and empowering the Legislature to confer the elective franchise upon the colored man. Their Legislature has already voted to ratify the constitutional amendment recently passed by Congress, abolishing slavery throughout the nation. These twelve thousand persons are thus fully committed to the Union, and to perpetual freedom in the state – committed to the very things, and nearly all the things the nation wants – and they ask the nation's recognition, and its assistance to make good their committal. Now, if we reject, and spurn them, we do our utmost to disorganize and disperse them. We in effect say to the white men, "You are worthless, or worse – we will neither help you, nor be helped by you." To the blacks we say, "This cup of liberty which these, your old masters, hold to your lips, we will dash from you, and leave you to the chances of gathering the spilled and scattered contents in some vague and undefined when, where, and how." If this course, discouraging and paralyzing both white and black, has any tendency to bring Louisiana into proper practical relations with the Union, I have, so far, been unable to perceive it. If, on the contrary, we recognize, and sustain the new government of Louisiana, the converse of all this is made true. We encourage the hearts, and nerve the arms of the twelve thousand to adhere to their work, and argue for it, and proselyte for it, and fight for it, and feed it, and grow it, and ripen it to a complete success. The colored man too, in seeing all united for him, is inspired with vigilance, and energy, and daring, to the same end. Grant that he desires the elective franchise, will he not attain it sooner by saving the already advanced steps toward it, than by running backward over them? Concede that the new government of Louisiana is only to what it should be as the egg is to the fowl, we shall sooner have the fowl by hatching the egg than by smashing it. Again, if we reject Louisiana, we also reject one vote in favor of the proposed amendment to the national constitution. To meet this proposition, it has been argued that no more than three fourths of those States which have not attempted secession are necessary to validly ratify the amendment. I do not commit myself against this, further than to say that such a ratification would be questionable, and sure to be persistently questioned; while a ratification by three fourths of all the States would be unquestioned and unquestionable.

I repeat the question. "Can Louisiana be brought into proper practical relation with the Union sooner by *sustaining* or by *discarding* her new State Government?"

What has been said of Louisiana will apply generally to other States. And yet so great peculiarities pertain to each state, and such important and sudden changes occur in the same state; and, withal, so new and unprecedented is the whole case, that no exclusive, and inflexible plan can safely be prescribed . . . .

Such [an] exclusive, and inflexible plan, would surely become a new entanglement. Important principles may, and must, be inflexible.

In the present "situation" as the phrase goes, it may be my duty to make some new announcement to the people of the South. I am considering, and shall not fail to act, when satisfied that action will be proper.

Document 6

Proclamation on Reorganizing Constitutional Government in Mississippi
President Andrew Johnson
June 13, 1865

When President Abraham Lincoln was assassinated on April 14, 1865, Vice President Andrew Johnson (1808–1875), a Unionist wartime governor of Tennessee, became president. President Johnson would be directing Reconstruction as president, making demands on and recognizing Southern governments as they brought themselves into a proper relation with the Union. Johnson released his own Proclamation of Amnesty and Reconstruction on May 29, 1865. Johnson's approach to amnesty in this proclamation was not substantially different from Lincoln's, though Johnson did require those with over $20,000 in net assets to apply for special pardon. Johnson did not say anything about how states would be reconstructed in the proclamation; he was thus silent on whether he would require voting rights for freedmen or the protection of civil rights for the states to be readmitted into the Union. None of the state governments that Lincoln had helped to create in Louisiana, Arkansas, Virginia, and Tennessee extended the franchise to blacks, and Johnson recognized those governments. As states begged back into the Union, Johnson directed a process for states to re-adopt constitutions consistent with Union. Johnson appointed a provisional governor of North Carolina on May 29, 1865. The next state government Johnson undertook to reconstruct was Mississippi. It was difficult to find Southerners loyal to the aims of Reconstruction and willing to carry out the Union's orders, even though they would be backed, initially, at least, with the force of the Union army.

Source: Andrew Johnson, "Proclamation 136 – Reorganizing a Constitutional Government in Mississippi," June 13, 1865. Online by Gerhard Peters and John T. Woolley, The American Presidency Project. https://goo.gl/XLjiRC.

Whereas the fourth section of the fourth article of the Constitution of the United States declares that the United States shall guarantee to every State in the Union a republican form of government and shall protect each of them against invasion and domestic violence; and

Whereas the President of the United States is by the Constitution made Commander in Chief of the Army and Navy, as well as chief civil executive officer of the United States, and is bound by solemn oath faithfully to execute the office of President of the United States and to take care that the laws be faithfully executed; and

Whereas the rebellion which has been waged by a portion of the people of the United States against the properly constituted authorities of the Government thereof in the most violent and revolting form, but whose organized and armed forces have now been almost entirely overcome, has in its revolutionary progress deprived the people of the State of Mississippi of all civil government; and

Whereas it becomes necessary and proper to carry out and enforce the obligations of the United States to the people of Mississippi in securing them in the enjoyment of a republican form of government:

Now, therefore, . . . I, Andrew Johnson . . . do hereby appoint William L. Sharkey,[1] of Mississippi, provisional governor of the State of Mississippi, whose duty it shall be, at the earliest practicable period, to prescribe such rules and regulations as may be necessary and proper for convening a convention composed of delegates to be chosen by that portion of the people of said State who are loyal to the United States . . . for the purpose of . . . amending the constitution thereof, and with authority to exercise within the limits of said State all the powers necessary and proper to enable such loyal people of the State of Mississippi to restore said State to its constitutional relations to the Federal Government and to present . . . a republican form of State government . . . : Provided, That in any election that may be hereafter held for choosing delegates to any State convention as aforesaid no person shall be qualified as an elector or shall be eligible as a member of such convention unless he shall have previously taken and subscribed the oath of amnesty as set forth in the President's proclamation of May 29, A. D. 1865, and is a voter qualified as prescribed by the constitution and laws of the State of Mississippi in force immediately before the 9th of January, A. D. 1861, the date of the so-called ordinance of secession: and the said convention, when convened, or the legislature that may be thereafter assembled, will prescribe the qualification of electors and the eligibility of persons to hold office under the constitution and laws of the State . . . .

---

[1] William Sharkey (1798–1873) was a prominent Whig planter who retired from political affairs after secession.

And I do hereby direct –

First. That the military commander of the department and all officers and persons in the military and naval service aid and assist the said provisional governor in carrying into effect this proclamation; and they are enjoined to abstain from in any way hindering, impeding, or discouraging the loyal people from the organization of a State government as herein authorized.

...

Fifth. That the district judge for the judicial district in which Mississippi is included proceed to hold courts within said State in accordance with the provisions of the act of Congress. The Attorney-General will instruct the proper officers to libel and bring to judgment, confiscation, and sale property subject to confiscation and enforce the administration of justice within said State in all matters within the cognizance and jurisdiction of the Federal courts.

...

Document 7

"Grasp of War"
Richard Henry Dana
June 21, 1865

Richard Henry Dana (1815-1882) was a Boston blue blood – from a family of long standing. After gaining notoriety as an author, he became a lawyer. He practiced maritime law and assisted fugitive slaves in gaining as much protection as they could in antebellum America. When the Civil War broke out, he served in the Attorney General's office. He successfully argued the government's position in The Prize Cases, *arguing that the Union blockade of Southern ports was justified within the Constitution and the laws of war. He resigned his office after President Abraham Lincoln was assassinated, fearing President Andrew Johnson would not push the issue of reconstruction far enough. When Johnson announced his reconstruction policies for North Carolina and Mississippi (Document 6), Dana, then a private citizen, put forward a powerful critique of them at a public meeting in Boston.*

Source: Richard Henry Dana, "Grasp of War," in Speeches in Stirring Times and Letters to a Son *(New York: Houghton Mifflin, 1910), pp. 243-259.*

... We wish to know, I suppose, first, What are our powers? That is the first question – what are our just powers? Second – What ought we to do? Third – How ought we to do it? . . . .

. . . [*First*], what are those powers and rights? What is a war? War is not an attempt to kill, to destroy; but it is *coercion for a purpose*. When a nation goes into war, she does it to secure an end, and the war does not cease until the end is secured. A boxing-match, a trial of strength or skill, is over when one party stops. A war is over when its purpose is secured. It is a fatal mistake to hold that this war is over, because the fighting has ceased. [Applause.] This war is not over. We are in the attitude and in the *status* of war to-day. There is the solution of this question. Why, suppose a man has attacked your life, my friend, in the highway, at night, armed, and after a death-struggle, you get him down – what then? When he says he has done fighting, are you obliged to release him? Can you not hold him until you have got some security against his weapons?

[Applause.] Can you not hold him until you have searched him, and taken his weapons from him? Are you obliged to let him up to begin a new fight for your life? The same principle governs war between nations. When one nation has conquered another, in a war, the victorious nation does not retreat from the country and give up possession of it, because the fighting has ceased. No; it holds the conquered enemy in the grasp of war until it has secured whatever it has a right to require. [Applause.] I put that proposition fearlessly – *The conquering part may hold the other in the grasp of war until it has secured whatever it has a right to require.*

But what have we a right to require? ... We have a right to require whatever the public safety and public faith make necessary. [Applause.] That is the proposition. Then, we come to this: *We have a right to hold the rebels in the grasp of war until we have obtained whatever the public safety and the public faith require.* [Applause, and cries of "good."] Is not that a solid foundation to stand upon? Will it not bear examination? and are we not upon it to-day?

I take up my [second] question. ... What [*is it*] that the public safety and the public faith demand? Is there a man here who doubts? In the progress of this war, we found it necessary to proclaim the emancipation of every slave. [Applause.] ... I would undertake to maintain ... the proposition that we have to-day an adequate military occupation of the whole rebel country, sufficient to effect the emancipation of every slave, by admitted laws of war. ...

The slaves are emancipated. In form, this is true. But the public faith stands pledged to them, that they and their posterity forever shall have a complete and perfect freedom. [Prolonged applause.] .... Then, *how* shall we secure to them a complete and perfect freedom? The constitution of every slave state is cemented in slavery. Their statute-books are full of slavery. It is the corner-stone of every rebel state. If you allow them to come back at once, without condition, into the exercise of all their state functions, what guaranty have you for the complete freedom of the men you emancipate? There must, therefore, not merely be an emancipation of the actual, living slaves, but there must be an abolition of the slave system. [Applause.] ...

But, my fellow citizens, is that enough? ...

We have a right to require, my friends, that the freedmen of the South shall have the right to hold land. [Applause.] ... We have a right to require that they shall be allowed to testify in the state courts. [Applause.] ... We have a right to demand that they shall bear arms as soldiers in the militia. [Applause.] ... We have a right to demand that there shall be an impartial ballot. [Great applause.] ...

Now, my friends, let us be frank with one another. On what ground are we going to put our demand for the ballot for freedmen? . . . [*Dana notes that in the South, Confederates who do not take the loyalty oath are not to be allowed to vote; while in the North, women are not allowed to vote.*] There is no such doctrine as that every human being has a right to vote. Society must settle the right to a vote upon this principle – "The greatest good of the greatest number" must decide it. The greatest good of society must decide it. On what ground, then, do we put it? We put it upon the ground that the public safety and the public faith require that there shall be no distinction of color. [Applause.] . . .

Now comes my third question – How do you propose to accomplish it? . . .

You find the answer in my first proposition. . . . We hold each state in the grasp of war until the state does what we have a right to require of her. [Applause.] . . . We have a military occupation. . . .

I ask, again, how shall we obtain what we have a right to acquire? The changes we require are changes of their constitutions, are they not? The changes must be fundamental. The people are remitted to their original powers. They must meet in conventions and form constitutions, and those constitutions must be satisfactory to the republic. [Loud applause.] . . .

. . . Suppose the states do not do what we require – what then? . . . Suppose President Johnson's experiment in North Carolina and Mississippi fails, and the white men are determined to keep the black men down – what then? Mr. President, I hope we shall never be called upon to answer, practically, that question. . . . But if we come to it . . . I, for one, am prepared with an answer. I believe that if you come to the ultimate right of the thing, the ultimate law of the case, it is this: that this war – no not the war, *the victory in the war* – places, not the person, nor the life, not the private property of the rebels – they are governed by other considerations and rules – I do not speak of them – *but the political systems of the rebel states, at the discretion of the republic.* [Great applause.] . . . It is the necessary result of conquest, with military occupation, in a war of such dimensions, such a character, and such consequences as this. . . .

When a man accepts a challenge to a duel, what does he put at stake? He puts his life at stake, does he not? And is it not childish, after the fatal shot is fired, to exclaim, "Oh, death and widowhood and orphanage are fearful things!" . . . When a nation allows itself to be at war, or when a people make war, they put at stake their national existence. [Applause.] . . . The conqueror must choose between two courses – to permit the political institutions, the body politic, to go on, and treat with it, or obliterate it. We have destroyed and obliterated their central government. Its existence was treason. As to their states, we mean to adhere to the first course. We mean to say the states shall remain, with new constitutions, new systems. We do not mean to exercise sovereign civil jurisdiction over them in our Congress. Fellow citizens, it is not merely out of tenderness to them; it would be the most dangerous possible course for us. Our system is a planetary system; each planet revolving round its orbit, and all round a common sun. This system is held together by a balance of powers – centripetal and centrifugal forces. We have established a wise balance of forces. Let not that balance be destroyed. If we should undertake to exercise sovereign civil jurisdiction over those states, it would be as great a peril to our system as it would be a hardship upon them. We must not, we will not undertake it, except as the last resort of the thinking and the good – as the ultimate final remedy, when all others have failed. . . .

Document 8

Black Codes of Mississippi
October – December, 1865

Mississippi was the first state to assemble a constitutional convention, doing so in mid-August 1865. In August, President Andrew Johnson wrote William Sharkey, his provisional governor (see Document 6), as the convention opened. Mississippi's new constitution, Johnson wrote, would not be approved unless it adopted the 13th Amendment (Document 4), nullified the state's previous act of secession, and repudiated war debts accumulated by its rebel government. The convention accomplished these goals after some controversy. Mississippi's Constitution skirted the issue of voting rights for blacks, delegating that issue and any others to the legislature that would be elected in October 1865. Elections were held in October 1865, bringing many old Confederates into office. Most prominent among them was Benjamin G. Humphreys (1808-1882), an officer in the Confederate Army, who was elected governor. Johnson pardoned the new governor ten days after he was elected. Humphreys convened the legislature, which passed a series of laws, known as black codes, to regulate the labor, movements, and activities of the recently freed slaves during the first months of its session.

Source: Laws of the State of Mississippi, passed at a Regular Session of the Mississippi Legislature, held in the City of Jackson, October, November and December, 1865 (Jackson: J. J. Shannon & Co., State Printers, 1866), 82–85, 86–89, 90–91, 165–167. Available at https://goo.gl/cJfW5k.

An Act to Confer Civil Rights on Freedmen, and for Other Purposes

Section 1. Be it Enacted by the Legislature of the State of Mississippi, That all freedmen, free Negroes, and mulattoes may sue and be sued, . . . may acquire personal property . . . and may dispose of the same in the same manner and to the same extent that white persons may: [*but no*] freedman, free Negro, or mulatto [*shall*] rent or lease any lands or tenements, except in incorporated towns or cities, in which places the corporate authorities shall control the same.

Sec 2. Be it further enacted, That all freedmen, free Negroes, and mulattoes may intermarry with each other in the same manner and under the same regulations that are provided by law for white persons....

Sec 3. Be it further enacted, That all freedmen, free negroes, and mulattoes who do now and have heretofore lived and cohabited together as husband and wife shall be taken and held in law as legally married, and the issue shall be taken and held as legitimate for all purposes. That it shall not be lawful for any freedman, free Negro, or mulatto to intermarry with any white person; nor for any white person to intermarry with any freedman, free Negro, or mulatto; and any person who shall so intermarry shall be deemed guilty of felony and, on conviction thereof, shall be confined in the state penitentiary for life; and those shall be deemed freedmen, free Negroes, and mulattoes who are of pure Negro blood; and those descended from a Negro to the third generation inclusive, though one ancestor of each generation may have been a white person.

Sec 4. Be it further enacted, That in addition to cases in which freedmen, free negroes, or mulattoes are now by law competent witnesses, freedmen, free negroes, and mulattoes shall be competent in civil cases when a party or parties to the suit ... also in cases where a white person or persons is or are the opposing parties [and] in all criminal prosecutions where the crime charged is alleged to have been committed by a white person upon or against the person or property of a freedman, free Negro, or mulatto....

Sec 5. Be it further enacted, That Every freedman, free Negro, and mulatto shall ... have a lawful home or employment, and shall have a written evidence thereof, as follows, to wit: if living in any incorporated city, town, or village, a license from the mayor thereof; and if living outside of any incorporated city, town, or village, from the member of the board of police of his beat, authorizing him or her to do irregular and job work, or a written contract, as provided in Section 6 of this act, which licenses may be revoked for cause, at any time, by the authority granting the same.

Sec 6. Be it further enacted, That All contracts for labor made with freedmen, free Negroes, and mulattoes for a longer period than one month shall be in writing and in duplicate, attested and read to said freedman, free Negro, or mulatto by a beat, city, or county officer, or two disinterested white persons of the county in which the labor is to be performed, of which each party shall have one; ... and if the laborer shall quit the service of the employer before expiration of his term of service without good cause, he shall forfeit his wages for that year, up to the time of quitting.

Sec 7. Be it further enacted, That every civil officer shall, and every person may, arrest and carry back to his or her legal employer any freedman, free Negro, or mulatto who shall have quit the service of his or her employer before the expiration of his or her term of service without good cause, and said officer and person shall be entitled to receive for arresting and carrying back every deserting employee aforesaid the sum of five dollars . . . and the same shall be paid by the employer, and held as a setoff for so much against the wages of said deserting employee . . . .

. . .

Sec 9. Be if further enacted, That if any person shall persuade or attempt to persuade, entice, or cause any freedman, free Negro, or mulatto to desert from the legal employment of any person before the expiration of his or her term of service . . . he or she shall be guilty of a misdemeanor . . . .

An Act to Regulate the Relation of Master and Apprentice, as relates to Freedmen, Free Negroes, and Mulattoes

Section 1. Be it enacted by the Legislature of the State of Mississippi, That it shall be the duty of all sheriffs, justices of the peace, and other civil officers of the several counties in this state to report to the Probate courts of their respective counties semiannually, at the January and July terms of said courts, all freedmen, free Negroes, and mulattoes under the age of eighteen within their respective counties, beats, or districts who are orphans, or whose parent or parents have not the means, or who refuse to provide for and support said minors; and thereupon it shall be the duty of said Probate Court to order the clerk of said court to apprentice said minors to some competent and suitable person, on such terms as the court may direct, having a particular care to the interest of said minors: *Provided,* that the former owner of said minors shall have the preference when, in the opinion of the court, he or she shall be a suitable person for that purpose.

. . .

Sec 3. Be it further enacted, That in the management and control of said apprentices, said master or mistress shall have power to inflict such moderate corporeal chastisement as a father or guardian is allowed to inflict on his or her child or ward at common law: Provided that in no case shall cruel or inhuman punishment be inflicted.

Sec 4. Be it further enacted, That if any apprentice shall leave the employment of his or her master or mistress without his or her consent, said master or mistress may pursue and recapture said apprentice and bring him or her before any justice of the peace of the county, whose duty it shall be to remand said apprentice to the service of his or her master or mistress . . . .

Sec 5. Be it further enacted, That if any person entice away any apprentice from his or her master or mistress, or shall knowingly employ an apprentice, or furnish him or her food or clothing, without the written consent of his or her master or mistress, or shall sell or give said apprentice ardent spirits, without such consent, said person so offending shall be deemed guilty of a high misdemeanor, and shall, on conviction thereof before the county court, be punished as provided for the punishment of persons enticing from their employer hired freedmen, free Negroes, or mulattoes.

. . .

Sec 8. Be it further enacted, That in case any master or mistress of any apprentice, bound to him or her under this act, shall be about to remove, or shall have removed to any other state of the United States by the laws of which such apprentice may be an inhabitant thereof, the Probate Court of the proper county may authorize the removal of such apprentice to such state, upon the said master or mistress entering into bond, with security, in a penalty to be fixed by the judge, conditioned that said master or mistress will, upon such removal, comply with the laws of such state in such cases . . . .

. . .

An Act to Amend the Vagrant Laws of the State

Section 1. Be it enacted by the Legislature of the State of Mississippi, That all rogues and vagabonds, idle and dissipated persons, beggars, jugglers, or persons practicing unlawful games or plays, runaways, common drunkards, common nightwalkers, pilferers, lewd, wanton, or lascivious persons, in speech or behavior, common railers and brawlers, persons who neglect their calling or employment, misspend what they earn, or do not provide for the support of themselves or their families or dependents, and all other idle and disorderly persons, including all who neglect all lawful business, or habitually misspend their time by frequenting houses of ill-fame, gaming houses, or tippling shops, shall be deemed and considered vagrants under the provisions of this act; and, on conviction thereof shall be fined not exceeding $100 . . . and be imprisoned at the discretion of the court not exceeding ten days.

Sec 2. Be it further enacted, That all freedmen, free Negroes, and mulattoes in this state over the age of eighteen years found . . . with no lawful employment or business, or found unlawfully assembling themselves together . . . and all white persons so assembling with freedmen, free Negroes, or mulattoes, or usually associating with freedmen, free Negroes, or mulattoes on terms of equality, or living in adultery or fornication with a freedwoman, free Negro, or mulatto, shall be deemed vagrants; and, on conviction thereof, shall be fined in the sum of not exceeding, in the case of a freedman, free Negro, or mulatto, fifty dollars, and a white man, two hundred dollars, and imprisoned at the discretion of the court, the free Negro not exceeding ten days, and the white man not exceeding six months.

Sec 3. Be it further enacted, That all justices of the peace, mayors, and aldermen of incorporated towns and cities of the several counties in this state shall have jurisdiction to try all questions of vagrancy in their respective towns, counties, and cities; and it is hereby made their duty, whenever they shall ascertain that any person or persons in their respective towns, counties, and cities are violating any of the provisions of this act, to have said party or parties arrested and brought before them and immediately investigate said charge; and, on conviction, punish said party or parties as provided for herein. . . .

An Act to Punish Certain Offenses Herein Named, and for Other Purposes

Section 1. Be it enacted by the Legislature of the State of Mississippi, That no freedman, free Negro, or mulatto not in the military service of the United States government, and not licensed so to do by the board of police of his or her county, shall keep or carry firearms of any kind, or any ammunition, dirk, or Bowie knife . . . .

Sec 2. Be it further enacted, That any freedman, free Negro, or mulatto committing riots, routs, affrays, trespasses, malicious mischief, cruel treatment to animals, seditious speeches, insulting gestures, language, or acts, or assaults on any person, disturbance of the peace, exercising the function of a minister of the Gospel, without a license from some regularly organized church, vending spirituous or intoxicating liquors, or committing any other misdemeanor the punishment of which is not specifically provided for by law shall, upon conviction thereof in the county court, be fined not less than ten dollars and not more than one hundred dollars, and may be imprisoned, at the discretion of the court, not exceeding thirty days.

. . .

Sec 4. Be it further enacted, that all the penal and criminal laws now in force in this State, defining offenses and prescribing the mode of punishment for crimes and misdemeanors committed by slaves, free negroes or mulattoes, be and the same re-enacted, and declared to be in full force and effect, against freedmen, free negroes and mulattoes, except so far as the mode and manner of trial and punishment have been changed or altered by law.

Sec 5. Be it further enacted, That if any freedman, free Negro, or mulatto convicted of any of the misdemeanors provided against in this act shall fail or refuse, for the space of five days after conviction, to pay the fine and costs imposed, such person shall be hired out by the sheriff or other officer ... to any white person who will pay said fine and all costs and take such convict for the shortest time....

Document 9

First Annual Address
Andrew Johnson
December 4, 1865

Several states had elections under restored state constitutions during the fall of 1865, and service in the Confederate army was a veritable requirement to be elected throughout the former Confederacy. States were doing the minimum to satisfy President Johnson's demands for an abolition of slavery, a renunciation of secession, and a repudiation of Confederate debts (Document 8). Localities across the South were adopting black codes, while Mississippi and South Carolina passed them at the state level (Document 8). Johnson at times recognized the problem these developments posed for sectional harmony and a just reconstruction that made the war worth its bloodshed. Commenting in a letter to one of his generals, James B. Steedman, about the election of Alexander Stephens (1812-1883), the Confederacy's Vice President, to the United States Senate following Georgia's 1865 elections, Johnson noted, "There seems, in many of the elections something like defiance, which is all out of place at this time."

Nevertheless, Johnson pardoned thousands of former rebels, allowing them to serve in state governments. Johnson seemed committed to stimulating Unionist sentiment in the South through returning Southern states to self-government as quickly as possible, relying on the gratitude of the pardoned to reconcile the country. Those elected in the Republican landslide of 1864, who were just taking their seats for the first time in December 1865, opposed these policies. Johnson's First Annual Address, therefore, was his greatest opportunity to defend his policy of restoration before the Congress that would have to support it through legislative action.

Source: Andrew Johnson, First Annual Message, December 4, 1865. Online by Gerhard Peters and John T. Woolley, The American Presidency Project. https://goo.gl/75QPNa.

... The best security for the perpetual existence of the States is the "supreme authority" of the Constitution of the United States. The perpetuity of the Constitution brings with it the perpetuity of the States; their mutual relation makes us what we are, and in our political system their connection is indissoluble. The whole cannot exist without the parts, nor the parts without the whole. So long as the Constitution of the United States endures, the States will endure. The destruction of the one is the destruction of the other; the preservation of the one is the preservation of the other.

I have thus explained my views of the mutual relations of the Constitution and the States.... It has been my steadfast object to escape from the sway of momentary passions and to derive a healing policy from the fundamental and unchanging principles of the Constitution.

I found the States suffering from the effects of a civil war.... The United States had recovered possession of their forts and arsenals, and their armies were in the occupation of every State which had attempted to secede. Whether the territory within the limits of those States should be held as conquered territory, under military authority emanating from the President as the head of the Army, was the first question that presented itself for decision.

Now military governments, established for an indefinite period, would have offered no security for the early suppression of discontent, would have divided the people into the vanquishers and the vanquished, and would have envenomed hatred rather than have restored affection. Once established, no precise limit to their continuance was conceivable. They would have occasioned an incalculable and exhausting expense. Peaceful emigration to and from that portion of the country is one of the best means that can be thought of for the restoration of harmony, and that emigration would have been prevented; for what emigrant from abroad, what industrious citizen at home, would place himself willingly under military rule?... The powers of patronage and rule which would have been exercised under the President, over a vast and populous and naturally wealthy region are greater than, unless under extreme necessity, I should be willing to entrust to any one man. They are such as for myself, I could never, unless on occasions of great emergency, consent to exercise. The willful use of such powers, if continued through a period of years, would have endangered the purity of the general administration and the liberties of the States which remained loyal.

Besides, the policy of military rule over a conquered territory would have implied that the States whose inhabitants may have taken part in the rebellion had by the act of those inhabitants ceased to exist. But the true theory is that all pretended acts of secession were from the beginning null and void. The States cannot commit treason nor screen the individual citizens who may have committed treason any more than they can make valid treaties or engage in lawful commerce with any foreign power. The States attempting to secede placed themselves in a condition where their vitality was impaired, but not extinguished; their functions suspended, but not destroyed.

But if any State neglects or refuses to perform its offices there is the more need that the General Government should maintain all its authority and as soon as practicable resume the exercise of all its functions. On this principle, I have acted, and have gradually and quietly, and by almost imperceptible steps, sought to restore the rightful energy of the General Government and of the States. To that end provisional governors have been appointed for the States, conventions called, governors elected, legislatures assembled, and Senators and Representatives chosen to the Congress of the United States. At the same time the courts of the United States, as far as could be done, have been reopened, so that the laws of the United States may be enforced through their agency. The blockade has been removed and the custom-houses reestablished in ports of entry, so that the revenue of the United States may be collected. The Post-Office Department renews its ceaseless activity, and the General Government is thereby enabled to communicate promptly with its officers and agents. The courts bring security to persons and property; the opening of the ports invites the restoration of industry and commerce; the post-office renews the facilities of social intercourse and of business. And is it not happy for us all that the restoration of each one of these functions of the General Government brings with it a blessing to the States over which they are extended? Is it not a sure promise of harmony and renewed attachment to the Union that after all that has happened the return of the General Government is known only as a beneficence?

I know very well that this policy is attended with some risk; that for its success it requires at least the acquiescence of the States which it concerns; that it implies an invitation to those States, by renewing their allegiance to the United States, to resume their functions as States of the Union. But it is a risk that must be taken. In the choice of difficulties, it is the smallest risk; and to diminish and if possible to remove all danger, I have felt it incumbent on me to assert one other power of the General Government – the power of pardon.... In exercising that power I have taken every precaution to connect it with the clearest recognition of the binding force of the laws of the United States and an unqualified acknowledgment of the great social change of condition in regard to slavery which has grown out of the war.

The next step which I have taken to restore the constitutional relations of the States has been an invitation to them to participate in the high office of amending the Constitution. Every patriot must wish for a general amnesty at the earliest epoch consistent with public safety. For this great end, there is need of a

concurrence of all opinions and the spirit of mutual conciliation. All parties in the late terrible conflict must work together in harmony. It is not too much to ask, in the name of the whole people, that on the one side the plan of restoration shall proceed in conformity with a willingness to cast the disorders of the past into oblivion, and that on the other the evidence of sincerity in the future maintenance of the Union shall be put beyond any doubt by the ratification of the proposed amendment to the Constitution, which provides for the abolition of slavery forever within the limits of our country. So long as the adoption of this amendment is delayed, so long will doubt and jealousy and uncertainty prevail.
. . .

The amendment to the Constitution being adopted, it would remain for the States whose powers have been so long in abeyance to resume their places in the two branches of the National Legislature, and thereby complete the work of restoration. Here it is for you, fellow-citizens of the Senate, and for you, fellow-citizens of the House of Representatives, to judge . . . of the elections, returns, and qualifications of your own members. . . .

The relations of the General Government toward the 4,000,000 inhabitants whom the war has called into freedom have engaged my most serious consideration. On the propriety of attempting to make the freedmen electors by the proclamation of the Executive I took for my counsel the Constitution itself, the interpretations of that instrument by its authors and their contemporaries, and recent legislation by Congress. When, at the first movement toward independence, the Congress of the United States instructed the several States to institute governments of their own, they left each State to decide for itself the conditions for the enjoyment of the elective franchise. During the period of the Confederacy there continued to exist a very great diversity in the qualifications of electors in the several States, and even within a State a distinction of qualifications prevailed with regard to the officers who were to be chosen. The Constitution of the United States recognizes these diversities when it enjoins that in the choice of members of the House of Representatives of the United States "the electors in each State shall have the qualifications requisite for electors of the most numerous branch of the State legislature." . . .

. . . [E]very danger of conflict is avoided when the settlement of the question is referred to the several States. . . . In my judgment, the freedmen, if they show patience and manly virtues, will sooner obtain a participation in the elective franchise through the States than through the General Government, even if it had power to intervene. When the tumult of emotions that have been raised by the suddenness of the social change shall have subsided, it may prove that they will receive the kindest usage from some of those on whom they have heretofore most closely depended.

But while I have no doubt that now, after the close of the war, it is not competent for the General Government to extend the elective franchise in the several States, it is equally clear that good faith requires the security of the freedmen in their liberty and their property, their right to labor, and their right to claim the just return of their labor. . . . We must equally avoid hasty assumptions of any natural impossibility for the two races to live side by side in a state of mutual benefit and good will. The experiment involves us in no inconsistency; let us, then, go on and make that experiment in good faith . . . . The country is in need of labor, and the freedmen are in need of employment, culture, and protection. While their right of voluntary migration and expatriation is not to be questioned, I would not advise their forced removal and colonization. Let us rather encourage them to honorable and useful industry, where it may be beneficial to themselves and to the country; and . . . let there be nothing wanting to the fair trial of the experiment. The change in their condition is the substitution of labor by contract for the status of slavery. The freedman cannot fairly be accused of unwillingness to work so long as a doubt remains about his freedom of choice in his pursuits and the certainty of his recovering his stipulated wages. . . . And if the one ought to be able to enforce the contract, so ought the other. The public interest will be best promoted if the several States will provide adequate protection and remedies for the freedmen. Until this is in some way accomplished there is no chance for the advantageous use of their labor, and the blame of ill success will not rest on them.

I know that sincere philanthropy is earnest for the immediate realization of its remotest aims; but time is always an element in reform. It is one of the greatest acts on record to have brought 4,000,000 people into freedom. . . . Now that slavery is at an end, or near its end, the greatness of its evil in the point of view of public economy becomes more and more apparent. Slavery was essentially a monopoly of labor, and as such locked the States where it prevailed against the incoming of free industry. Where labor was the property of the capitalist, the white man was excluded from employment, or had but the second-best chance of finding it; and the foreign emigrant turned away from the region where his condition would be so precarious. With the destruction of the monopoly free labor will hasten from all parts of the civilized world to assist in developing various and immeasurable resources which have hitherto lain dormant. . . . The removal of the monopoly of slave labor is a pledge that those regions will be peopled by a numerous and enterprising population, which will vie with any in the Union in compactness, inventive genius, wealth, and industry.

... Monopolies, perpetuities, and class legislation are contrary to the genius of free government, and ought not to be allowed. Here there is no room for favored classes or monopolies; the principle of our Government is that of equal laws and freedom of industry. Wherever monopoly attains a foothold, it is sure to be a source of danger, discord, and trouble. We shall but fulfill our duties as legislators by according "equal and exact justice to all men," special privileges to none. The Government is subordinate to the people; but, as the agent and representative of the people, it must be held superior to monopolies, which in themselves ought never to be granted, and which, where they exist, must be subordinate and yield to the Government....

Document 10

Report on the Condition of the South
Carl Schurz
December 19, 1865

In his First Annual Address, President Andrew Johnson seemed to think that restoration of Southern states was by and large completed (Document 9). Constitutional conventions had been held. Elections were conducted. New governments met. All, according to Johnson, seemed to be going about as well as could be hoped. No less an authority than General Ulysses S. Grant, the Union's victorious general, concluded that "the mass of thinking men in the South accept the present situation of affairs in good faith." Yet doubts about Johnson's understanding of the state of things lingered: there was genuine disagreement about what the Southerners were thinking and doing and about what could be realistically hoped for. Northern Republicans saw Black Codes passed, rebels elected to offices high and low, and Union men attacked in the South and worried that the situation was still a low-level rebellion. An adequate evaluation of Johnson's policy of quick restoration depended on accurate knowledge of what was going on in the South.

Enter Carl Schurz (1829-1908), a German immigrant and Union general from Missouri, who would later be elected senator. Johnson sent Schurz on a fact-finding mission to the South during the summer of 1865. Schurz fell out with Johnson along the way, as Johnson adopted a policy of relatively easy restoration for Southern states and allowed several states to organize their own militias. Schurz opposed these policies openly. Schurz delivered his report to the U.S. Senate, setting the stage for the criticisms of Johnson's plans and for the rise of an alternative mode of reconstruction that tried to hold states to a much higher standard.

Source: Carl Schurz, "Report on the Condition of the South," in Speeches, Correspondences, and Political Papers of Carl Schurz, Edited by Frederic Bancroft (New York: G. T. Putnam's Sons, 1913), Volume I, 279, 281–82, 283–86, 289–90, 292–93, 302–04, 306, 309, 311, 327–28, 329, 331, 332–33, 343–44, 346–47, 354, 356–358, 359.

... You did me the honor of selecting me for a mission to the States lately in rebellion, for the purpose of inquiring into the existing condition of things, of laying before you whatever information of importance I might gather, and of suggesting to you such measures as my observations would lead me to believe advisable....[1]

Condition of Things Immediately After the Close of the War

In the development of the popular spirit in the South since the close of the war two well-marked periods can be distinguished. The first commences with the sudden collapse of the confederacy and the dispersion of its armies, and the second with the first proclamation indicating the "reconstruction policy" of the Government. Of the first period I can state the characteristic features only from the accounts I received partly from Unionists who were then living in the South, partly from persons that had participated in the rebellion. When the news of Lee's and Johnston's surrenders burst upon the southern country the general consternation was extreme. People held their breath, indulging in the wildest apprehensions as to what was now to come. Men who had occupied positions under the Confederate Government, or were otherwise compromised in the rebellion, ran before the Federal columns as they advanced and spread out to occupy the country, from village to village, from plantation to plantation hardly knowing whether they wanted to escape or not. Others remained at their homes, yielding themselves up to their fate....

Such was, according to the accounts I received, the character of that first period. The worst apprehensions were gradually relieved as day after day went by without bringing the disasters and inflictions which had been vaguely anticipated, until at last the appearance of the North Carolina proclamation[2] substituted new hopes for them. The development of this second period I was called upon to observe on the spot, and it forms the main subject of this report.

---

[1] Although Schurz, having broken with President Johnson's policies before completing his report, would deliver it not to the president but to the Senate, he nevertheless wrote it as if it were addressed to the President.

[2] See Document 6: The North Carolina Proclamation, President Johnson's first on May 29, 1865, was structurally identical to the Mississippi Proclamation, which he submitted days later. For the North Carolina Proclamation, see https://goo.gl/gg1ugD.

Returning Loyalty

... The white people at large being, under certain conditions, charged with taking the preliminaries of "reconstruction" into their hands, the success of the experiment depends upon the spirit and attitude of those who either attached themselves to the secession cause from the beginning, or, entertaining originally the opposite views, at least followed its fortunes from the time that their States had declared their separation from the Union.

The first Southern men of this class with whom I came into contact immediately after my arrival in South Carolina expressed their sentiments almost literally in the following language: "We acknowledge ourselves beaten, and we are ready to submit to the results of the war. The war has practically decided that no State shall secede and that the slaves are emancipated. We cannot be expected at once to give up our principles and convictions of right, but we accept facts as they are, and desire to be reinstated as soon as possible in the enjoyment and exercise of our political rights." This declaration was repeated to me hundreds of times in every State I visited, with some variations of language, according to the different ways of thinking or the frankness or reserve of the different speakers....

Upon the ground of these declarations, and other evidence gathered in the course of my observations, I may group the Southern people into four classes, each of which exercises an influence upon the development of things in that section:

1. Those who, although having yielded submission to the National Government only when obliged to do so, have a clear perception of the irreversible changes produced by the war, and honestly endeavor to accommodate themselves to the new order of things. Many of them are not free from traditional prejudices but open to conviction, and may be expected to act in good faith whatever they do. This class is composed, in its majority, of persons of mature age – planters, merchants, and professional men; some of them are active in the reconstruction movement, but boldness and energy are, with a few individual exceptions, not among their distinguishing qualities.

2. Those whose principal object is to have the States without delay restored to their position and influence in the Union and the people of the States to the absolute control of their home concerns. They are ready, in order to attain that object, to make any ostensible concession that will not prevent them from arranging things to suit their taste as soon as that object is attained. This class comprises a considerable number, probably a large majority, of the professional politicians who are extremely active in the reconstruction movement. They are loud in their praise of the President's reconstruction policy, and clamorous for

the withdrawal of the Federal troops and the abolition of the Freedmen's Bureau.

3. The incorrigibles, who still indulge in the swagger which was so customary before and during the war, and still hope for a time when the Southern Confederacy will achieve its independence. This class consists mostly of young men, and comprises the loiterers of the towns and idlers of the country. They persecute Union men and Negroes whenever they can do so with impunity, insist clamorously upon their "rights," and are extremely impatient of the presence of the Federal soldiers. A good many of them have taken the oaths of allegiance and amnesty, and associated themselves with the second class in their political operations. This element is by no means unimportant; it is strong in numbers, deals in brave talk, addresses itself directly and incessantly to the passions and prejudices of the masses, and commands the admiration of the women.

4. The multitude of people who have no definite ideas about the circumstances under which they live and about the course they have to follow; whose intellects are weak, but whose prejudices and impulses are strong, and who are apt to be carried along by those who know how to appeal to the latter.

Much depends upon the relative strength and influence of these classes. In the course of this report you will find statements of facts which may furnish a basis for an estimate. But whatever their differences may be, on one point they are agreed: further resistance to the power of the National Government is useless, and submission to its authority a matter of necessity....

. . . .

Feeling Toward the Soldiers and the People of the North

... [E]vidence of "returning loyalty" would be a favorable change of feeling with regard to the government's friends and agents, and the people of the loyal States generally. I mentioned above that all organized attacks upon our military forces stationed in the South have ceased; but there are still localities where it is unsafe for a man wearing the federal uniform or known as an officer of the Government to be abroad outside of the immediate reach of our garrisons. The shooting of single soldiers and Government couriers was not unfrequently reported while I was in the South....

... [N]o instance has come to my notice in which the people of a city or a rural district cordially fraternized with the army.... Upon the whole, the soldier of the Union is still looked upon as a stranger, an intruder – as the "Yankee," "the enemy." It would be superfluous to enumerate instances of insult offered to our soldiers, and even to officers high in command....

Situation of Unionists

... It struck me soon after my arrival in the South that the known Unionists – I mean those who during the war had been to a certain extent identified with the National cause – were not in communion with the leading social and political circles; and the further my observation extended the clearer it became to me that their existence in the South was of a rather precarious nature....

Even Governor Sharkey [of Mississippi], in the course of a conversation I had with him ... admitted that, if our troops were then withdrawn, the lives of Northern men in Mississippi would not be safe....

....

What Has Been Accomplished

While the generosity and toleration shown by the government to the people lately in rebellion have not met with a corresponding generosity shown by those people to the Government's friends, it has brought forth some results which, if properly developed, will become of value. It has facilitated the re-establishment of the forms of civil government, and led many of those who had been active in the rebellion to take part in the act of bringing back the states to their constitutional relations....

But as to the moral value of these results, we must not indulge in any delusions. There are two principal points to which I beg to call your attention. In the first place, the rapid return to power and influence of so many of those who but recently were engaged in a bitter war against the Union, has had one effect which was certainly not originally contemplated by the Government. Treason does, under existing circumstances, not appear odious in the South. The people are not impressed with any sense of its criminality. And, secondly, there is, as yet among the Southern people *an utter absence of national feeling*. I made it a business, while in the South, to watch the symptoms of "returning loyalty" as they appeared not only in private conversation, but in the public press and in the speeches delivered and the resolutions passed at Union meetings. Hardly ever was there an expression of hearty attachment to the great republic, or an appeal to the impulses of patriotism; but whenever submission to the National authority was declared and advocated, it was almost uniformly placed upon two principal grounds: That, under present circumstances, the Southern people could "do no better"; and then that submission was the only means by which they could rid themselves of the Federal soldiers and obtain once more control of their own affairs....

The re-organization of civil government is relieving the military, to a great extent, of its police duties and judicial functions; but at the time I left the South it was still very far from showing a satisfactory efficiency in the maintenance of order and security. In many districts robbing and plundering were going on with perfect impunity; the roads were infested by bands of highwaymen; numerous assaults occurred and several stage lines were considered unsafe. . . .

The Negro Question – First Aspects

The principal cause of that want of national spirit which has existed in the South so long and at last gave birth to the rebellion, was, that the Southern people cherished, cultivated, idolized their peculiar interests and institutions in preference to those which they had in common with the rest of the American people. Hence the importance of the Negro question as an integral part of the question of union in general, and the question of reconstruction in particular. . . .

Opinions of the Whites

. . . [A] large majority of the Southern men with whom I came into contact announced their opinions with so positive an assurance as to produce the impression that their minds where fully made up. In at least nineteen cases of twenty the reply I received to my inquiry about their views on the new system was uniformly this: "You cannot make the Negro work without physical compulsion." I heard this hundreds of times, heard it wherever I went, heard it in nearly the same words from so many different persons, that at last I came to the conclusion that this is the prevailing sentiment among the Southern people. . . .

Effects of Such Opinions, and General Treatment of the Negro

A belief, conviction, or prejudice, or whatever you may call it, so widely spread and apparently so deeply rooted as this, that the Negro will not work without physical compulsion, is certainly calculated to have a very serious influence upon the conduct of the people entertaining it. It naturally produced a desire to preserve slavery in its original form as much and as long as possible – and you may, perhaps, remember the admission made by one of the provisional governors, over two months after the close of the war, that the people of his State still indulged in a lingering hope slavery might yet be preserved – or to introduce into the new system that element of physical compulsion which would make the Negro work. . . . In many instances Negroes who walked away from the plantations, or were found upon the roads, were shot or otherwise severely punished, which was calculated to produce the impression among those remaining with their masters that an attempt to escape from slavery would result in certain destruction. . . .

Education of the Freedmen

. . . As popular education is the true ground upon which the efficiency and the successes of free-labor society grow, no man who rejects the former can be accounted a consistent friend of the latter. It is also evident that the education of the Negro, to become general and effective after the full restoration of local government in the South, must be protected and promoted as an integral part of the educational systems of the States.

. . . [T]he popular prejudice is almost as bitterly set against the Negro's having the advantage of education as it was when the negro was a slave. There may be an improvement in that respect, but it would prove only how universal the prejudice was in former days. Hundreds of times I heard the old assertion repeated, that "learning will spoil the nigger for work," and that "Negro education will be the ruin of the South." Another most singular notion still holds a potent sway over the minds of the masses – it is, that the elevation of the blacks will be the degradation of the whites. . . .

The consequence of the prejudice prevailing in the Southern States is that colored schools can be established and carried on with safety only under the protection of our military forces, and that where the latter are withdrawn the former have to go with them. . . .

The Freedmen

The first Southern man with whom I came into contact after my arrival at Charleston designated the general conduct of the emancipated slaves as surprisingly good. Some went even so far as to call it admirable. . . . A great many colored people while in slavery had undoubtedly suffered much hardship and submitted to great wrongs, partly inseparably connected with the condition of servitude, and partly aggravated by the individual willfulness and cruelty of their masters and over seers. They were suddenly set free; and not only that: their masters, but a short time ago almost omnipotent on their domains, found themselves, after their defeat in the war, all at once face to face with their former, slaves as a conquered and powerless class. Never was the temptation to indulge in acts of vengeance for wrongs suffered more strongly presented than to the colored people of the South; but no instance of such individual revenge was then on record, nor have I since heard of any case of violence that could be traced to such motives. . . . This was the first impression I received after my arrival in the South, and I received it from the mouths of late slaveholders.

But at that point the unqualified praise stopped and the complaints began: the Negroes would not work; they left their plantations and went wandering from place to place, stealing by the way; they preferred a life of idleness and vagrancy to that of honest and industrious labor; they either did not show any willingness to enter into contracts, or, if they did, showed a stronger disposition to break them than to keep them; they were becoming insubordinate and insolent to their former owners; they indulged in extravagant ideas about their rights and relied upon the Government to support them without work; in one word, they had no conception of the rights freedom gave, and of the obligations freedom imposed upon them. . . .

Prospective – the Reactionary Tendency

I stated above that, in my opinion, the solution of the social problem in the South did not depend upon the capacity and conduct of the Negro alone, but in the same measure upon the ideas and feelings entertained and acted upon by the whites. What their ideas and feelings were while under my observation, and how they affected the contact of the two races, I have already set forth. The question arises, what policy will be adopted by the "ruling class" when all restraint imposed upon them by the military power of the National Government is withdrawn, and they are left free to regulate matters according to their own tastes? It would be presumptuous to speak of the future with absolute certainty; but it may safely be assumed that the same causes will always tend to produce the same effect. As long as a majority of the Southern people believe that "the Negro will not work without physical compulsion," and that "the blacks at large belong to the whites at large," that belief will tend to produce a system of coercion, the enforcement of which will be aided by the hostile feeling against the Negro now prevailing among the whites, and by the general spirit of violence which in the South was fostered by the influence slavery exercised upon the popular character. It is, indeed, not probable that a general attempt will be made to restore slavery in its old form, on account of the barriers which such an attempt would find in its way; but there are systems intermediate between slavery as it formerly existed in the South, and free labor as it exists in the North, but more nearly related to the former than to the latter, *the introduction of which will be attempted.* I have already noticed some movements in that direction, which were made under the very eyes of our military authorities, and of which the Opelousas and St. Landry ordinances[3] were the most significant. . . .

---

[3] Schurz is referring to the locales that passed black codes.

It is worthy of note that the convention of Mississippi – and the conventions of other States have followed its example – imposed upon subsequent legislatures the obligation not only to pass laws for the protection of the freedmen in person and property, but also *to guard against the dangers arising from sudden emancipation.* This language is not without significance; not the blessings of a full development of free labor, but only the dangers of emancipation are spoken of. It will be observed that this clause is so vaguely worded as to authorize the legislatures to place any restriction they may see fit upon the emancipated Negro, in perfect consistency with the amended State Constitutions; for it rests with them to define what the dangers of sudden emancipation consist in, and what measures may be required to guard against them. It is true, the clause does not authorize the legislatures to reestablish slavery in the old form; but they may pass whatever laws they see fit, stopping short only one step of what may strictly be defined as "slavery." Peonage of the Mexican pattern, or serfdom of some European pattern, may under that clause be considered admissible; . . . it appears not only possible, but eminently probable, that the laws which will be passed to guard against the dangers arising from emancipation will be directed against the spirit of emancipation itself. . . .

. . .

The True Problem – Difficulties and Remedies

. . . [I]t is not only the Political machinery of the States and their constitutional relations to the General Government, but the whole organism of Southern society that must be reconstructed, or rather constructed anew, so as to bring it in harmony with the rest of American society. . . .

The true nature of the difficulties of the situation is this: The General Government of the republic has, by proclaiming the emancipation of the slaves, commenced a great social revolution in the South, but has, as yet, not completed it. . . .

. . . It is, indeed, difficult to imagine circumstances more unfavorable for the development of a calm and unprejudiced public opinion than those under which the Southern people are at present laboring. The war has not only defeated their political aspirations, but it has broken up their whole social organization. When the rebellion was put down, they found themselves not only conquered in a political and military sense, but economically ruined. . . . The planters . . . are partly laboring under the severest embarrassments, partly reduced to absolute poverty. Many who are stripped of all available means, and have nothing but their land, cross their arms in gloomy despondency . . . . Others, who still possess means, are at a loss how to use them, as their old way of doing things is, by the abolition of slavery, rendered impracticable, at least where the military arm of the government has enforced emancipation. . . . A large number of the plantations . . . [are] under heavy mortgages, and the owners know that, unless they retrieve their fortunes in a comparatively short space of time, their property will pass out of their hands. . . . Besides, the Southern soldiers, when returning from the war, did not, like the Northern soldiers, find a prosperous community which merely waited for their arrival to give them remunerative employment. [Many] found their homesteads destroyed, their farms devastated, their families in distress; and [others found] an impoverished and exhausted community which had but little to offer them. . . . [A] nervous anxiety to hastily repair broken fortunes, and to prevent still greater ruin and distress, embraces nearly all classes . . . .

. . . The practical question presents itself: Is the immediate restoration of the late rebel States to absolute self-control so necessary that it must be done even at the risk of endangering one of the great results of the war, and of bringing on in those States insurrection or anarchy, or would it not be better to postpone that restoration until such dangers are passed? If, as long as the change from slavery to free labor is known to the Southern people only by its destructive results, these people must be expected to throw obstacles in its way, would it not seem necessary that the movement of social "reconstruction" be kept in the right channel by the hand of the power which originated the change, until that change can have disclosed some of its beneficial effects? . . .

. . . One reason why the southern people are so slow in accommodating themselves to the new order of things is, that they confidently expect soon to be permitted to regulate matters according to their own notions. Every concession made to them by the government has been taken as an encouragement to preserve in this hope, and, unfortunately for them, this hope is nourished by influences from other parts of the country. Hence their anxiety to have their State governments restored *at once*, to have the troops withdrawn. . . .

Document 11

Reply of the Colored Delegation to the President
Frederick Douglass
February 7, 1866

Frederick Douglass (1818-1895) and other black leaders met with President Andrew Johnson in the White House on February 7, 1866, in an effort to persuade Johnson that his approach to restoration was causing untold damage to the freedmen in the South and to the hopes for national reconciliation on the basis of freedom. Douglass and the others in this meeting pressed Johnson to support a union of poor whites and freedmen into a "party... among the poor." This new party, they hoped, would be able to win elections under the restored Southern constitutions and govern it toward protection for freedmen and the dismantling of the Southern slave-based oligarchy. This coalition would require that the vote be extended to freedmen. In response, Johnson expressed great skepticism about such a prospect and about extending the vote to freedmen. He was loath to require that states extend the vote to blacks. Black civil rights, Johnson held, came at the expense of poor southern whites and the latter were the true victims of the late war. "The Negro will vote with the late master, whom he does not hate," Johnson predicted, "rather than with the non-slaveholding white, whom he does hate."

After President Johnson made clear that he would not be argued out of this opinion, the delegation thanked Johnson for the audience and departed. Afterwards, Douglass wrote the following open letter for publication in the newspapers.

Source: **University of Rochester Frederick Douglass Project,** *a collaboration of the Department of Rare Books, Special Collections, and Preservation at the University of Rochester and The Frederick Douglass Institute at West Chester University of Pennsylvania. https://goo.gl/c7J5j8.*

Mr. President: . . . Believing as we do that the views and opinions you expressed in that address[1] are entirely unsound and prejudicial to the highest interest of our race as well as our country at large, we cannot do other than expose the same, and, as far as may be in our power, arrest their dangerous influence. It is not necessary at this time to call attention to more than two or three features of your remarkable address:

1. The first point to which we feel especially bound to take exception is your attempt to found a policy opposed to our enfranchisement, upon the alleged ground of an existing hostility on the part of the former slaves toward the poor white people of the South. We admit the existence of this hostility, and hold that it is entirely reciprocal. But you obviously commit an error by drawing an argument from an incident of a state of slavery, and making it a basis for a policy adapted to a state of freedom. The hostility between the whites and blacks of the South . . . . has its root and sap in the relation of slavery, and was incited on both sides by the cunning of the slave masters. Those masters secured their ascendency over both the poor whites and the blacks by putting enmity between them. They divided both to conquer each. There was no earthly reason why the blacks should not hate and dread the poor whites when in a state of slavery, for it was from this class that their masters received their slave-catchers, slave-drivers, and overseers. They were the men called in upon all occasions by the masters when any fiendish outrage was to be committed upon the slave. Now . . . the cause of this hatred removed, the effect must be removed also. Slavery is abolished. The cause of antagonism is removed, and you must see that it is altogether illogical . . . to legislate from slave-holding and slave-driving premises for a people whom you have repeatedly declared your purpose to maintain in freedom.

2. Besides, even if it were true, as you allege, that the hostility of the blacks toward the poor whites must necessarily project itself into a state of freedom, and that this enmity between the two races is even more intense in a state of freedom than in a state of slavery, in the name of Heaven, we reverently ask, how can you, in view of your professed desire to promote the welfare of the black man, deprive him of all means of defense, and clothe him whom you regard as his enemy in the panoply of political power? Can it be that you would recommend a policy which would arm the strong and cast down the defenseless? . . . Experience proves that those are oftenest abused who can be abused with the

---

[1] Douglass refers to the off-the-cuff lecture Johnson had given, privately, to the delegation who met with him on February 7th to ask for his support of voting rights for freedmen.

greatest impunity. Men are whipped oftenest who are whipped easiest. Peace between races is not to be secured by degrading one race and exalting another, by giving power to one race and withholding it from another; but by maintaining a state of equal justice between all classes....

3. On the colonization theory you were pleased to broach, very much could be said. It is impossible to suppose, in view of the usefulness of the black man in time of peace as a laborer in the South, and in time of war as a soldier at the North, and the growing respect for his rights among the people, and his increasing adaptation to a high state of civilization in this his native land, there can ever come a time when he can be removed from this country without a terrible shock to its prosperity and peace. Besides, the worst enemy of the nation could not cast upon its fair name a greater infamy than to suppose that Negroes could be tolerated among them in a state of the most degrading slavery and oppression, and must be cast away, driven into exile, for no other cause than having been freed from their chains.

Document 12

Address Before the General Assembly of the State of Georgia
Alexander H. Stephens
February 22, 1866

Alexander Stephens had been a Whig Congressman from Georgia in the 1840s and 1850s. He opposed Georgia's secession from the Union. Yet, as Georgia followed the rest of the South in secession from the Union, Stephens was elected Vice President of the Confederacy. As Vice President, he delivered the famous "Cornerstone speech" in March 1861, arguing that the Confederacy was the first government based on "great physical, philosophical, and moral truth" that "the Negro is not equal to the white man" and that a black's "subordination to the superior race is his natural and normal condition." Stephens was captured and imprisoned after the Union victory. President Andrew Johnson paroled Stephens after about five months in prison. Soon after his release, under Georgia's new constitution made pursuant to Johnson's restoration policy (Document 6), the Georgia legislature elected Stephens as senator. Accepting the seat as Georgia's Senator, Stephens delivered the speech excerpted here, outlining the policies that would guide his service.

The U.S. Congress, however, would not seat Stephens (as a former Confederate, he was disqualified from serving). The election of Stephens was a crucial piece of evidence for Republicans in Congress that Johnson's policies were far too lenient. This diagnosis paved the way for the Reconstruction Acts (Document 17) and other more radical measures.

Source: Alexander H. Stephens, In Public and Private, With Letters and Speeches, Before, During, and Since the War, *ed. Henry Cleveland (Philadelphia: National Publishing Company, 1866), 804, 805–06, 807, 810–11, 812, 813–14, 816–17, 817–18.*

The great object with me now, is to see a restoration, if possible, of peace, prosperity, and constitutional liberty in this once happy, but now disturbed, agitated, and distracted country. To this end, all my energies and efforts, to the extent of their powers, will be devoted.

You ask my views on the existing state of affairs; our duties at the present, and the prospects of the future? ...

Can these evils upon us – the absence of law; the want of protection and security of person and property ... be removed? Or can those greater ones which threaten our very political existence, be averted? These are the questions.

It is true we have not the control of all the remedies.... Our fortunes and destiny are not entirely in our own hands. Yet there are some things that we may, and can, and ought, in my judgment, to do, from which no harm can come, and from which some good may follow, in bettering our present condition....

The first great duty, then, I would enjoin at this time, is the exercise of the simple, though difficult and trying, but nevertheless indispensable quality of patience. Patience requires of those afflicted to bear and to suffer with fortitude whatever ills may befall them.... We are in the condition of a man with a dislocated limb, or a broken leg, and a very bad compound fracture at that. How it became broken should not be with him a question of so much importance, as how it can be restored to health, vigor, and strength. This requires of him as the highest duty to himself to wait quietly and *patiently* in splints and bandages, until nature resumes her active powers – until the vital functions perform their office. ... We must or ought now, therefore, in a similar manner to discipline ourselves to the same or like degree of patience.... I know how trying it is to be denied representation in Congress, while we are paying our proportion of the taxes – how annoying it is to be even partially under military rule – and how injurious it is to the general interest and business of the country to be without post-offices and mail communications;[1] to say nothing of divers other matters on the long list of our present inconveniences and privations. All these, however, we must patiently bear and endure for a season....

Next to this, another great duty we owe to ourselves is the exercise of a liberal spirit of forbearance amongst ourselves.

The first step toward local or general harmony is the banishment from our breasts of every feeling and sentiment calculated to stir the discords of the past. Nothing could be more injurious or mischievous to the future of this country, than the agitation, at present, of questions that divided the people anterior to, or during the existence of the late war. On no occasion, and especially in the bestowment of office, ought such differences of opinion in the past ever to be

---

[1] President Johnson had said that the mails were running in his First Annual Address (Document 9).

mentioned, either for or against any one, otherwise equally entitled to confidence. These ideas or sentiments of other times and circumstances are not the germs from which hopeful organizations can now arise. . . . Great disasters are upon us and upon the whole country, and without inquiring how these originated . . . let us now as common sharers of common misfortunes, on all occasions, consult only as to the best means . . . to secure the best ends toward future amelioration. . . .

This view should also be born in mind, that whatever differences of opinion existed before the late fury of the war, they sprung mainly from differences as to the best means to be used . . . to secure the great controlling object of all – which was GOOD GOVERNMENT. Whatever may be said of the loyalty or disloyalty of any, in the late most lamentable conflict of arms, I think I may venture safely to say, that there was, on the parts of the great mass of the people of Georgia, and of the entire South, no *disloyalty* to the principles of the constitution of the United States. To that system of representative government; of delegated and limited powers; that establishment in a new phase, on this continent, of all the essentials of England's *Magna Charta*, for the protection and security of life, liberty and property; with the additional recognition of the principle as a fundamental truth, that all political power resides in the people. With us it was simply a question as to where our allegiance was due in the maintenance of these principles – which authority was paramount in the last resort – State or federal. . . . It was with this view and this purpose secession was tried. That has failed. . . .

. . . Our only alternative now is, either to give up all hope of constitutional liberty, or to retrace our steps, and to look for its vindication and maintenance in the forums of reason and justice, instead of on the arena of arms – in the courts and halls of legislation, instead of on the fields of battle.

I am frank and candid in telling you right here, that our surest hopes, in my judgement, of these ends, are in the restoration policy of the President of the United States [*Andrew Johnson*].

. . .

I could enjoin no greater duty upon my countrymen now, North and South, than the exercise of that degree of forbearance which would enable them to conquer their prejudices. . . .

I say to you, and if my voice could extend throughout this vast country . . . among the first [*of duties*], looking to restoration of peace, prosperity and harmony in this land, is the great duty of exercising that degree of forbearance which will enable them to conquer their prejudices. Prejudices against communities as well as individuals.

And next to that, the indulgence of a Christian spirit of charity....

... The exercise of patience, forbearance, and charity, therefore, are the three first duties I would at this time enjoin – and of these three, "the greatest is charity."[2]

But to proceed. Another one of our present duties, is this: we should accept the issues of the war, and abide by them in good faith.... The people of Georgia have in convention revoked and annulled her ordinance of 1861, which was intended to sever her from the compact of Union of 1787.... Whether Georgia, by the action of her convention of 1861, was ever rightfully out of the Union or not, there can be no question that she is now in, so far as depends upon her will and deed....

But with this change comes a new order of things. One of the results of the war is a total charge in our whole internal policy. Our former social fabric has been entirely subverted.... The relation heretofore, under our old system, existing between the African and European races, no longer exists. Slavery, as it was called, or the *status* of the black race, their subordination to the white, upon which all our institutions rested, is abolished forever, not only in Georgia, but throughout the limits of the United States. This change should be received and accepted as an irrevocable fact....

All changes of systems or proposed reforms are but experiments and problems to be solved. Our system of self-government was an experiment at first. Perhaps as a problem it is not yet solved. Our present duty on this subject is not with the past or the future; it is with the present....

This duty of giving this new system a fair and just trial will require of you, as legislators of the land, great changes in our former laws in regard to this large class of population. Wise and humane provisions should be made for them. It is not for me to go into detail. Suffice it to say on this occasion, that ample and full protection should be secured to them, so that they may stand equal before the law, in the possession and enjoyment of all rights of person, liberty and property. Many considerations claim this at your hands. Among these may be stated their fidelity in times past. They cultivated your fields, ministered to your personal wants and comforts, nursed and reared your children; and even in the hour of danger and peril they were, in the main, true to you and yours. To them we owe a debt of gratitude, as well as acts of kindness. This should also be done because they are poor, untutored, uninformed; many of them helpless, liable to be imposed upon, and need it. Legislation should ever look to the protection of the weak against the strong. Whatever may be said of the equality of races, or their

---

[2] 1 Corinthians 13:13.

natural capacity to become equal, no one can doubt that at this time this race among us is not equal to the Caucasian. This inequality does not lessen the moral obligations on the part of the superior to the inferior, it rather increases them. From him who has much, more is required than from him who has little.[3] The present generation of them, it is true is far above their savage progenitors, who were at first introduced into this country, in general intelligence, virtue, and moral culture. This shows capacity for improvement. But in all the higher characteristics of mental development, they are still very far below the European type. What further advancement they may make, or to what standard they may attain, under a different system of laws every way suitable and wisely applicable to their changed condition, time alone can disclose. I speak of them as we now know them to be; having no longer the protection of a master, or legal guardian, they now need all the protection which the shield of the law can give.

But, above all, this protection should be secured, because it is right and just that it should be, upon general principles. All governments in their organic structure, as well as in their administration, should have this leading object in view: the good of the governed. . . . In legislation, therefore, under the new system, you should look to the best interest of all classes; their protection, security, advancement and improvement, physically, intellectually, and morally. All obstacles, if there be any, should be removed, which can possibly hinder or retard, the improvement of the blacks to the extent of their capacity. All proper aid should be given to their own efforts. Channels of education should be opened up to them. Schools, and the usual means of moral and intellectual training, should be encouraged among them. This is the dictate, not only of what is right and proper, and just in itself, but it is also the promptings of the highest considerations of interest. It is difficult to conceive a greater evil or curse, that could befall our country, stricken and distressed as it now is, than for so large a portion of its population, as this class will quite probably constitute amongst us, hereafter, to be reared in ignorance, depravity and vice. In view of such a state of things well might the prudent even now look to its abandonment. . . . The most vexed questions of the age are social problems. These we have heretofore had but little to do with; we were relieved from them by our peculiar institution. Emancipation of the blacks, with its consequences, was ever considered by me with much more interest as a social question, one relating to the proper status of the different elements of society, and their relations toward each other, looking to the best interest of all, than in any other light. . . . This problem . . . is now

---

[3] Stephens paraphrases Luke 12:48: "For unto whomsoever much is given, of him shall be much required."

upon us, presenting one of the most perplexing questions of the sort that any people ever had to deal with. Let us resolve to do the best we can with it....

... [L]et all patriots ... rally, in all elections everywhere, to the support of him, be he who he may, who bears the standard with "Constitutional Union" emblazoned on its fold. President Johnson is now, in my judgment, the chief great standard-bearer of these principles, and in his efforts at restoration should receive the cordial support of every well-wisher of his country.

In this consists, on this rests, my only hope. Should he be sustained, and the government be restored to its former functions, all the States brought back to their practical relations under the constitution, our situation will be greatly changed from what it was before. A radical and fundamental change ... has been made in that organic law.[4] We shall have lost what was known as our "peculiar institution" which was so intertwined with the whole framework of our State body politic. We shall have lost nearly half the accumulated capital of a century. But we shall have still left all the essentials of free government, contained and embodied in the old constitution.... With these, even if we had to begin entirely anew, the prospect before us would be much more encouraging than the prospect was before them, when they fled from the oppressions of the old world, and sought shelter and homes in this then wilderness land. The liberties we begin with, they had to achieve....

The old Union was based upon the assumption, that it was for the best interest of the people of all the States to be united as they were, each State faithfully performing to the people of the other States all their obligations under the common compact. I always thought this assumption was founded upon broad, correct, and statesman-like principles. I think so yet.... And now, after the severe chastisements of war, if the general sense of the whole country shall come back to the acknowledgment of the original assumption, that it is for the best interests of all the States to be so united, as I trust it will; the States still being "separate as the billows but one as the sea;" I can perceive no reason why, under such restoration, we as a whole, with "peace, commerce, and honest friendship with all nations and entangling alliances with none,"[5] may not enter upon a new career, exciting increased wonder in the old world, by grander achievements hereafter to be made, than any heretofore attained, by the peaceful and harmonious workings of our American institutions of self-government....

---

[4] the fundamental system of laws or principles that defines the way a nation is governed
[5] a phrase from Thomas Jefferson's First Inaugural Address

Document 13

An Act to Protect All Persons in the United States in Their Civil Rights, and Furnish the Means of their Vindication
(Civil Rights Act)
April 9, 1866

An alliance between the old leaders of the South and President Andrew Johnson emerged from the reconstruction he directed. Johnson accepted every restored Southern government and liberally pardoned those who participated in the rebellion. He did not confiscate their estates. He did little to protect the freedmen. Under his direction, the South was restored but not reformed.

The Republicans elected in 1864 did not stand idly by and watch what they viewed as the squandering of the Union victory. Late in 1865 they established the Joint Committee on Reconstruction to ascertain what was going on in the South. What they learned was consistent with Carl Schurz's Report on the Condition of the South (Document 10). Most concerning to the Republicans was the complacent acceptance of an only nominal freedom for the former slaves. In February 1866, Congress passed, over Johnson's veto, a bill extending the life and increasing the powers of the Freedman's Bureau. This bill allowed the national government to continue its direct assistance to freed slaves. Republicans then saw that it was necessary to ensure that states would protect the basic civil rights of all their citizens. They took up the monumental issue of the national government protecting civil rights, the protection of which had long been considered the domain of state governments. The Senate passed the bill in February (33-12), while the House passed it in mid-March (111-38). Johnson vetoed it. But by April 9 both the House (122-41) and the Senate (33-15) overrode Johnson's veto and the bill became law. This bill exemplifies the approach to reform that came to be called Radical Reconstruction.

Source: Statutes at Large, Thirty-ninth Congress, First Session, April 9, 1866, p. 27. https://goo.gl/iHGJMQ.

Be it enacted by the Senate and House of Representatives of the United States of America in Congress assembled, That all persons born in the United States and not subject to any foreign power, excluding Indians not taxed, are hereby declared to be citizens of the United States; and such citizens, of every race and color, without regard to any previous condition of slavery or involuntary servitude, except as a punishment for crime whereof the party shall have been duly convicted, shall have the same right, in every State and Territory in the United States, to make and enforce contracts, to sue, be parties, and give evidence, to inherit, purchase, lease, sell, hold, and convey real and personal property, and to full and equal benefit of all laws and proceedings for the security of person and property, as is enjoyed by white citizens, and shall be subject to like punishment, pains, and penalties, and to none other, any law, statute, ordinance, regulation, or custom, to the contrary notwithstanding.

Sec. 2. *And be it further enacted,* That any person who, under color of any law, statute, ordinance, regulation, or custom, shall subject, or cause to be subjected, any inhabitant of any State or Territory to the deprivation of any right secured or protected by this act, or to different punishment, pains, or penalties on account of such person having at any time been held in a condition of slavery or involuntary servitude, except as a punishment for crime whereof the party shall have been duly convicted, or by reason of his color or race, than is prescribed for the punishment of white persons, shall be deemed guilty of a misdemeanor and, on conviction, shall be punished by fine not exceeding one thousand dollars, or imprisonment not exceeding one year, or both . . . .

Sec. 3. *And be it further enacted,* That the district courts of the United States . . . shall have, exclusively of the courts of the several States, cognizance of all crimes and offences committed against the provisions of this act, and also, concurrently with the circuit courts of the United States, of all causes, civil and criminal, affecting persons who are denied or cannot enforce in the courts or judicial tribunals of the State or locality where they may be any of the rights secured to them by the first section of this act. . . .

Sec. 4. *And be it further enacted,* That the district attorneys, marshals, and deputy marshals of the United States, the commissioners appointed by the circuit and territorial courts of the United States, with powers of arresting, imprisoning, or bailing offenders against the laws of the United States . . . and every other officer who may be specially empowered by the President of the United States, shall be . . . specially authorized and required, at the expense of the United States, to institute proceedings against . . . every person who shall violate the provisions of this act, and cause him or them to be arrested and imprisoned, or bailed . . . for trial before such court of the United States or territorial court as by this act has cognizance of the offence. . . .

. . .

Sec. 6. *And be it further enacted*, That any person who shall knowingly and willfully obstruct, hinder, or prevent any officer . . . charged with the execution of any warrant . . . or shall rescue or attempt to rescue such person from the custody of the officer . . . or shall aid, abet, or assist any person so arrested . . . to escape from the custody of the officer . . . or shall harbor or conceal any person for whose arrest a warrant or process shall have been issued . . . so as to prevent his discovery and arrest after notice or knowledge of the fact that a warrant has been issued for the apprehension of such person, shall . . . be subject to a fine . . . and imprisonment not exceeding six months. . . .

. . .

Sec. 8. *And be it further enacted*, That whenever the President of the United States shall have reason to believe that offences have been or are likely to be committed against the provisions of this act . . . it shall be lawful for him . . . to direct the judge, marshal, and district attorney . . . to attend at such place . . . for the purpose of the more speedy arrest and trial of persons charged with a violation of this act; and it shall be the duty of every judge or other officer, when any such requisition shall be received by him, to attend at the place and for the time therein designated.

Sec. 9. *And be it further enacted*, That it shall be lawful for the President of the United States, or such person as he may empower for that purpose, to employ such part of the land or naval forces of the United States, or of the militia, as shall be necessary to prevent the violation and enforce the due execution of this act.

Sec. 10. *And be it further enacted*, That upon all questions of law arising in any cause under the provisions of this act a final appeal may be taken to the Supreme Court of the United States.

Document 14

Congressional Debate on the 14th Amendment
February – May, 1866

As Republicans were passing the Civil Rights Act of 1866 (Document 13), they were concerned to make sure that its protection for freedmen would be secure within the Constitution. The 13th Amendment did not seem to provide Congress with sufficient new powers to protect freedmen and others from the black codes (Document 8) and unequal enforcement of the laws happening under Johnson's restored state governments. How could the U.S. Constitution be amended to ensure that the state governments provided justice and the protection of rights to all citizens? As the Supreme Court had ruled in Barron v. Baltimore (1833), the original ten amendments to the Constitution limited the power only of Congress, leaving the states free to violate the rights protected in the Bill of Rights or to honor them only with regard to some of their citizens. The issue of protecting the freedmen from state abuses and neglect thus became part of larger deliberations among Republicans about how to correct this defect in the constitutional system. How could the national government protect the rights of individual citizens?

Representative John Bingham (1815-1900), a Republican from Ohio and the principal sponsor of the 14th amendment, first brought it to the floor in February, 1866. Action on it was postponed after Republicans became leery of its language (reproduced below as part of the speeches on the Amendment), and Congress's attention turned to the Civil Rights Act. Once that act passed in April 1866, Bingham turned to winning support for a revised amendment that would support the Civil Rights Act specifically and, more broadly, fix what Republicans saw as the defect in the original Constitution. The debates from February and April illuminate the approach to protecting rights found in the 14th Amendment. The amendment cleared the Senate on June 8, 1866 (33-11) and the House on June 13, 1866 (120-32). It was ratified by three-quarters of the state legislatures on July 28, 1868. Below, selected speeches from key actors in the 14th Amendment debates are presented after excerpts from amendment in its final adopted form.

Source: *14th Amendment*, Statutes at Large, 39th Congress, 1st Session, 358–59, https://goo.gl/TraZUU; *Congress Debates the 14th Amendment*, Congressional Globe, 39th Congress, 1st Session, pp. 1083, 1095, 2459, 2462, 2542, 2765.

14th Amendment

Section 1. All persons born or naturalized in the United States, and subject to the jurisdiction thereof, are citizens of the United States and of the state wherein they reside. No state shall make or enforce any law which shall abridge the privileges or immunities of citizens of the United States; nor shall any state deprive any person of life, liberty, or property, without due process of law; nor deny to any person within its jurisdiction the equal protection of the laws.

Section 2. Representatives shall be apportioned among the several states according to their respective numbers, counting the whole number of persons in each state, excluding Indians not taxed. But when the right to vote at any election for the choice of electors for President and Vice President of the United States, Representatives in Congress, the executive and judicial officers of a state, or the members of the legislature thereof, is denied to any of the male inhabitants of such state . . . and citizens of the United States, or in any way abridged, except for participation in rebellion, or other crime, the basis of representation therein shall be reduced in the proportion which the number of such male citizens shall bear to the whole number of male citizens twenty-one years of age in such state.

Section 3. No person shall be a Senator or Representative in Congress, or elector of President and Vice President, or hold any office, civil or military, under the United States, or under any state, who, having previously taken an oath, as a member of Congress, or as an officer of the United States, or as a member of any state legislature, or as an executive or judicial officer of any state, to support the Constitution of the United States, shall have engaged in insurrection or rebellion against the same, or given aid or comfort to the enemies thereof. But Congress may by a vote of two-thirds of each House, remove such disability.

. . .

Section 5. The Congress shall have power to enforce, by appropriate legislation, the provisions of this article.

Key Speeches on the 14th Amendment

[Representative John Bingham proposed the following Amendment to the Constitution in February.]

"The Congress shall have the power to make all laws necessary and proper to secure to citizens of each state all privileges and immunities of citizens in the several states, and to all persons in the several states equal protection of life, liberty and property."[1]

[Representative Giles W. Hotchkiss, R-NY (1815-1878) moved that Congress postpone consideration of this amendment on February 28, 1866.]

Mr. HOTCHKISS. My excuse for detaining the House is simply that I desire to explain why I shall vote [to postpone consideration, which] may be regarded as inconsistent with my usual votes in this House.

I have no doubt that I desire to secure every privilege and every right to every citizen in the United States that the gentleman who reports this resolution desires to secure. As I understand it, [*Representative Bingham's*] object in offering this resolution and proposing this amendment is to provide that no State shall discriminate between its citizens and give one class of citizens greater rights than it confers upon another. If this amendment secured that, I should vote very cheerfully for it today; but as I do not regard it as permanently securing these rights, I shall vote to postpone its consideration until there can be a further conference between the friends of the measure, and we can devise some means whereby we shall secure these rights beyond a question.

I understand the amendment as now proposed by its terms to authorize Congress to establish uniform laws throughout the United States upon the subject named, the protection of life, liberty, and property. I am unwilling that Congress shall have any such power. Congress already has the power to establish a uniform rule of naturalization and uniform laws upon the subject of bankruptcy. That is as far as I am willing that Congress shall go. The object of a Constitution is not only to confer power upon the majority, but to restrict the power of the majority and to protect the rights of the minority. It is not indulging in imagination to any great stretch to suppose that we may have a Congress here who would establish such rules in my State as I should be unwilling to be governed by. Should the power of this Government, as the gentleman from

---

[1] *Congressional Globe*, 39th Congress, 1st Session, p. 1083. https://goo.gl/j9q7mE

Ohio fears, pass into the hands of the rebels, I do not want rebel laws to govern and be uniform throughout this Union.

Mr. BINGHAM. The gentleman will pardon me. The amendment is exactly in the language of the Constitution; that is to say, it secures to the citizens of each of the States all the privileges and immunities of citizens of the several States. It is not to transfer the laws of one State to another State at all. It is to secure to the citizen of each State all the privileges and immunities of citizens of the United States in the several States. If the State laws do not interfere, those immunities follow under the Constitution.

Mr. HOTCHKISS. Constitutions should have their provisions so plain that it will be unnecessary for courts to give construction to them; they should be so plain that the common mind can understand them.

The first part of this amendment to which the gentleman alludes, is precisely like the present Constitution; it confers no additional powers. It is the latter clause wherein Congress is given the power to establish these uniform laws throughout the United States. Now, if the gentleman's object is, as I have no doubt it is, to provide against a discrimination to the injury or exclusion of any class of citizens in any State from the privileges which other classes enjoy, the right should be incorporated into the Constitution. It should be a constitutional right that cannot be wrested from any class of citizens, or from the citizens of any State by mere legislation. But this amendment proposes to leave it to the caprice of Congress; and your legislation upon the subject would depend upon the political majority of Congress, and not upon two thirds of Congress and three fourths of the States.

Now, I desire that the very privileges for which the gentleman is contending shall be secured to the citizens; but I want them secured by a constitutional amendment that legislation cannot override. Then if the gentleman wishes to go further, and provide by laws of Congress for the enforcement of these rights, I will go with him.

. . . . Place these guarantees in the Constitution in such a way that they cannot be stripped from us by any accident, and I will go with the gentleman.

Mr. Speaker, I make these remarks because I do not wish to be placed in the wrong upon this question. I think the gentleman from Ohio [Mr. BINGHAM] is not sufficiently radical in his views upon this subject. I think he is a conservative. [Laughter.] I do not make the remark in any offensive sense. But I want him to go to the root of this matter.

His amendment is not as strong as the Constitution now is. The Constitution now gives equal rights to a certain extent to all citizens. This amendment provides that Congress may pass laws to enforce these rights. Why not provide by an amendment to the Constitution that no State shall discriminate against any class of its citizens; and let that amendment stand as a part of the organic law of the land, subject only to be defeated by another constitutional amendment. We may pass laws here to-day, and the next Congress may wipe them out. Where is your guarantee then?

Let us have a little time to compare our views upon this subject, and agree upon an amendment that shall secure beyond question what the gentleman desires to secure. It is with that view, and no other, that I shall vote to postpone this subject for the present.

[Congress rejected a call to table the amendment but agreed to postpone consideration by a 110-37 vote.[2] On April 30, 1866, members of the Joint Committee on Reconstruction reported to Congress a new 14th Amendment, substantially the same as the final amendment. Debate began a week later.]

May 8, 1866

Representative Thaddeus Stevens, R-PA:

... I can hardly believe that any person can be found who will not admit that every one of these provisions is just. They are all asserted, in some form or other, in our DECLARATION or organic law.[3] But the Constitution limits only the action of Congress, and is not a limitation on the States. This amendment supplies that defect, and allows Congress to correct the unjust legislation of the States, so far that the law which operates upon one man shall operate *equally* upon all. Whatever law punishes a white man for a crime shall punish the black man precisely in the same way and to the same degree. Whatever law protects the white man shall afford "equal" protection to the black man. Whatever means of redress is afforded to one shall be afforded to all. Whatever law allows the white man to testify in court shall allow the man of color to do the same. These are great advantages over their present codes. Now, different degrees of punishment are inflicted, not on account of the magnitude of the crime, but according to the color of the skin. Now, color disqualifies a man from testifying in courts, or being tried in the same way as white men. I need not enumerate

---

[2] Tabling would have effectively killed the bill, but postponing consideration meant that it would come up in Congress without a return to the committee.

[3] By "organic law," Stevens refers to the fundamental law of the US, written or unwritten. He seems to view the Declaration as establishing this fundamental law later established in the Constitution.

these partial and oppressive laws. Unless the Constitution should restrain them those States will all, I fear, keep up this discrimination, and crush to death the hated freedmen....

Rep. James Garfield, R-OH:
... I am glad to see this first section here which proposes to hold over every American citizen, without regard to color, the protecting shield of law. The gentleman who has just taken his seat [Mr. FINCK, D-OH] undertakes to show that because we propose to vote for this section we therefore acknowledge that the civil rights bill was unconstitutional. He was anticipated in that objection by the gentleman from Pennsylvania, [Mr. STEVENS]. The civil rights bill is now a part of the law of the land. But every gentleman knows it will cease to be a part of the law whenever the mad moment arrives when that gentleman's party comes into power. It is precisely for that reason that we propose to lift that great and good law above the reach of political strife, beyond the reach of the plots and machinations of any party.... For this reason, and not because I believe the civil rights bill unconstitutional, I am glad to see that first section here....

May 10, 1866

Representative John Bingham:
... The necessity for the first section of this amendment to the Constitution, Mr. Speaker, is one of the lessons that have been taught to your committee and taught to all the people of this country by the history of the past four years of terrific conflict – that history in which God is, and in which He teaches the profoundest lessons to men and nations. There was a want hitherto, and there remains a want now, in the Constitution of our country, which the proposed amendment will supply. What is that? It is the power in the people, in the whole people of the United States, by express authority of the Constitution to do that by congressional enactment which hitherto they have not had the power to do, and have never even attempted to do; that is, to protect by national law the privileges and immunities of all the citizens of the Republic and the inborn rights of every person within its jurisdiction whenever the same shall be abridged or denied by the unconstitutional acts of any State.

... This amendment takes from no State any right that ever pertained to it. No State ever had the right, under the forms of law or otherwise, to deny to any freeman the equal protection of the laws or to abridge the privileges or immunities of any citizen of the Republic, although many of them have assumed and exercised the power, and that without remedy....

May 23, 1866

Senator Jacob Howard, R-MI:
... It will be observed that this is a general prohibition upon all the States, as such, from abridging the privileges and immunities of the citizens of the United States. That is its first clause, and I regard it as very important. It also prohibits each one of the States from depriving any person of life, liberty, or property without due process of law, or denying to any person within the jurisdiction of the State the equal protection of its laws.

The first clause of this section relates to the privileges and immunities of citizens of the United States as such, and as distinguished from all other persons not citizens of the United States. It is not, perhaps, very easy to define with accuracy what is meant by the expression, "citizen of the United States."... A citizen of the United States is held by the courts to be a person who was born within the limits of the United States and subject to their laws....

It would be a curious question to solve what are the privileges and immunities of citizens of each of the States in the several States. I do not propose to go at any length into that question at this time.... [I]t is certain the clause was inserted in the Constitution for some good purpose.... [W]e may gather some intimation of what probably will be the opinion of the judiciary by referring to a case adjudged many years ago in one of the circuit courts of the United States by Judge [Bushrod] Washington.[4] ... It is the case of *Corfield vs. Coryell*.... Judge Washington says: ...

> The inquiry is, what are the privileges and immunities of citizens in the several States? We feel no hesitation in confining these expressions to those privileges and immunities which are in their nature fundamental, which belong of right to the citizens of all free Governments, and which have at all times been enjoyed by the citizens of the several States which compose this Union from the time of their becoming free, independent, and sovereign. What these fundamental principles are it would, perhaps, be more tedious than difficult to enumerate. They may, however, be all comprehended under the following general heads: protection by the Government, the enjoyment of life and liberty, with the

---

[4] Bushrod Washington (1762-1829) was an Associate Justice of the Supreme Court from 1798 through 1829 and a nephew of George Washington.

right to acquire and possess property of every kind, and to pursue and obtain happiness and safety, subject nevertheless to such restraints as the Government may justly prescribe for the general good of the whole. The right of a citizen of one State to pass through or to reside in any other State, for purposes of trade, agriculture, professional pursuits, or otherwise; to claim the benefit of the writ of *habeas corpus*; to institute and maintain notions of any kind in the courts of the State; to take, hold, and dispose of property, either real or personal, and an exemption from higher taxes or impositions than are paid by the other citizens of the State, may be mentioned as some of the particular privileges and immunities of citizens which are clearly embraced by the general description of privileges deemed to be fundamental, to which may be added the elective franchise, as regulated and established by the laws or constitution of the State in which it is to be exercised....

Such is the character of the privileges and immunities spoken of in the second section of the fourth article of the Constitution. To these privileges and immunities, whatever they may be – for they are not and cannot be fully defined in their entire extent and precise nature – to these should be added the personal rights guaranteed and secured by the first eight amendments of the Constitution; such as the freedom of speech and of the press; the right of the people peaceably to assemble and petition the Government for a redress of grievances, a right appertaining to each and all the people; the right to keep and to bear arms; the right to be exempted from the quartering of soldiers in a house without the consent of the owner; the right to be exempt from unreasonable searches and seizures, and from any search or seizure except by virtue of a warrant issued upon a formal oath or affidavit; the right of an accused person to be informed of the nature of the accusation against him, and his right to be tried by an impartial jury of the vicinage; and also the right to be secure against excessive bail and against cruel and unusual punishments....

Document 15

"The One Man Power vs. Congress!"
Senator Charles Sumner
October 2, 1866

The first stages of what came to be known as Radical Republicanism included the Civil Rights Act of 1866 (Document 13) and the 14th Amendment (Document 14). As these measures were debated and passed, race riots in Memphis during May and in New Orleans in July killed scores of blacks. State governments did little to find those guilty of the crimes. President Andrew Johnson spoke vociferously against the civil rights measures in the run up to the midterm elections of 1866, and he did not execute these important laws with zeal or efficiency. The Republicans took their case to the people in the elections of 1866 and won a decisive victory. With their veto-proof majorities in both the House and the Senate, the Republicans sought to expand and deepen Reconstruction in the South with the aim of better securing civil rights and making race riots a thing of the past. In time, Republicans would pass Reconstruction acts (Document 17) that superseded the existing Southern governments brought back under Johnson's plan (Documents 6 and 9). They acted so that rebels would have less of a place in the new order. They also extended the franchise to blacks in Washington D.C. and tried to end state racial discrimination in voting (Document 22). Many other more extensive proposals were made.

Still, Johnson would be the one to implement any laws and his heart was clearly not in it. Something had to be done about his dogged opposition to Reconstruction, or so Republicans thought. This line of criticism would, a year or so later, lead to Johnson's impeachment. For now, Charles Sumner (1811-1874) Republican Senator of Massachusetts, long one of the chief advocates in the Senate for emancipation, extended his criticisms of Johnson in a speech to the people of Boston in the fall of 1866.

Source: Charles Sumner, "The One Man Power vs. Congress!" Address of the Honorable Charles Sumner at the Music Hall, Boston, October 2, 1866 (Boston: Wright & Potter, State Printers, 1866). Available at https://goo.gl/E4npRT.

It is now more than a year since I last had the honor of addressing my fellow-citizens of Massachusetts. On that occasion, I dwelt on what seemed to be the proper policy towards the States recently in rebellion – insisting that it was our duty ... to obtain at least security for the future; and this security ... could be found only in the exclusion of ex-rebels from political power, and in irreversible guarantees especially applicable to ... the freedman. During the intervening months, the country has been agitated by this question, which was perplexed by an unexpected difference between the President and Congress. The President insists upon installing ex-rebels in political power, and sets at naught the claim of guarantees and the idea of security for the future, while he denies to Congress any control over this question, and takes it all to himself. Congress has asserted its control, and has endeavored to shut out ex-rebels from political power and to establish guarantees, to the end that there might be security for the future. Meanwhile, the States recently in rebellion, with the exception of Tennessee, are without representation in Congress. Thus stands the case.

The Two Parties in the Controversy

The two parties in the controversy are the President on the one side, and the people of the United States in Congress assembled on the other side.... It is the *One Man Power* vs. *Congress*. Of course, each of these performs its part in the government; but, until now, it has always been supposed that the Legislative *gave the law* to the Executive, and not that the Executive *gave the law* to the Legislative. Perhaps this irrational assumption becomes more astonishing when it is considered that the actual President, besides being the creature of an accident, is inferior in ability and character, while the House of Representatives is eminent in both respects.... Thus, in looking at the parties, we are tempted to exclaim: Such a President dictating to such a Congress! ...

Irreversible Guarantees Must Be Had

The question at issue is one of the vastest ever presented for practical decision.... It is a question of statesmanship. We are to secure by counsel what was won by war. Failure now will make the war itself a failure; surrender now will undo all our victories....

... [T]oday, I protest again against any admission of ex-rebels to the great partnership of this Republic, and I renew the claim of irreversible guarantees especially applicable to the national creditor and the national freedman.... Our first duty is to provide safeguards for the future. This can be only by provisions ... which shall fix forever the results of the war – the obligations of government – and the equal rights of all. Such is the suggestion of common prudence and of self-defense.... States which precipitated themselves out of Congress must not be permitted to precipitate themselves back. They must not be allowed to enter those halls which they treasonably deserted, until we have every reasonable assurance of future good conduct....

A Lost Opportunity

From all quarters we learn that after the surrender of Lee, the rebels were ready for any terms, if they could escape with their lives. They were vanquished, and they knew it.... Had the national government merely taken advantage of this plastic condition, it might have stamped Equal Rights upon the whole people, as upon molten wax, while it fixed the immutable conditions of permanent peace. The question of reconstruction would have been settled before it arose. It is sad to think that this was not done. Perhaps in all history there is no instance of such an opportunity lost....

The Presidential Policy Founded on Two Blunders

Glance, if you please, at that Presidential Policy ... and you will find that it pivots on at least two alarming blunders ... *first*, in setting up the *One Man Power*, as the source of jurisdiction over this great question; and *secondly*, in using the *One Man Power* for the restoration of rebels to place and influence, so that good Unionists, whether white or black, are rejected, and the rebellion itself is revived in the new governments....

The One Man Power

[First]... [T]he President has assumed legislative power, even to the extent of making laws and constitutions for States. You all know that at the close of the war, when the rebel states were without lawful governments, he assumed to supply them. In this business of reconstruction he assumed to determine who should vote, and also to affix conditions for adoption by the conventions....

... [I]t is one thing to govern a State temporarily by military power, and quite another thing to create a constitution for a State which shall continue *when the military power has expired*. The former is a military act, and belongs to the President. The latter is a civil act, and belongs to Congress. On this distinction I stand....

Giving Power to Ex-Rebels

The other blunder is ... giving power to ex-rebels, at the expense of constant Unionists, white or black, and employing them in the work of reconstruction, so that the new governments continue to represent the rebellion....

... [T]he President began his work of reconstruction by appointing civilians to an office absolutely unknown to the law, when besides they could not take the required oath of office; and to complete the disregard of Congress he fixed their salary and paid it out of the funds of the War Department....

... From top to bottom these States were organized by men who had been warring on their country. Ex-rebels were appointed by the governor or chosen by the people everywhere. Ex-rebels sat in conventions and in legislatures. Ex-rebels became judges, justices of the peace, sheriffs and everything else, while the faithful Unionist, white or black, was rejected....

Partisans of the Presidential "policy" are in the habit of declaring that it is a continuation of the policy of the martyred Lincoln. This is a mistake. Would that he could rise from his bloody shroud to repel the calumny! But he has happily left his testimony behind, in words which all who have ears to hear can hear. On one occasion the martyr presented the truth bodily when he said, in a suggestive metaphor, that we must "build up from the sound material;"[1] but his successor insists upon building from materials rotten with treason and gaping with rebellion. On another occasion the martyr said that "an attempt to guarantee and protect a *revived* State government, constructed in whole or in *preponderating part* from the *very element* against whose hostility and violence it is to be protected, is *simply absurd.*"[2] But this is the very thing which the President is now attempting. He is constructing State governments, not merely in preponderating part, *but in whole* from the hostile element. Therefore, he departs openly from the policy of the martyred Lincoln....

The President Inconsistent With Himself.

Such are two pivotal blunders of the President. It is not easy to see how he has fallen into these – so strong were his early professions the other way. The powers of Congress he had distinctly admitted. Thus, as early as 24th July, 1865, he had sent to Sharkey, acting by his appointment as Provisional Governor of Mississippi, this despatch: "It must, however, be distinctly understood, that the restoration to which your proclamation refers will be subject to the will of

---

[1] We have not identified the source of this Lincoln quotation. It may be a reference to the Lyceum Address.
[2] Abraham Lincoln, Third Annual Message, December 8, 1863.

Congress." ... He was equally positive against the restoration of rebels to power. You do not forget that, in accepting his nomination as Vice-President, he rushed forward to declare that the rebel States must be remodelled; that confiscation must be enforced, and that rebels must be excluded from the work of reconstruction. His language was plain and unmistakable. Announcing that "government must be fixed on the principles of eternal justice" he went on to declare, that, "if the man who gave his influence and his means to destroy the government should be permitted to participate in the great work of reorganization, then all the precious blood so freely poured out will have been wantonly spilled, and all our victories go for naught." . . . Then, in words of surpsising energy, he cried out, that "the great plantations must be seized and divided into small farms," and that "traitors should take a back seat in the work of restoration." . . .

How the President Fell

. . . Then ensued a strange sight. Instead of faithful Unionists, recent rebels thronged the Presidential ante-chambers, rejoicing in a new-found favor. They made speeches at the President, and he made speeches at them. A mutual sympathy was manifest. On one occasion the President announced himself a "Southern man," with "Southern sympathies," thus quickening that sectional flame which good men hoped to see quenched forever. . . . Instead of telling the ex-rebels that thronged the Presidential ante-chambers, as he should have done, that he was their friend ; that he wished them well from the bottom his heart; that he longed to see their fields yield an increase and peace in all their borders, and that, to this end, he counselled them to devote themselves to agriculture, commerce and manufactures, and for the present to say nothing about politics;—instead of this, he sent them away talking and thinking of nothing but politics, and frantic for the re-establishment of a sectional power. Instead of designating officers of the army as military governors, which I had supposed he would do, he appointed ex-rebels, who could not take the oath required by Congress of all officers of the United States, and they in turn appointed ex-rebels to office under them, so that participation in the rebellion found its reward, and treason, instead of being made odious, became a passport to power. . . .

The Presidential Madness

. . . The evil that he has done already is on such a scale that it is impossible to measure it, unless as you measure an arc of the globe. I doubt if in all history there is any ruler, who in the same brief space of time has done so much. There have been kings and emperors, proconsuls and satraps, who have exercised a tyrannical power; but the facilities of communication now lend swiftness and extension to all evil influences, so that the President has been able to do in a year what in other days would have taken a life. Nor is the evil that he has done confined to any narrow spot. It is co-extensive with the Republic. Next to Jefferson Davis stands Andrew Johnson as its worst enemy. The whole has suffered; but it is the rebel region which has suffered most. He should have sent peace; instead, he sent a sword. . . .

What Remains To Be Done

. . . [L]et me tell you plainly what must be done. In the first place, Congress must be sustained in its conflict with the *One Man Power*, and in the second place, ex-rebels must not be restored to power. Bearing these two things in mind the way will be easy. Of course, the constitutional amendment must be adopted. As far as it goes, it is well; but it does not go far enough. More must be done. Impartial suffrage must be established.[3] A homestead must be secured to every freedman . . . If to these is added education, there will be a new order of things, with liberty of the press, liberty of speech and liberty of travel. . . . Our present desires may be symbolized by four "E's," standing for *Emancipation, Enfranchisement, Equality and Education.* Let these be secured and all else will follow. . . .

Impartial Suffrage Must Be Secured by the Nation and Not Left to the States

You are aware, that from the beginning I have insisted upon impartial suffrage as the only certain guarantee of security and reconciliation. I renew this persistence and mean to hold on to the end. Every argument, every principle, every sentiment is in its favor. But there is one reason, which at this moment I place above all others; it is the *necessity of the case.* You will require the votes of colored persons in the rebel States in order to sustain the Union itself. Without their votes you cannot build securely for the future. . . . Give the ballot to the colored citizen and he will be not only assured in his own rights, but he will be the timely defender of yours. . . .

But it is said, leave this question to the States; and State rights are pleaded against the power of Congress. This has been the cry – at the beginning to

---

[3] Sumner refers to the 14th Amendment (Document 14), not yet ratified in October 1866, and what would become the 15th Amendment guaranteeing that the right to vote will not be abridged "on account of race, color or previous condition of servitude." See Document 22.

prevent efforts against the Rebellion, and now, at the end, to prevent efforts against the revival of the Rebellion....

But there are powers of Congress, not derived from the rebellion, which are adequate to this exigency, and now is the time to exercise them and thus complete the work that has been begun. It was the nation that decreed emancipation, and the nation must see to it, by every obligation of honor and justice, that emancipation is secured. It is not enough that slavery is abolished in name. The Baltimore platform, on which President Johnson was elected, requires "the utter and complete extirpation of Slavery from the soil of the Republic ;" but his can be accomplished only by the eradication of every inequality and caste, so that all shall be equal before the law....

. . . Surely it is not natural to suppose that people, who have claimed property in their fellow-men – who have indulged that wild and guilty fantasy that man can hold property in man – will become at once the kind and just legislators of freedmen. It is contrary to nature to expect it. Even if they have made up their minds to emancipation, they are, from inveterate habit and prejudice, incapable of doing justice to the colored race. . . . People do not change suddenly or completely....

I claim this power for the nation. If it be said that the power has never been exercised, then, I say, that the time has come when it should be exercised. I claim it on at least three several grounds.

(1.) There is the *Constitutional Amendment*.[4] . . . Every argument . . . by which you assert the power for the protection of colored person in what are called their *civil* rights, is equally strong for their protection in what are called their *political* rights. In each case you legislate to the same end, that the freedman may be maintained in that liberty which has so tardily been accorded to him, and the legislation is just as "appropriate" in one case as in the other.

(2.) There is also that distinct clause of the Constitution, requiring the United States "to guarantee to every State in the Union a *republican form of government."* . . . Let it be declared, that a State which disfranchises any portion of its citizens by a discrimination in its nature insurmountable, as in the case of color, cannot be considered a republican government. The principle is obvious, and its practical adoption would ennoble the country and give to mankind a new definition of republican government.

(3.) But there is another reason which is with me peremptory. There is no discrimination of color in the allegiance which you require. Colored citizens,

---

[4] Sumner refers to an amendment protecting the vote, what would become the 15th Amendment. See Document 22.

like white citizens, owe allegiance to the United States; therefore, they may claim protection as an equivalent. In other words, allegiance and protection must be reciprocal....

In this cause I cannot be frightened by words. There is a cry against "centralization," "consolidation," "imperialism," all of which are bad enough when dedicated to any purpose of tyranny. As the House of Representatives is renewed every two years, it is inconceivable to suppose that such a body ... can become a tyranny, especially when it seeks safeguards for Human Rights.... There can be no danger in Liberty assured by central authority; nor can there be any danger in any powers to uphold Liberty. Such a centralization, such a consolidation – aye, Sir, such an imperialism would be to the whole country a well-spring of security, prosperity and renown. To find danger in it is to find danger in the Declaration of Independence and the Constitution itself, which speaks with central power; it is to find danger in those central laws which govern the moral and material world, binding men together in society and keeping the planets wheeling in their spheres....

Document 16

Speech on Reconstruction
Thaddeus Stevens
January 3, 1867

Republicans won veto-proof majorities in both Houses of Congress in the 1866 elections. Seeing this victory as support, within limits, of their approach to reconstruction, a leading radical Republican, Representative Thaddeus Stevens (R-PA; 1792-1868), took the floor of the House of Representatives to outline his vision of Reconstruction and to support the Reconstruction Acts (Document 17) that Congress was considering. Like Senator Charles Sumner (Document 15), Stevens was pushing for national efforts beyond the Civil Rights Act of 1866 (Document 13) and the 14th Amendment (Document 14).

Source: Congressional Globe, 39th Cong., 2nd sess., Jan. 3, 1867, pp. 251-253. Available at A Century of Lawmaking for a New Nation: U.S. Congressional Documents and Debates, 1774–1875, American Memory, an online collection of the Library of Congress, https://goo.gl/uiPKjL.

... This is a bill designed to enable loyal men, so far as I could discriminate them in these States, to form governments which shall be in loyal hands, that they may protect themselves from ... outrages ... In states that have never been restored since the rebellion from a state of conquest, and which are this day held in captivity under the laws of war, the military authorities, under this decision and its extension into disloyal states, dare not order the commanders of departments to enforce the laws of the country....

Since the surrender of the armies of the confederate States of America a little has been done toward establishing this Government upon the true principles of liberty and justice.... But in what have we enlarged their liberty of thought? In what have we taught them the science and granted them the privilege of self-government? ... Call you this a free Republic when four millions are subjects but not citizens? ... I pronounce it no nearer to a true Republic now when twenty-five million of a privileged class exclude five million[1] from all participation in the rights of government....

What are the great questions which now divide the nation? In the midst of the political Babel which has been produced by the intermingling of secessionists, rebels, pardoned traitors, hissing Copperheads,[2] and apostate Republicans, such a confusion of tongues is heard that it is difficult to understand either the questions that are asked or the answers that are given. Ask, what is the "President's policy?" and it is difficult to define it. Ask, what is the "policy of Congress?" and the answer is not always at hand.

A few moments may be profitably spent in seeking the meaning of each of these terms. Nearly six years ago a bloody war arose between different sections of the United States. Eleven States, possessing a very large extent of territory, and ten or twelve million people, aimed to sever their connection with the Union, and to form an independent empire, founded on the avowed principle of human slavery and excluding every free State from this confederacy.... The two powers mutually prepared to settle the question by arms....

President Lincoln, Vice President Johnson, and both branches of Congress repeatedly declared that the belligerent States could never again intermeddle with the affairs of the Union, or claim any right as members of the United States Government until the legislative power of the Government should declare them entitled thereto.... For whether their states were out of the Union as they declared, or were disorganized and "out of their proper relations" to the Government, as some subtle metaphysicians contend, their rights under the Constitution had all been renounced and abjured under oath, and could not be resumed on their own mere motion....

The Federal arms triumphed. The confederate armies and government surrendered unconditionally. The law of nations then fixed their condition. They were subject to the controlling power of the conquerors. No former laws, no former compacts or treaties existed to bind the belligerents. They had all been melted and consumed in the fierce fires of the terrible war. The United States ... appointed military provisional governors to regulate their municipal institutions until the law-making power of the conqueror should fix their

---

[1] Stevens gives two different numbers for the African American population in the South. Perhaps he refers in the latter instance to African Americans in the nation in general. The 1860 census counted about 4.5 million African Americans residing in the US. About 3.5 million of these lived in the Southern states that would secede, while a half million lived in the border states.

[2] Copperheads, or Peace Democrats, were those who had opposed war with the South.

condition and the law by which they should be permanently governed.... No one then supposed that those States had any governments, except such as they had formed under their rebel organization.... Whoever had then asserted that those States [were] entitled to all the rights and privileges which they enjoyed before the rebellion and were on a level with their loyal conquerors would have been deemed a fool....

In this country the whole sovereignty rests with the people, and is exercised through their Representatives in Congress assembled.... No Government official, from the president and the Chief Justice down, can do any one single act which is not prescribed and directed by the legislative power....

... This I take to be the great question between the President and Congress. He claims the right to reconstruct by his own power. Congress denies him all power in the matter, except those of advice, and has determined to maintain such denial....

... [President Johnson] desires that the States created by him shall be acknowledged as valid States, while at the same time he inconsistently declares that the old rebel States are in full existence, and always have been, and have equal rights with the loyal States....

Congress refuses to treat the States created by him as of any validity, and denies that the old rebel States have any existence which gives them any rights under the Constitution.... Congress denies that any State lately in rebellion has any government or constitution known to the Constitution of the United States ....

It is to be regretted that inconsiderate[3] and incautious Republicans should ever have supposed that the slight amendments already proposed to the Constitution, even when incorporated into that instrument, would satisfy the reforms necessary for the security of the Government. Unless the rebel States, before admission, should be made republican in spirit, and placed under the guardianship of loyal men, all our blood and treasure will have been spent in vain. I waive now the question of punishment which, if we are wise, will still be inflicted by moderate confiscations, both as a reproof and example. Having these States, as we all agree, entirely within the power of Congress, it is our duty to take care that no injustice shall remain in their organic laws.[4] Holding them "like clay in the hands of the potter,"[5] we must see that no vessel is made for destruction. Having now no governments, they must have enabling acts....

---

[3] over-hasty; acting without forethought
[4] the fundamental system of laws or principles that defines the way a nation is governed
[5] Jeremiah 8:16; Isaiah 64:8.

Impartial suffrage, both in electing the delegates and ratifying their proceedings, is now the fixed rule. There is more reason why colored voters should be admitted in the rebel States than in the Territories. In the States they form the great mass of the loyal men. Possibly with their aid loyal governments may be established in most of those States. Without it all are sure to be ruled by traitors; and loyal men, black and white, will be oppressed, exiled, or murdered. There are several good reasons for the passage of this bill. In the first place, it is just. I am now confining my arguments to Negro suffrage in the rebel States. Have not loyal blacks quite as good a right to choose rulers and make laws as rebel whites? In the second place, it is a necessity in order to protect the loyal white men in the seceded States. The white Union men are in a great minority in each of those States. With them the blacks would act in a body; and it is believed that in each of said States, except one, the two united would form a majority, control the States, and protect themselves. Now they are the victims of daily murder. They must suffer constant persecution or be exiled.....

Another good reason is, it would insure the ascendancy of the Union party. Do you avow the party purpose? exclaims some horror-stricken demagogue. I do. For I believe, on my conscience, that on the continued ascendancy of that party depends the safety of this great nation. If impartial suffrage is excluded in the rebel States then everyone of them is sure to send a solid rebel representative delegation to Congress, and cast a solid rebel electoral vote. They, with their kindred Copperheads of the North, would always elect the President and control Congress. While slavery sat upon her defiant throne, and insulted and intimidated the trembling North, the South frequently divided on questions of policy between Whigs and Democrats,[6] and gave victory alternately to the sections. Now, you must divide them between loyalists, without regard to color, and disloyalists, or you will be the perpetual vassals of the free-trade, irritated, revengeful South. For these, among other reasons, I am for Negro suffrage in every rebel State. If it be just, it should not be denied; if it be necessary, it should be adopted; if it be a punishment to traitors, they deserve it.

But it will be said, as it has been said, "This is Negro equality!" What is Negro equality. . .? It means . . . just this much, and no more: every man, no matter what his race or color; every earthly being who has an immortal soul, has an equal right to justice, honesty, and fair play with every other man; and the law should secure him these rights. The same law which condemns or acquits an African should condemn or acquit a white man. The same law which gives a

---

[6] The two principal parties in antebellum America, until the Republicans replaced the Whigs.

verdict in a White man's favor should give a verdict in a black man's favor on the same state of facts. Such is the law of God and such ought to be the law of man. This doctrine does not mean that a Negro shall sit on the same seat or eat at the same table with a white man. That is a matter of taste which every man must decide for himself. . . . If there be any who are afraid of the rivalry of the black man in office or in business, I have only to advise them to try and beat their competitor in knowledge and business capacity, and there is no danger that his white neighbors will prefer his African rival to himself. . . .

Document 17

Reconstruction Acts

March 2, 1867, March 23, 1867, and July 19, 1867

By the spring of 1867, Republican frustration with the governments restored under President Johnson's approach was palpable. Considering these governments illegitimate, both the House and the Senate refused to admit those elected by these restored states to their seats in Congress. Their unwillingness to give Congressional power to those they considered unreformed secessionists was accompanied by alarm at President Johnson's lax enforcement of the Civil Rights Act passed the year before. The president's delayed, minimalist enforcement of the law subverted the goals of giving aid to freedmen and protecting the civil rights of freedmen and loyalists in the South. The President seemed to be abetting the effort of the Southern states to restore the social system that prevailed before the war.

The Republicans elected in the landslides of 1864 and 1866 took a new approach. The First Reconstruction Bill (also known as "An Act to Provide More Efficient Government of the Rebel States") was passed in the waning days of the 39th Congress, and President Johnson could have pocket vetoed it as President Lincoln had pocked vetoed the Wade-Davis Bill (Document 3). Instead, President Johnson vetoed it and Congress overrode that veto (Document 18). The 40th Congress began its session on March 4 and in short order passed supplementary Reconstruction Acts empowering the United States military to accomplish additional tasks in the reconstruction of the Southern governments and adding detail to the First Reconstruction Act. These efforts attempted to bypass President Johnson as the one charged with executing the law. President Johnson vetoed both of these bills and both were overridden. This open battle between Johnson and Congressional Republicans marked a new level in executive and legislative conflict over reconstruction.

Portions of all three acts are excerpted below. Together, they constitute an ambitious interventionist approach to reconstruction.

Source: Statutes at Large, 39th Congress, Second Session, March 2, 1867, 428–29, https://goo.gl/Vwb6wM; Statutes at Large, 40th Congress, First Session, 2–4; https://goo.gl/7CXom3; Statutes at Large, 40th Congress, First Session, 14–16, https://goo.gl/4AD1kp.

An Act to Provide for the More Efficient Government of the Rebel States
March 2, 1867

WHEREAS no legal State governments or adequate protection for life or property now exists in the rebel States of Virginia, North Carolina, South Carolina, Georgia, Mississippi, Alabama, Louisiana, Florida, Texas, and Arkansas; and whereas it is necessary that peace and good order should be enforced in said States until loyal and republican State governments can be legally established: Therefore,

Be it enacted by the Senate and House of Representatives of the United States of America in Congress assembled, That said rebel States shall be divided into military districts and made subject to the military authority of the United States.
...

SEC. 2. *And be it further enacted,* That it shall be the duty of the President to assign to the command of each of said districts an officer of the army ... and to detail a sufficient military force to enable such officer to perform his duties and enforce his authority within the district to which he is assigned.

SEC. 3. *And be it further enacted,* That it shall be the duty of each officer assigned as aforesaid, to protect all persons in their rights of person and property, to suppress insurrection, disorder, and violence, and to punish, or cause to be punished, all disturbers of the public peace and criminals; and to this end he may allow local civil tribunals to take jurisdiction of and to try offenders, or, when in his judgment it may be necessary for the trial of offenders, he shall have power to organize military commissions or tribunals for that purpose, and all interference under color of State authority with the exercise of military authority under this act, shall be null and void.
...

SEC. 5. *And be it further enacted,* That when the people of any one of said rebel States shall have formed a constitution of government in conformity with the Constitution of the United States in all respects, framed by a convention of delegates elected by the male citizens of said State, twenty-one years old and upward, of whatever race, color, or previous condition, who have been resident in said State for one year previous to the day of the election, except such as may be disfranchised for participation in the rebellion or for felony at common law, and when such constitution shall provide that the elective franchise shall be enjoyed by all such persons as have the qualifications herein stated for electors of delegates, and when such constitution shall have been submitted to Congress for examination and approval, and Congress shall have approved the same, and when said State, by a vote of its legislature elected under said constitution, shall have adopted the [14th] amendment... and when said article shall have become a part of the Constitution of the United States, said State shall be declared entitled to representation in Congress, and senators and representatives shall be admitted therefrom on their taking the oath prescribed by law, and then and thereafter the preceding sections of this act shall be inoperative in said State....

SEC. 6. *And be it further enacted,* That, until the people of said rebel States shall be by law admitted to representation in the Congress of the United States, any civil governments which may exist therein shall be deemed provisional only, and in all respects subject to the paramount authority of the United States at any time to abolish, modify, control, or supersede the same....

An Act supplemental to an Act entitled "An Act to provide for the more efficient Government of the Rebel States,"... to facilitate Restoration
March 23, 1867

Be it enacted by the Senate and House of Representatives of the United States in Congress assembled, That before . . . September [1, 1867], the commanding general in each district . . . shall cause a registration to be made of male citizens of the United States, twenty-one years of age and upwards, resident in each county or parish in the State or States included in his district, which registration shall include only those persons who are qualified to vote for delegates by the [first Reconstruction act], and who shall have taken and subscribed the following oath or affirmation: "I, ___, do solemnly swear (or affirm), in the presence of Almighty God, that I am a citizen of the State of ___; that I have resided in said State for ___ months next preceding this day, and now reside in the county of ___ or the parish of ___, in said State (as the case may be); that I am twenty-one years old; that I have not been disfranchised for participation in any rebellion or civil war against the United States, nor for felony committed against the laws of any State or of the United States; that I have never been a member of any State legislature, nor held any executive or judicial office in any State and afterwards engaged in insurrection or rebellion against the United States, or given aid or comfort to the enemies thereof; . . . that I will faithfully support the Constitution and obey the laws of the United States, and will, to the best of my ability, encourage others so to do, so help me God"; which oath or affirmation may be administered by any registering officer.

SEC. 2. *And be it further enacted,* That after the completion of the registration hereby provided for in any State, at such time and places therein as the commanding general shall appoint and direct, of which at least thirty days' public notice shall be given, an election shall be held of delegates to a convention for the purpose of establishing a constitution and civil government for such State loyal to the Union....

SEC. 3. *And be it further enacted*, That at said election the registered voters of each State shall vote for or against a convention to form a constitution therefor under this act.... The persons appointed to superintend said election, and to make return of the votes given thereat, as herein provided, shall count and make return of the votes given for and against a convention; and the commanding general to whom the same shall have been returned shall ascertain and declare the total vote in each State for and against a convention. If a majority of the votes given on that question shall be for a convention, then such convention shall be held as hereinafter provided; but if a majority of said votes shall be against a convention, then no such convention shall be held under this act....

SEC. 4. *And be it further enacted*, That the commanding general of each district shall appoint as many boards of registration as may be necessary, consisting of three loyal officers or persons, to make and complete the registration, superintend the election, and make return to him of the votes, list of voters, and of the persons elected as delegates by a plurality of the votes cast at said election; and upon receiving said returns he shall open the same, ascertain the persons elected as delegates according to the returns of the officers who conducted said election, and make proclamation thereof; and if a majority of the votes given on that question shall be for a convention, the commanding general, within sixty days from the date of election, shall notify the delegates to assemble in convention, ... and said convention, when organized, shall proceed to frame a constitution and civil government according to the provisions of this act, and the act to which it is supplementary; and when the same shall have been so framed, said constitution shall be submitted by the convention for ratification to the persons registered under the provisions of this act at an election to be conducted by the officers or persons appointed or to be appointed by the commanding general ... and to be held after the expiration of thirty days from the date of notice thereof, to be given by said convention; and the returns thereof shall be made to the commanding general of the district.

SEC. 5. *And be it further enacted*, That if, according to said returns, the constitution shall be ratified by a majority of the votes of the registered electors qualified ..., the president of the convention shall transmit a copy of the same duly certified to the President of the United States, who shall forthwith transmit the same to Congress ... ; and if it shall moreover appear to Congress that the election was one at which all the registered and qualified electors in the State had an opportunity to vote freely and without restraint, fear, or the influence of fraud, and if the Congress shall be satisfied that such constitution meets the approval of a majority of all the qualified electors in the State, and if the said constitution shall be declared by Congress to be in conformity with the provisions of the act . . . , and the said constitution shall be approved by Congress, the State shall be declared entitled to representation, and senators and representatives shall be admitted therefrom. . . .

An Act supplementary to an Act entitled "An Act to provide for the more efficient Government of the Rebel States," passed on [March 2, 1867], and the Act supplementary thereto, passed on [March 23, 1867]
July 19, 1867

Be it enacted by the Senate and House of Representatives of the United States of America in Congress assembled, That it is hereby declared to have been the true intent and meaning of the act[s] of [March 2, 1867] and [March 23, 1867], that the governments then existing in the rebel States of Virginia, North Carolina, South Carolina, Georgia, Mississippi, Alabama, Louisiana, Florida, Texas, and Arkansas were not legal State governments. . . .

SEC. 2. *And be it further enacted,* That the commander of any district named in said act shall have power, subject to the disapproval of the General of the army of the United States . . . to suspend or remove from office . . . any officer or person holding or exercising . . . any civil or military office or duty in such district under any power, election, appointment or authority derived from, or granted by, or claimed under, any so-called State or the government thereof, or any municipal or other division thereof. . . .

SEC. 3. *And be it further enacted,* That the General of the army of the United States shall be invested with all the powers of suspension, removal, appointment, and detail granted in the preceding section to district commanders.

. . .

SEC. 5. *And be it further enacted,* That the boards of registration provided for in the [earlier acts] shall have power, and it shall be their duty before allowing the registration of any person, to ascertain, upon such facts or information as they can obtain, whether such person is entitled to be registered under said act, and the oath required by said act shall not be conclusive on such question, and no person shall be registered unless such board shall decide that he is entitled thereto; and such board shall also have power to examine, under oath . . . any one touching the qualification of any person claiming registration; but in every case of refusal by the board to register an applicant . . . the board shall make a note or memorandum . . . setting forth the grounds of such refusal or such striking from the list. . . .

. . .

SEC. 11. *And be it further enacted,* That all the provisions of [these acts] . . . shall be construed liberally, to the end that all the intents thereof may be fully and perfectly carried out.

Document 18

Veto of the First Reconstruction Act
President Andrew Johnson
March 2, 1867

President Andrew Johnson, opposed to the comparatively mild intervention represented in the Freedman's Bureau and the Civil Rights Act of 1866 (Document 13), took the unusual step of campaigning against the Republican Congress during the elections of 1866. He warned the country about the "Africanizing" tendencies of Republican policies and of the ways that, he believed, the Republicans were subverting the constitutional order. Nevertheless, Republicans swept to victory. Worried that their previous attempts at Reconstruction were not meeting with success, they now had veto-proof majorities with which to do something about it. The problems were manifold. First, Johnson opposed the Civil Rights Act and was lax in his administration of it. Second, riots and low-level rebellion cropped up in major southern cities such as Memphis and New Orleans, leaving dozens of freedmen dead or wounded. Third and most important, the "reconstructed" southern states refused to ratify the 14th Amendment or to act in ways generally consistent with its strictures. Voluntary or semi-voluntary reconstruction was not bettering the condition of freedmen, nor was it leading to a revival of Union sentiments. Republicans, invigorated by the electorate's rejection of Johnson, started reconstruction all over again, in a sense, with the Reconstruction Act of March 2, 1867, passed on the last day of the 39th Congress, and its progeny, passed in the first days of the 40th Congress (Document 17). These bills divided the South into five military districts, each under the supervision of a general who was charged with reconstructing the Southern constitutions to comport with the strictures of the 14th Amendments and with taking steps to allow blacks to vote. Even though the Reconstruction Acts passed Congress overwhelmingly, Johnson vetoed all of them; and Congress overrode all his vetoes. The selection below, representative of Johnson's objections to all the Reconstruction Acts, comes from his veto of the first one.

Source: Andrew Johnson, "Veto Message," March 2, 1867. Online by Gerhard Peters and John T. Woolley, The American Presidency Project, https://goo.gl/LbX7C2.

I have examined the bill "to provide for the more efficient government of the rebel States" with the care and anxiety which its transcendent importance is calculated to awaken. I am unable to give it my assent for reasons so grave that I hope a statement of them may have some influence on the minds of the patriotic and enlightened men with whom the decision must ultimately rest.

The bill places all the people of the ten States therein named under the absolute domination of military rulers; and the preamble ... declares that there exists in those States no legal governments and no adequate protection for life or property, and asserts the necessity of enforcing peace and good order within their limits. Is this true as matter of fact? ...

The provisions which these governments have made for the preservation of order, the suppression of crime, and the redress of private injuries are in substance and principle the same as those which prevail in the Northern States and in other civilized countries. . . . All the information I have on the subject convinces me that the masses of the Southern people and those who control their public acts, while they entertain diverse opinions on questions of Federal policy, are completely united in the effort to reorganize their society on the basis of peace and to restore their mutual prosperity as rapidly and as completely as their circumstances will permit.

The bill, however, would seem to show upon its face that the establishment of peace and good order is not its real object. The fifth section declares that the preceding sections shall cease to operate in any State where certain events shall have happened. . . . All these conditions must be fulfilled before the people of any of these States can be relieved from ... military domination; but when they are fulfilled, then immediately the pains and penalties of the bill are to cease, no matter whether there be peace and order or not, and without any reference to the security of life or property. . . . The military rule which it establishes is plainly to be used, not for any purpose of order or for the prevention of crime, but solely as a means of coercing the people into the adoption of principles and measures to which it is known that they are opposed, and upon which they have an undeniable right to exercise their own judgment.

I submit to Congress whether this measure is not in its whole character, scope, and object without precedent and without authority, in palpable conflict with the plainest provisions of the Constitution, and utterly destructive to those great principles of liberty and humanity for which our ancestors on both sides of the Atlantic have shed so much blood and expended so much treasure.

The ten States named in the bill are divided into five districts. For each district an officer of the Army ... is to be appointed to rule over the people; and he is to be supported with an efficient military force to enable him to perform his duties and enforce his authority. Those duties and that authority, as defined by the third section of the bill, are "to protect all persons in their rights of person and property, to suppress insurrection, disorder, and violence, and to punish or cause to be punished all disturbers of the public peace or criminals." The power thus given to the commanding officer over all the people of each district is that of an absolute monarch. His mere will is to take the place of all law. . . . He alone is permitted to determine what are rights of person or property, and he may protect them in such way as in his discretion may seem proper. It places at his free disposal all the lands and goods in his district, and he may distribute them . . . to whom he pleases. . . .

I come now to a question which is, if possible, still more important. Have we the power to establish and carry into execution a measure like this? I answer, Certainly not, if we derive our authority from the Constitution and if we are bound by the limitations which it imposes.

This proposition is perfectly clear, that no branch of the Federal Government – executive, legislative, or judicial – can have any just powers except those which it derives through and exercises under the organic law[1] of the Union. Outside of the Constitution we have no legal authority more than private citizens, and within it we have only so much as that instrument gives us. This broad principle limits all our functions and applies to all subjects. It protects not only the citizens of States which are within the Union, but it shields every human being who comes or is brought under our jurisdiction. We have no right to do in one place more than in another that which the Constitution says we shall not do at all. If, therefore, the Southern States were in truth out of the Union, we could not treat their people in a way which the fundamental law forbids.

Some persons assume that the success of our arms in crushing the opposition which was made in some of the States to the execution of the Federal laws reduced those States and all their people, the innocent as well as the guilty, to the condition of vassalage and gave us a power over them which the Constitution does not bestow or define or limit. No fallacy can be more transparent than this. Our victories subjected the insurgents to legal obedience, not to the yoke of an arbitrary despotism. . . .

Invasion, insurrection, rebellion, and domestic violence were anticipated when the Government was framed, and the means of repelling and suppressing them were wisely provided for in the Constitution; but it was not thought necessary to declare that the States in which they might occur should be expelled from the Union. Rebellions . . . occurred prior to that out of which these

---

[1] the fundamental system of laws or principles that defines the way a nation is governed

questions grow; but the States continued to exist and the Union remained unbroken....

I need not say to the representatives of the American people that their Constitution forbids the exercise of judicial power in any way but one – that is, by the ordained and established courts. It is equally well known that in all criminal cases a trial by jury is made indispensable by the express words of that instrument.... To what extent a violation of it might be excused in time of war or public danger may admit of discussion, but we are providing now for a time of profound peace, when there is not an armed soldier within our borders except those who are in the service of the Government. It is in such a condition of things that an act of Congress is proposed which, if carried out, would deny a trial by the lawful courts and juries to 9,000,000 American citizens and to their posterity for an indefinite period. It seems to be scarcely possible that anyone should seriously believe this consistent with a Constitution which declares in simple, plain, and unambiguous language that all persons shall have that right and that no person shall ever in any case be deprived of it....

The United States are bound to guarantee to each State a republican form of government.[2] Can it be pretended that this obligation is not palpably broken if we carry out a measure like this, which wipes away every vestige of republican government in ten States and puts the life, property, liberty, and honor of all the people in each of them under the domination of a single person clothed with unlimited authority?...

The purpose and object of the bill – the general intent which pervades it from beginning to end – is to change the entire structure and character of the State governments and to compel them by force to the adoption of organic laws and regulations which they are unwilling to accept if left to themselves. The Negroes have not asked for the privilege of voting; the vast majority of them have no idea what it means. This bill not only thrusts it into their hands, but compels them, as well as the whites, to use it in a particular way. If they do not form a constitution with prescribed articles in it and afterwards elect a legislature which will act upon certain measures in a prescribed way, neither blacks nor whites can be relieved from the slavery which the bill imposes upon them.

Without pausing here to consider the policy or impolicy of Africanizing the southern part of our territory, I would simply ask the attention of Congress to that manifest, well-known, and universally acknowledged rule of constitutional law which declares that the Federal Government has no jurisdiction, authority, or power to regulate such subjects for any State. To force the right of suffrage

---

[2] U.S. Constitution, Article IV, section 4.

out of the hands of the white people and into the hands of the Negroes is an arbitrary violation of this principle....

That the measure proposed by this bill does violate the Constitution in the particulars mentioned and in many other ways which I forbear to enumerate is too clear to admit of the least doubt....

It is a part of our public history which can never be forgotten that both Houses of Congress, in July, 1861, declared in the form of a solemn resolution that the war was and should be carried on for no purpose of subjugation, but solely to enforce the Constitution and laws, and that when this was yielded by the parties in rebellion the contest should cease, with the constitutional rights of the States and of individuals unimpaired.[3] This resolution was adopted and sent forth to the world unanimously by the Senate and with only two dissenting voices in the House. It was accepted by the friends of the Union in the South as well as in the North as expressing honestly and truly the object of the war. On the faith of it many thousands of persons in both sections gave their lives and their fortunes to the cause. To repudiate it now by refusing to the States and to the individuals within them the rights which the Constitution and laws of the Union would secure to them is a breach of our plighted honor for which I can imagine no excuse and to which I cannot voluntarily become a party....

---

[3] Johnson refers to the Crittenden-Johnson or War Aims Resolution, of which he was one of the sponsors. He does not mention that the Resolution was repealed in December 1861, as public opinion in the North turned against the South.

Document 19

"Damages to Loyal Men"
Representative Thaddeus Stevens
March 19, 1867

The years 1867 and 1868 marked the most creative, ambitious time for the radical Republicans. Early in March 1867 they passed, over President Andrew Johnson's veto, the Reconstruction Acts (Document 17), which imposed military rule on the defeated southern states while they engaged in new constitution making. The radicals specified what should be in these new constitutions, including the requirement to enfranchise blacks and to ratify the 14th Amendment. How far should the radicals go? This, in essence, is the issue raised in this speech by Representative Thaddeus Stevens (1792–1868). Stevens did not think a political revolution would suffice; he thought it would be necessary to restructure the southern economy so that a social revolution protecting racial equality could follow. Stevens's speech, made nearly two years after the conclusion of the war, raises the genuinely radical, fundamental question of land redistribution. Taking land from the old Confederates and redistributing it to loyal men might, he hoped, be the best way to punish traitors and reward loyalty. His proposal would take land belonging to state governments that had seceded, or to the Confederal government and lands belonging to those whose lands could be confiscated under the Confiscation Act of July 1862, and transfer the lands to freed slaves and loyal Union men.

Source: The text is taken from a copy of the speech in the Library of Congress, "Speech Of Hon. T. Stevens, of Pennsylvania, Delivered in the House Of Representatives, March 19, 1867, on the Bill (H. R. No. 20) Relative to Damages to Loyal Men, And for Other Purposes," available online at https://goo.gl/fRv68y.

... To this issue I desire to devote the small remnant of my life. I desire to make the issue before the people of my own State, and should be glad if the issue were to extend to other States. I desire the verdict of the people upon this great question.

This bill is important to several classes of people....

It is important to the loyal men, North and South, who have been plundered and impoverished by rebel raiders and rebel Legislatures:

It is important to four millions of injured, oppressed, and helpless men, whose ancestors for two centuries have been held in bondage and compelled to earn the very property, a small portion of which we propose to restore to them, and who are now destitute, helpless, and exposed to want and starvation, under the deliberate cruelty of their former masters.

It is also important to the delinquents whose property it takes as a fine – a punishment for the great crime of making war to destroy the Republic, and for prosecuting the war in violations of all the rules of civilized warfare. It is certainly too small a punishment for so deep a crime, and too slight a warning to future ages....

This bill, it seems to me, can be condemned only by the criminals and their immediate friends, and by that unmanly kind of men whose intellectual and moral vigor has melted into a fluid weakness which they mistake for mercy, and which is untempered with a single grain of justice....

I proceed to consider the bill. By the act of 17th July, 1862,[1] treason is made punishable by death or some smaller punishment, at the discretion of the court. Before punishment can be inflicted for treason or misprision of treason[2] the party must be duly convicted in a court of the United States. Not so with the balance of the bill. All the rest of that law (after the first four sections) refers to persons engaged in the belligerent army, or officially connected with the government known as the "Confederate States of America," or to those who voluntarily aided that power....

The fifth section enacts that – "To insure the speedy termination of the present rebellion, it shall be the duty of the President of the United States to cause the seizure of all the estates and property, money, stocks, credits, and effects of the persons hereinafter named in this section, and apply and use the same and the proceeds thereof for the support of the Army of the United States."

Then follow the enumeration of all the officers of the army and navy of the confederate government: all civil officers of said government; all persons engaged in the army or navy, less they laid down their arms within a given time. ...

This law is unrepealed. It is in full force, and stands on the statute-book as one of the laws which the President swore to execute. (Would to God he had obeyed his oath! Let us see that we obey ours.)

---

[1] The Second Confiscation Act
[2] concealing what one knows about an act of treason

It may be objected that the Government is stretching its powers in making such confiscations. That was a question well considered when the act of 1862 was passed.... I will briefly review some of the arguments in favor of the right. We are treating these belligerents simply as enemies, and their property as enemies' property now in the possession and power of the conqueror. By the law of nations in its most stringent provision all the property, liberty, and lives of a conquered enemy who has waged an unjust war are at the disposal of the victor. Modern civilization will seldom justify the exercise of the extreme right. The lives, the liberty, and, in most cases, the real property of the vanquished are left untouched. The property, however, of the vanquished is held in some shape liable to pay the expenses and damages sustained by the injured party.... Where there is no government capable of making terms of peace the law-making power of the conqueror must fix the terms. This gives [the conqueror] sufficient right to take just such property as it may deem proper. Where the subdued belligerent is composed of traitors, their personal crimes aggravate their belligerent offence and justify severer treatment just as a tribe of savages are treated with more rigor than civilized foes.

... The cause of the war was slavery. We have liberated the slaves. It is our duty to protect them, and provide for them while they are unable to provide for themselves. Have we not a right... "to do ourselves justice respecting the object which has caused the war," by taking lands for homesteads [for] these "objects" of the war?

Have we not a right, if we chose to go to that extent, to indemnify ourselves for the expenses and damages caused by the war?...

We could be further justified in inflicting severe penalties upon this whole hostile people as "a fierce and savage people," as an "obstinate enemy," whom it is a duty to tame and punish. Our future safety requires stern justice....

But it matters not what you may think of the efficiency of the act of July 17, 1862. The laws of war authorize us to take this property by our sovereign power – by a law now to be passed. We have a subdued enemy in our power; we have all their property and lives at our disposal. No peace has been formed. No terms of peace or of reconciliation have been yet proclaimed, unless the proclamation of the President can make peace and war. The Constitution denies him any power in either case. Then, unless Andrew Johnson be king, the terms of peace are yet to be proclaimed. Among those terms, as we have shown, we have a right to impose confiscation of all their property – to "impoverish" them, as Andrew Johnson has told us; to "divide their large farms and sell them to industrious men." This is strict law and good common sense....

... I must earnestly pray that [the provision granting land to freedmen] may not be defeated. On its success, in my judgment, depends not only the happiness and respectability of the colored race, but their very existence. Homesteads to them are far more valuable than the immediate right of suffrage, though both are their due.

Four million of persons have just been freed from a condition of dependence, wholly unacquainted with business transactions, kept systematically in ignorance of all their rights and of the common elements of education, without which none of any race are competent to earn an honest living, to guard against the frauds which will always be practiced on the ignorant, or to judge of the most judicious manner of applying their labor. But few of them are mechanics, and none of them skilled manufacturers. They must necessarily, therefore, be the servants and victims of others, unless they are made in some measure independent of their wiser neighbors. The guardianship of the Freedmen's Bureau, that benevolent institution, cannot be expected long to protect them. It encounters the hostility of the old slaveholders, whether in official or private station, because it deprives these dethroned tyrants of the luxury of despotism. In its nature it is not calculated for a permanent institution. Withdraw that protection and leave them a prey to the legislation and treatment of their former masters, and the evidence already furnished shows that they will soon become extinct, or driven to defend themselves by civil war. Withhold from them all their rights, and leave them destitute of the means of earning a livelihood, the victims of the hatred or cupidity of the rebels whom they helped to conquer, and it seems probable that the war of races might ensue which the President feared would arise from kind treatment and restoration of their rights. I doubt not that hundreds of thousands would annually be deposited in secret, unknown graves. Such is already the course of their rebel murderers; and it is done with impunity. The clearest evidence of that fact has already been shown by the testimony taken by the "Central Directory."[3] Make them independent of their old masters, so that they may not be compelled to work for them upon unfair terms, which can only be done by giving them a small tract of land to cultivate for themselves, and you remove all this danger. You also elevate the character of the freedman. Nothing is so likely to make a man a good citizen as to make him a freeholder. Nothing will so multiply the productions of the South

---

[3] "Central Directory" was a term that Andrew Johnson used to describe the Committee on Reconstruction, a committee of the 39th Congress (March, 1865 – March, 1867) formed to consider conditions in the Southern states. Stevens was a member of the Committee.

as to divide it into small farms. Nothing will make men so industrious and moral as to let them feel that they are above want and are the owners of the soil which they till. It will also be of service to the white inhabitants. They will have constantly among them industrious laborers, anxious to work for fair wages. How is it possible for them to cultivate their lands if these people were expelled? If Moses should lead or drive them into exile, or carry out the absurd idea of colonizing them, the South would become a barren waste.

Document 20

Party Platforms of 1868
Republican and Democratic Parties
May 20, 1868 and July 4, 1868

Political parties pass platforms at their quadrennial conventions as they prepare to nominate presidential candidates. Such platforms, as old as such conventions in the United States, convey a party's principles and policies, in the hopes that voters will know what each party stands for and rally to its pledged approach. Party platforms also must take into account political realities, so to a certain extent they gauge public opinion – or the direction in which public opinion is tending or can be led by party leadership. The presidential election of 1868 was the first held after the war, and each party laid out its principles and policies especially concerning Reconstruction. The Republican Party nominated General U.S. Grant (1822–1885) at its party convention in Chicago, and it generally set out to defend the Radical approach to Reconstruction contained in the Reconstruction Acts (Document 17) and to condemn the approach President Andrew Johnson had taken. The Democratic Party nominated former New York Governor Horatio Seymour (1810–1886) in New York City six weeks later. The Democrats appealed to what they called the "conservative" element in the country – those who would keep the Constitution as it was. Grant won a sweeping electoral victory in 1868, winning 214 electoral votes to Seymour's 80 and winning over 300,000 votes more than Seymour.

Source: *Republican Party Platform of 1868*, May 20, 1868. Online by Gerhard Peters and John T. Woolley, The American Presidency Project, https://goo.gl/ncuoou; *1868 Democratic Party Platform*, July 4, 1868. Online by Gerhard Peters and John T. Woolley, The American Presidency Project, https://goo.gl/eHM8id.

Republican Platform of 1868

The National Union Republican Party of the United States, assembled in National Convention, in the city of Chicago, on the 20th day of May, 1868, make the following declaration of principles:

First – We congratulate the country on the assured success of the reconstruction policy of Congress, as evinced by the adoption, in the majority of the States lately in rebellion, of constitutions securing equal civil and political rights to all, and regard it as the duty of the Government to sustain those constitutions, and to prevent the people of such States from being remitted to a state of anarchy or military rule.

Second – The guaranty by Congress of equal suffrage to all loyal men at the South was demanded by every consideration of public safety, of gratitude, and of justice, and must be maintained; while the question of suffrage in all the loyal States properly belongs to the people of those States.

...

Eighth – We profoundly deplore the untimely and tragic death of Abraham Lincoln, and regret the accession of Andrew Johnson to the Presidency, who has acted treacherously to the people who elected him and the cause he was pledged to support; has usurped high legislative and judicial functions; has refused to execute the laws; has used his high office to induce other officers to ignore and violate the laws; has employed his executive powers to render insecure the property, the peace, the liberty, and life of the citizen; has abused the pardoning power; has denounced the National Legislature as unconstitutional; has persistently and corruptly resisted, by every means in his power, every proper attempt at the reconstruction of the States lately in rebellion; has perverted the public patronage into an engine of wholesale corruption; and has been justly impeached for high crimes and misdemeanors, and properly pronounced guilty thereof by the vote of thirty-five senators.[1]

...

Thirteenth – We highly commend the spirit of magnanimity and forgiveness with which men who have served in the rebellion, but now frankly and honestly co-operate with us in restoring the peace of the country, and reconstructing the Southern State Governments upon the basis of impartial justice and equal rights, are received back into the communion of the loyal people; and we favor the removal of the disqualifications and restrictions

---

[1] The House of Representatives approved the articles of impeachment March, 1868. The Senate voted for impeachment 35-19, but this fell one vote short of the two-thirds vote required for conviction.

imposed upon the late rebels, in the same measure as the spirit of disloyalty will die out, and as may be consistent with the safety of the loyal people.

Fourteenth – We recognize the great principles laid down in the immortal Declaration of Independence as the true foundation of Democratic Government; and we hail with gladness every effort toward making these principles a living reality on every inch of American soil.

Democratic Platform of 1868

The Democratic party in National Convention assembled, reposing its trust in the intelligence, patriotism, and discriminating justice of the people; standing upon the Constitution as the foundation and limitation of the powers of the government, and the guarantee of the liberties of the citizen; and recognizing the questions of slavery and secession as having been settled for all time to come by the war, or the voluntary action of the Southern States in Constitutional Conventions assembled, and never to be renewed or reagitated; does, with the return of peace, demand,

First. Immediate restoration of all the States to their rights in the Union, under the Constitution, and of civil government to the American people.[2]

Second. Amnesty for all past political offenses, and the regulation of the elective franchise in the States, by their citizens.

...

Sixth. Economy in the administration of the government, the reduction of the standing army and navy; the abolition of the Freedmen's Bureau; and all political instrumentalities designed to secure negro supremacy; ... the repeal of all enactments for enrolling the State militia into national forces in time of peace.

...

...

In demanding these measures and reforms we arraign the Radical party for its disregard of right, and the unparalleled oppression and tyranny which have marked its career.

After the most solemn and unanimous pledge of both Houses of Congress to prosecute the war exclusively for the maintenance of the government and the preservation of the Union under the Constitution, it has repeatedly violated that most sacred pledge, under which alone was rallied that noble volunteer army which carried our flag to victory.

---

[2] When the Democratic Party passed its platform, South Carolina, Mississippi, Alabama, Georgia, Louisiana, Texas, and Virginia had not yet been re-admitted into the Union, though South Carolina, Alabama and Louisiana would be re-admitted later in July 1868.

Instead of restoring the Union, it has, so far as in its power, dissolved it, and subjected ten States, in time of profound peace, to military despotism and Negro supremacy.

It has nullified there the right of trial by jury; it has abolished the habeas corpus, that most sacred writ of liberty; it has overthrown the freedom of speech and of the press; it has substituted arbitrary seizures and arrests, and military trials and secret star-chamber inquisitions, for the constitutional tribunals; it has disregarded in time of peace the right of the people to be free from searches and seizures; it has entered the post and telegraph offices, and even the private rooms of individuals, and seized their private papers and letters without any specific charge or notice of affidavit, as required by the organic law;[3] ... it has established a system of spies and official espionage to which no constitutional monarchy of Europe would now dare to resort.... [I]t has stripped the President of his constitutional power of appointment, even of his own Cabinet....[4]

And we do declare and resolve, That ever since the people of the United States threw off all subjection to the British crown, the privilege and trust of suffrage have belonged to the several States, and have been granted, regulated, and controlled exclusively by the political power of each State respectively, and that any attempt by Congress, on any pretext whatever, to deprive any State of this right, or interfere with its exercise, is a flagrant usurpation of power, which can find no warrant in the Constitution; and if sanctioned by the people will subvert our form of government, and can only end in a single centralized and consolidated government, in which the separate existence of the States will be entirely absorbed, and an unqualified despotism be established in place of a federal union of co-equal States; and that we regard the reconstruction acts so-called, of Congress, as such an usurpation, and unconstitutional, revolutionary, and void....

That the President of the United States, Andrew Johnson, in exercising the power of his high office in resisting the aggressions of Congress upon the Constitutional rights of the States and the people, is entitled to the gratitude of the whole American people; and in behalf of the Democratic party, we tender him our thanks for his patriotic efforts in that regard.

---

[3] the fundamental set of laws and principles governing a country
[4] Congress had passed the Tenure in Office Act, which prevented the President from removing cabinet members before Congress had confirmed a successor. In this context, Congress passed such an act to keep Lincoln's pro-emancipation cabinet in place to secure the goals of Reconstruction against the wishes of Johnson. When Johnson disobeyed the act, he was impeached and nearly removed.

Upon this platform the Democratic party appeals to every patriot, including all the Conservative element, and all who desire to support the Constitution and restore the Union, forgetting all past differences of opinion, to unite with us in the present great struggle for the liberties of the people; and that to all such, to whatever party they may have heretofore belonged, we extend the right hand of fellowship, and hail all such co-operating with us as friends and brethren....

Document 21

Executive Documents on State of the Freedmen
November 20, 1868

Information about South's loyalties and about the state of the freedmen was crucial to the reconstruction efforts from the time of Carl Schurz's "Report on the Condition of the South" (Document 10). Any critique of President Andrew Johnson's policy depended, at least in part, on a demonstration that disloyal Southerners were coming to power and that they were not respecting the civil rights of freedmen. Some criticisms of the radical plans for military enforcement of Reconstruction depended on the claim that such extreme measures were unnecessary given the new loyalty among the Southerners and their willingness to accept the emancipation of the freedmen. Accurate information was, however, not easy to come by and not always accepted when it was gathered. One such source of information was Congress's Joint Committee on Reconstruction, which sent sub-committees throughout the South gathering information about conditions for freedmen and loyalists (Document 25). Another source of information was the army, which was in charge of registering voters, overseeing elections, and protecting freedmen while the Southern states were reconstructing themselves pursuant to the Reconstruction Acts (Document 17). A collection of such reports was delivered by the Secretary of War John Schofield (1831-1906), a former Union general, to Congress soon after President Ulysses S. Grant was elected in 1868 (Document 20) at the 3rd and final session of the 40th Congress. The reports detailed the conditions throughout the South. These excerpts describe Texas in the period following the war. Texas was one of three states that had not yet been re-admitted into the Union when Grant took his oath of office.

Source: Message of the President of the United States and Accompanying Documents to the Two Houses of Congress at the Commencement of the Third Session of the Fortieth Congress, Report of the Secretary of War, (Washington, DC: Government Printing Office, 1868), 705, 1051-1052.

Report of the Secretary of War

MR. PRESIDENT: I have the honor to submit a general report of the operations of this department since the last annual report of the Secretary of

War, with the reports of the chiefs of bureaus and military commanders for the same period....

The precise objects of the [secret] organizations cannot be readily explained, but seem, in this State, to be to disarm, rob, and in many cases murder Union men and negroes, and as occasion may offer, murder United States officers and soldiers; also to intimidate everyone who knows anything of the organization but who will not join it.

The civil law east of the Trinity River is almost a dead letter. In some counties the civil officers are all, or a portion of them, members of the Klan. In other counties where the civil officers will not join the Klan, or some other armed band, they have been compelled to leave their counties....

In many counties where the county officers have not been driven off, their influence is scarcely felt. What political end, if any, is aimed at by these bands I cannot say, but they attend in large bodies the political meetings (barbecues) which have been and are still being held in various parts of this State under the auspices of the democratic clubs of the different counties.

The speakers encourage their attendance, and in several counties men have been indicated by name from the speaker's stand, as those selected for murder. The men thus pointed out have no course left them but to leave their homes or be murdered on the first convenient opportunity.

The murder of Negroes is so common as to render it impossible to keep an accurate account of them.

Many of the members of these bands of outlaws are transient persons in the State, the absence of railroads and telegraphs and great length of time required to communicate between remote points facilitating their devilish purposes.

These organizations are evidently countenanced, or at least not discouraged, by a majority of the white people in the counties where the bands are most numerous. They could not otherwise exist.

I have given this matter close attention, and am satisfied that a remedy to be effective must be gradually applied and continued with the firm support of the army until these outlaws are punished or dispersed.

They cannot be punished by the civil courts until some examples by military commissions show that men can be punished in Texas for murder and kindred crimes. Perpetrators of such crimes have not heretofore, except in very rare instances, been punished in this State at all.

Free speech and a free press, as the terms are generally understood in other States, have never existed in Texas. In fact, the citizens of other States cannot appreciate the state of affairs in Texas without actually experiencing it. The official reports of lawlessness and crime, so far from being exaggerated, do not tell the whole truth.

Jefferson is the center from which most of the trade, travel, and lawlessness of eastern Texas radiate, and at this point or its vicinity there should be stationed about a regiment of troops. The recent murder at Jefferson of Hon. G. W. Smith, a delegate to the constitutional convention, has made it necessary to order more troops to that point. This movement weakens the frontier posts to such an extent as to impair their efficiency for protection against Indians, but the bold, wholesale murdering in the interior of the State seems at present to present a more urgent demand for the troops than Indian depredations. The frontier posts should, however, be re-enforced if possible, as it is not improbable that the Indians from the northwest, after having suffered defeat there, will make heavy incursions into Texas....

The educational work has been vigorously prosecuted. The measure of success attained is quite gratifying considering the obstacles that have been encountered – the poverty of the freedmen, the small amount of aid received from benevolent associations at the north, and, in the more remote sections, the prejudice and opposition of white citizens. In May the total number of schools in operation was 217, with 244 teachers and 10,971 pupils.

While the freedmen, as a class, exhibit a very general interest in religious matters, many of their habit still show the debasing influence of the slave system. Prominent among these is the want of a due appreciation of the obligations of the marriage contract. In this respect, however, their conduct is undergoing much improvement, and cases of desertion of wife and family are becoming rare.

The condition of society in the more remote and sparsely settled parishes is greatly disorganized. In some sections the treatment of the colored people has been deplorable. Outrage and crimes of every description have been perpetrated upon them with impunity. In these sections the character of the local magistracy is not as high as could be desired, and many of them have connived at the escape of offenders, while some have even participated in the outrages. In other sections lawless ruffians have overawed the civil authorities, "Vigilance Committees" and "Ku-klux Klans," disguised by night, have burned the dwellings and shed the blood of unoffending freedmen. In many cases of brutal murder brought before the civil authorities, verdicts of justifiable homicide in self-defense have been rendered. The agents of the bureau, in obedience to their instructions, have exerted all the powers confided to them for the protection of the freed people, first referring the cases to the civil officials, and then, if justice is not rendered, calling on the military authorities for their action. For a few months past the assistant commissioner reports a decrease in the number of outrages committed, and more efficient measures on the part of the civil authorities for the apprehension and punishment of the perpetrators....

The unsettled condition of this district has rendered necessary the distribution of a large military force over the State.

The commanding officers of military posts are also acting as agents of the bureau for their respective districts, so that a comparatively small force of civilian agents are on duty in this State. By these officers the operations of the bureau have been conducted as efficiently as circumstances would permit. They have power to hear and adjudicate cases to which freedmen are parties, and to impose and collect fines. Their mode of procedure has been conformed to that prescribed by State laws for justices of the peace, though their jurisdiction has not been limited by the amount in controversy. They are forbidden to receive fees for any services rendered by them. Sheriffs and constables have been directed to execute the process of the bureau. Appeal lies from the bureau agent to the assistant commissioner of the State.

The magistrates and judges of the higher courts of law are, in general, fair and impartial in the discharge of their duties, but juries in their verdicts, and in the weight they give to testimony, have almost always discriminated against the freedmen.

A fearful amount of lawlessness and ruffianism has prevailed in Texas during the past year. Armed bands styling themselves Ku-Klux, &c., have practiced barbarous cruelties upon the freedmen. Murders by the desperadoes who have long disgraced this State are of common occurrence. The civil authorities have been overawed, and, in many cases, even the bureau and military forces have been powerless to prevent the commission of these crimes. From information on file in the office of the assistant commissioner it appears that in the month of March the number of freedmen murdered was 21; of white men, 15; the number of freedmen assaulted with the intent to kill, 11; white men, 7. In July the number of freedmen murdered was 32; white men, 7. It has been estimated by reliable authority that in August 1868, there were probably 5,000 indictments pending in the State for homicide, in some of its various degrees, in most cases downright murder. Yet since the close of the war only in one solitary case (that of a freedman who was hung at Houston) has punishment to the full extent of the law been awarded.

In consequence of this condition of affairs a kind of a quiet prevails among the freed people, lacking but little in all the essentials of slavery. In the more remote districts, where bureau agents are 50 or 100 miles apart, and stations of troops still further distant, freedmen do not dare or presume to act in opposition to the will of their late masters. They make no effort to exercise rights conferred upon them by the acts of Congress, and few even of Union men are brave enough, or rather foolhardy enough, to advise them in anything antagonistic to the sentiments of the people lately in rebellion.

Document 22

The 15th Amendment
February 26, 1869 (passed)
February 2, 1870 (ratified)

States determine who can vote, for the most part, under the original Constitution of the United States. According to Article 1, Section 2, whoever can vote for the "most numerous branch of state legislatures" could vote for members of the House of Representatives. States decide who is eligible for those most numerous branches. States could, if they chose, impose voting restrictions based on property, race, sex, age and other characteristics. Soon after the Civil War, it became a question whether or not states and especially Southern states would continue to have the freedom to restrict the vote. President Abraham Lincoln seemed to imply that he favored granting of the vote to blacks in his Last Public Address (Document 5), but he stopped short of requiring such a provision in state constitutions. President Andrew Johnson opposed requiring that restored Southern governments give the vote to blacks (Document 9).

The Republican sweep of the 1866 election gave momentum to the idea of extending the vote. From early 1867, Representative Thaddeus Stevens (R-PA) favored extending the franchise to blacks and disenfranchising former rebels (Document 16). Senator Charles Sumner favored much the same scheme (Document 15). The invigorated Republican Congress took action where it could under the Constitution – in the nation's capital and in the territories. In January 1867, a bill enfranchising blacks in the District of Columbia passed over Johnson's veto. In short order, Congress extended the vote to all men in the territories. Military rule under the Reconstruction Acts (Document 17) was coming to an end in the South as President Grant took office in 1869. No longer would the military direct the politics of the South, and no longer would it provide protection for blacks. Republicans therefore approved the 15th amendment in February 1869, partly as a means to empower blacks to protect themselves with the vote.

Source: Statutes at Large, Fortieth Congress, Third Session, February 27, 1869, p. 346. https://goo.gl/zSQZPZ.

Section 1.

The right of citizens of the United States to vote shall not be denied or abridged by the United States or by any state on account of race, color, or previous condition of servitude.

Section 2.

The Congress shall have the power to enforce this article by appropriate legislation.

Document 23

The Enforcement Acts
May 31, 1870 and April 20, 1871

President Ulysses S. Grant accepted the Republican nomination for president in 1868 with the famous, ambiguous statement, "Let us have peace." After his victory, he pursued the goals of conciliating Southern whites and protecting the rights of the freed slaves. His first acts were conciliatory, urging Congress to recognize the new state governments in Southern states – Virginia, Mississippi and Texas – that had not been freed from military supervision under the Reconstruction Acts (Document 17). The recognition, Grant argued in his First Annual Message, would "close the work of reconstruction." Southerners seemed to reciprocate, beginning what was called a "new departure" of accepting the conclusions of the war and seeming to turn to other domestic issues like transportation.

Yet all was not well under these new governments and freedman rights were still insecure. The passage of the 15th Amendment (Document 22) pointed to a new way to protect the rights of freed slaves. They could protect their own rights through the ballot box: their sheer numbers would force the whites to pay attention to their interests. However, these self-governing states were not zealous in protecting the voting and civil rights of freed slaves and union men. In fact, states were so lax in protecting those rights that they allowed domestic crimes against freed slaves and union men to go unpunished and even uninvestigated. During this period, the Ku Klux Klan and kindred organizations terrorized blacks and other loyal citizens in many parts of the South (Document 21). About one-tenth of the blacks who had been members of the constitutional conventions organized under the Reconstruction Acts in 1867-1868 were murdered in the succeeding years, for instance. Republicans in Congress, with the blessing of Grant, sought to protect citizens in the South from acts of violence and intimidation through empowering the national government to protect civil rights and especially voting rights directly. The result was a series of Enforcement Acts (also known as the Ku Klux Klan Acts), which tried to identify the various ways in which criminal conspiracies threatened loyal citizens or threatened the public peace and the enforcement of the law. Such conspiratorial actions were made illegal and the President and courts allowed investigate, prosecute and try individuals for the illegal actions under this act. As the Klan changed the scope of its operations, the law and its scope expanded to capture more illegal activity. The scope of that activity can be gauged through tracing the development of these acts.

Source: Statutes at Large, *Forty First Congress, Second Session, May 31, 1870, 140–46*, https://goo.gl/Yuvqn8; Statutes at Large, *Forty Second Congress, First Session, April 20, 1871, 13–15*, https://goo.gl/gWhrko.

The Enforcement Act, 1870
An Act to enforce the Right of Citizens of the United States to vote in the several States of the Union, and for other Purposes

Be it enacted by the Senate and House of Representatives of the United States of America in Congress assembled, That all citizens of the United States who are ... qualified by law to vote at any election by the people in any State, Territory, district, county, city, parish, township ... shall be entitled and allowed to vote at all such elections without distinction of race, color, or previous condition of servitude; any constitution, law, custom, usage, or regulation of any State ... to the contrary notwithstanding.

SEC. 2. *And be it further enacted*, That if by or under the authority of the constitution or laws of any State, or the laws of any Territory, any act is or shall be required to be done as a prerequisite or qualification for voting, and by such constitution or laws persons or officers are or shall be charged with the performance of duties in furnishing to citizens an opportunity to perform such prerequisite, or to become qualified to vote, it shall be the duty of every such person and officer to give to all citizens of the United States the same and equal opportunity to perform such prerequisite, and to become qualified to vote without distinction of race, color, or previous condition of servitude; and if any such person or officer shall refuse or knowingly omit to give full effect to this section, he shall, for every such offence, forfeit and pay the sum of five hundred dollars to the person aggrieved thereby... and shall also, for every such offence, be deemed guilty of a misdemeanor, and shall, on conviction thereof, be fined not less than five hundred dollars, or be imprisoned not less than one month and not more than one year, or both, at the discretion of the court.

...

SEC. 4. *And be it further enacted*, That if any person, by force, bribery, threats, intimidation, or other unlawful means, shall hinder, delay, prevent, or obstruct, or shall combine and confederate with others to hinder, delay, prevent, or obstruct, any citizen from doing any act required to be done to qualify him to vote or from voting at any election as aforesaid, such person shall for every such offence forfeit and pay the sum of five hundred dollars to the person aggrieved thereby ... and shall, on conviction thereof, be fined not less than five hundred dollars, or be imprisoned not less than one month and not more than one year, or both, at the discretion of the court.

SEC. 5. *And be it further enacted,* That if any person shall prevent, hinder, control, or intimidate, or shall attempt to prevent, hinder, control, or intimidate, any person from exercising or in exercising by the right of suffrage, to whom right of suffrage is secured or guaranteed by the fifteenth amendment to the Constitution of the United States, by means of bribery, threats, or threats of depriving such person of employment or occupation, or of ejecting such person from rented house, lands, or other property, or by threats of refusing to renew leases or contracts for labor, or by threats of violence to himself or family, such person so offending shall be deemed guilty of a misdemeanor, and shall, on conviction thereof, be fined not less than five hundred dollars, or be imprisoned not less than one month and not more than one year, or both. . . .

SEC. 6. *And be it further enacted,* That if two or more persons shall band or conspire together, or go in disguise upon the public highway, or upon the premises of another, with intent to violate any provision of this act, or to injure, oppress, threaten, or intimidate any citizen with intent to prevent or hinder his free exercise and enjoyment of any right or privilege granted or secured to him by the Constitution or laws of the United Sates, or because of his having exercised the same, such persons shall be held guilty of felony, and, on conviction thereof, shall be fined or imprisoned, or both, . . . [and] shall. . . be thereafter ineligible to, and disabled from holding, any office or place of honor, profit, or trust crested by the Constitution or laws of the United States.

. . .

SEC. 8. *And be it further enacted,* That the district courts of the United States, within their respective districts, shall have, exclusively of the courts of the several States, cognizance of all crimes and offences committed against the provisions of this act. . .

SEC. 9. And be it further enacted, That the district attorneys, marshals, and deputy marshals of the United States. . . , and every other officer who may be specially empowered by the President of the United States, shall be, and they are hereby, specially authorized and required, at the expense of the United States, to institute proceedings against all and every person who shall violate the provisions of this act, and cause him or them to be arrested and imprisoned, or bailed, as the case may be, for trial before such court of the United States or territorial court as has cognizance of the offense. . . .

SEC. 10. And be it further enacted, That it shall be the duty of all marshals and deputy marshals to obey and execute all warrants and precepts issued under the provisions of this act, when to them directed; and should any marshal or deputy marshal refuse to receive such warrant or other process when tendered, or to use all proper means diligently to execute the same, he shall, on conviction thereof, be fined in the sum of one thousand dollars, to the use of the person deprived of the rights conferred by this act. And the better to enable the said commissioners to execute their duties faithfully ..., they are hereby authorized and empowered, within their districts ..., to appoint ... any one or more suitable persons, from time to time, to execute all such warrants and other process as may be issued by them in the lawful performance of their respective duties, and the persons so appointed to execute any warrant or process as aforesaid shall have authority to summon and call to their aid the bystanders or *posse comitatus*[1] of the proper county, or such portion of the land or naval forces of the United States, or of the militia, as may be necessary to the performance of the duty with which they are charged ....

SEC. 11. And be it further enacted, That any person who shall knowingly and willfully obstruct, hinder, or prevent any officer or other person charged with the execution of any warrant or process issued under the provisions of this act, ... or [who] shall rescue or attempt to rescue such person from the custody of the officer or other person or persons, or ... [who] shall aid, abet, or assist any persons so arrested as aforesaid, directly or indirectly, to escape from the custody of the officer or the other person legally authorized as aforesaid, or shall harbor or conceal any person for whose arrest a warrant or process shall have been issued as aforesaid ... shall, for either of said offences, be subject to a fine not exceeding one thousand dollars, or imprisonment not exceeding six months, or both ....

...

SEC. 13. And be it further enacted, That it shall be lawful for the President of the United States to employ such part of the land or naval forces of the United States, or the militia, as shall be necessary to aid in the execution of judicial process issued under this act.

...

SEC. 15. And be it further enacted, That any person who shall hereafter knowingly accept or hold any office under the United States, or any State to which he is ineligible under the third section of the fourteenth article of

---

[1] *Posse Commitatus* is the common law term for the authority of a county sheriff to conscript citizens to assist in carrying out legal duties.

amendment of the Constitution of the United States,[2] or who shall attempt to hold or exercise the duties of any such office, shall be deemed guilty of a misdemeanor against the United States, and, upon conviction thereof before the circuit or district court of the United States, shall be imprisoned not more than one year, or fined not exceeding one thousand dollars, or both...

. . . .

The Second Enforcement Act, 1871

An Act to enforce the Provisions of the Fourteenth Amendment to the Constitution of the United States, and for other Purposes

Be it enacted by the Senate and House of Representatives of the United States of America in Congress assembled, That any person who, under color of any law, statute, ordinance, regulation, custom, or usage of any State, shall subject ... any person ... to the deprivation of any rights, privileges, or immunities secured by the Constitution of the United States, any such law, statute, ordinance, regulation, custom, or usage of the State to the contrary notwithstanding, [*that person shall*] be liable to the party injured in, any action at law, suit in equity, or other proper proceeding for redress; such proceeding to be prosecuted in the several district or circuit courts of the United States ... under the provisions of [*The Enforcement Act of 1870*]...

SEC. 2. That if two or more persons within any State or Territory of the United States shall conspire together to overthrow, or to put down ... the government of the United States, or to levy war against the United States, or to oppose by force the authority of the government of the United States, or by force, intimidation, or threat to prevent, hinder, or delay the execution of any law of the United States, or by force to seize, take, or possess any property of the United States contrary to the authority thereof, or by force, intimidation, or threat to prevent any person from accepting or holding any office or trust or place of confidence under the United States, or from discharging the duties hereof, or by force, intimidation, or threat to induce any officer of the United States to leave any State, district, or place where his duties as such officer might lawfully be performed, or to injure him in his person or property on account of his lawful discharge of the duties of his office, or to injure his person while engaged in the lawful discharge of the duties of his office, or to injure his property so as to molest, interrupt, hinder, or impede him in the discharge of his

---

[2] This section excluded those who had broken an oath of office and joined a rebellion against the United States from holding office again.

official duty, or by force, intimidation, or threat to deter any party or witness in any court of the United States from attending such court, or from testifying in any matter pending in such court fully, freely, and truthfully, or to injure any such party or witness in his person or property on account of his having so attended or testified, or by force, intimidation, or threat to influence the verdict, presentment, or indictment, of any juror or grand juror in any court of the United States, or to injure such juror in his person or property on account of any verdict, presentment, or indictment lawfully assented to by him, or on account of his being or having been such juror, or shall conspire together, or go in disguise upon the public highway or upon the premises of another for the purpose, either directly or indirectly, of depriving any person or any class of persons of the equal protection of the laws, or of equal privileges or immunities under the laws, or for the purpose of preventing or hindering the constituted authorities of any State from giving or securing to all persons within such State the equal protection of the laws, or shall conspire together for the purpose of in any manner impeding, hindering, obstructing, or defeating the due course of justice in any State or Territory, with intent to deny to any citizen of the United States the due and equal protection of the laws, or to injure any person in his person or his property for lawfully enforcing the right of any person or class of persons to the equal protection of the laws, or by force, intimidation, or threat to prevent any citizen of the United States lawfully entitled to vote from giving his support or advocacy in a lawful manner towards or in favor of the election of any lawfully qualified person as an elector of President or Vice-President of the United States, or as a member of the Congress of the United States, or to injure any such citizen in his person or property on account of such support or advocacy, each and every person so offending shall be deemed guilty of a high crime, and, upon conviction thereof in any district or circuit court of the United States... having jurisdiction of similar offences, shall be punished by a fine not less than five hundred nor more than five thousand dollars, or by imprisonment, with or without hard labor, as the court may determine, for a period of not less than six months nor more than six years, as the court may determine, or by both such fine and imprisonment as the court shall determine....

SEC. 3. That in all cases where insurrection, domestic violence, unlawful combinations, or conspiracies in any State shall so obstruct or hinder the execution of the laws thereof, and of the United States, as to deprive any portion or class of the people of such State of any of the rights, privileges, or immunities, or protection, named in the Constitution and secured by this act, and the constituted authorities of such State shall either be unable to protect, or shall, from any cause, fail in or refuse protection of the people in such rights, such facts shall be deemed a denial by such State of the equal protection of the laws to which they are entitled under the Constitution of the United States; and in all such cases, . . . it shall be lawful for the President, and it shall be his duty to take such measures . . . as he may deem necessary for the suppression of such insurrection, domestic violence, or combinations . . . .

SEC. 4. That whenever in any State or part of a state the unlawful combinations named in the preceding section of this act shall be organized and armed and so numerous and powerful as to be able, by violence to either overthrow or set at defiance the constituted authorities of such State, and of the United States within such State, or when the constituted authorities are in complicity with, or shall connive at the unlawful purposes of, such powerful and armed combinations; . . . it shall be lawful for the President of the United States, when in his judgment the public safety shall require it, to suspend the privileges of the writ of habeas corpus, to the end that such rebellion may be overthrown. . . .

SEC. 5. That no person shall be a grand or petit juror in any court of the United States . . . who shall, in the judgment of the court, be in complicity with any such combination or conspiracy. . . .

SEC. 6. That any person or persons, having knowledge that any of the wrongs conspired to be done and mentioned in the second section this act are about to be committed, and having power to prevent or aid in preventing the same, shall neglect or refuse so to do, and such wrongful act shall be committed, such person or persons injured shall be liable to the person injured, or to his legal representatives, . . . for all damages caused by any such wrongful act . . . ; and such damages may be recovered in an action on the case in the proper circuit court of the United States . . . .

Document 24

Proclamation on Enforcement of the 14th Amendment
President Ulysses S. Grant
May 3, 1871

President Ulysses S. Grant issued this proclamation a few weeks after passage of what is known as the Second Enforcement Act (Document 23). The aims of the Enforcement Acts were to provide the national government with sufficient law enforcement powers to bring to justice individuals and groups who deprived their fellow citizens of their civil rights and, more specifically, their voting rights. Only if freedmen and Union men could feel confident that they could act in politics without fear of personal retribution would the vote be an effective guarantor of safety and liberty in the South. Grant understood that law enforcement would not be enough to make civil and voting rights effective. Citizens would also have to participate as jurors and witnesses, if members of the Ku Klux Klan and other groups who sought to deprive their fellow citizens of civil rights were to be charged and convicted under the law.

Source: Ulysses S. Grant: "Proclamation 199 – Enforcement of the Fourteenth Amendment to the United States Constitution" May 3, 1871. Online by Gerhard Peters and John T. Woolley, The American Presidency Project. https://goo.gl/1vQo6Y.

The act of Congress entitled "An act to enforce the provisions of the fourteenth amendment to the Constitution of the United States, and for other purposes," approved April 20, A. D. 1871, being a law of extraordinary public importance, I consider it my duty to issue this my proclamation calling the attention of the people of the United States thereto, enjoining upon all good citizens, and especially upon all public officers, to be zealous in the enforcement thereof, and warning all persons to abstain from committing any of the acts thereby prohibited.

This law of Congress applies to all parts of the United States and will be enforced everywhere to the extent of the powers vested in the Executive. But inasmuch as the necessity therefore is well known to have been caused chiefly by persistent violations of the rights of citizens of the United States by combinations of lawless and disaffected persons in certain localities lately the theater of insurrection and military conflict, I do particularly exhort the people of those parts of the country to suppress all such combinations by their own voluntary efforts through the agency of local laws and to maintain the rights of all citizens of the United States and to secure to all such citizens the equal protection of the laws.

Fully sensible of the responsibility imposed upon the executive by the act of Congress to which public attention is now called, and reluctant to call into exercise any of the extraordinary powers thereby conferred upon me except in cases of imperative necessity, I do, nevertheless, deem it my duty to make known that I will not hesitate to exhaust the powers thus vested in the executive whenever and wherever it shall become necessary to do so for the purpose of securing to all citizens of the United States the peaceful enjoyment of the rights guaranteed to them by the Constitution and laws.

It is my earnest wish that peace and cheerful obedience to law may prevail throughout the land and that all traces of our late unhappy civil strife may be speedily removed. These ends can be easily reached by acquiescence in the results of the conflict, now written in our Constitution, and by the due and proper enforcement of equal, just, and impartial laws in every part of our country.

The failure of local communities to furnish such means for the attainment of results so earnestly desired imposes upon the National Government the duty of putting forth all its energies for the protection of its citizens of every race and color and for the restoration of peace and order throughout the entire country.

In testimony whereof I have hereunto set my hand and caused the seal of the United States to be affixed.

Done at the city of Washington, this 3d day of May, A. D. 1871, and of the Independence of the United States the ninety-fifth.

Document 25

Charlotte Fowler's Testimony to Sub-Committee on Reconstruction in Spartanburg, South Carolina
July 6, 1871

The return of governance to the hands of Southerners raised a whole host of additional problems. The Republican Congress recognized these problems when it passed the Enforcement Acts (Document 23). Private organizations throughout the South, led by the Ku Klux Klan, were depriving freed slaves, blacks, and loyal union men of their lives and property. Southern governments allowed private organizations to operate with impunity. The House and Senate appointed a twenty-one member committee to investigate the Ku Klux Klan and other kindred organizations in 1871. Its aim was to discover how big a problem the Klan presented in the South so that legislation and funding could match the nature of the threat. A subcommittee of eight members received testimony in Washington D.C. and traveled through several of the former slaveholding states to receive more. The committee produced over 8,000 pages of testimony and reports, published in 35 volumes. These volumes tell a story of unpunished violence against the freedmen and loyal union men. According to political scientist Forrest Nabors, who ran analytics on the entire text of the committee's work, the word "shot" appears over 4,000 times and the word "kill" and its variants appears almost 9,500 times. It is an incredible documentary history of what happened under the redeemed Southern governments that no longer had a union military presence. The following excerpt is just one story from one witness delivered to the subcommittee during July 1871 in Spartanburg, South Carolina.

Source: Testimony Taken by the Joint Select Committee to Enquire into the Condition of Affairs in the Late Insurrectionary States, South Carolina, Volume 3 *(Washington, DC: Government Printing office, 1872), 386–392.* https://goo.gl/rSV6cr.

SPARTANBURGH, SOUTH CAROLINA, July 6, 1871

CHARLOTTE FOWLER (colored) sworn and examined.
By the CHAIRMAN:
Question. Where do you live?
Answer. On Mr. Moore's premises.... I did live in Spartanburg County with my husband, before the old man was killed; but now I live with my son.
Question. How long ago is it since your husband was killed?
Answer. It was the 1st of May.
Question. What was his name?
Answer. Wallace Fowler.
Question. Tell how he was killed.
Answer. The night he was killed – I was taken sick on Wednesday morning, and I laid on my bed Wednesday and Thursday. I didn't eat a mouthful; I couldn't do it, I was so sick; so he went out working on his farm.... When he came home he cooked something for me to eat, and said: "Old woman, if you don't eat something you will die." Says I: "I can't eat." Says he, "Then I will eat, and feed the little baby." That is the grandchild he meant. I says: "You take that little child and sleep in the bed; I think I have got the fever, and I don't want you to get it." He said, "No, I don't want to get the fever, for I have got too much to do." He got up and pulled off his clothes, and got in bed.... So he laid there for about a half an hour, and then I heard the dogs.... I reckon I did not lay in bed a half an hour before I heard somebody by the door; it was not one person, but two – ram! ram! ram! at the door. Immediately I was going to call him to open the door; but he heard it as quick as lightning, and he said to them: "Gentlemen, do not break the door down; I will open the door;" and just as he said that they said: "God damn you, I have got you now." I was awake, and I ... got out of the bed, and fell down on the floor. I was very much scared. The little child followed its grandfather to the door – you know in the night it is hard to direct a child. When he said, "God damn you, I have got you now," and he said, "Don't you run," and just then I heard the report of a pistol, and they shot him down; and this little child ran back to me before I could get out, and says, "Oh, grandma, they have killed my poor grandpappy." He was such an old gentleman that I thought they just shot over him to scare him; but sure enough, as quick as I got to the door, I raised my right hand and said, "Gentlemen, you have killed a poor, innocent man." My poor old man! Says he, "Shut up." I never saw but two of them, for, by that time, the others had vanished.
Question. How did you know there were any others there?

Answer. The little boy that was there when they shot his grandpappy ran into the house; he was there, and when they started I heard the horses' feet going from the gate. I was then a hallooing and screaming. After they shot the old man, they came back into the house – "Chup! Chup! Chup! make up a light." I said, "I am not able to make up a light; I have been sick two days." I called to the little girl, "Is there any light there?" She says, "No." But the mantel was there, where I could reach it, where they put the splinters, and I said, "Light that splinter;" and she lit the splinter. He said, "Hand it here;" and she handed it to him; and then he says, "March before me, march before me." That was done in the middle of my room. He says, "Hand me up your arms" – that is the guns. Says I, "There isn't any here, sir." Says he, "Hand me up that pistol." I says, "There is none here; the old man had none in slavery, and had none in all his freedom, and everybody on the settlement knows it." When he told me about the light he put that pistol up to my face – so – and says, "If you don't come here I will get you light out of this." He did that when I was a poor woman by myself.

Question. What else?

Answer. I didn't know that anybody had anything against the old man; everybody liked him but one man, and that was Mr. Thompson. Somewhere along summer before last he [*that is, Fowler*] had planted some watermelons in his patch; and he kept losing his watermelons, and one day he said he would go and lay, and see who took them; and sure enough he caught two little white boys; one was Mr. Thompson's boy and the other was Mr. Millwood's boy; both were white boys; they had cut up a whole lot of the melons. . . .

Question. Is that the reason you thought that Thompson did not like him?

Answer. Mr. Thompson is the only one in the whole settlement that has had anything against him. You may search the whole settlement over. . . .

[*Charlotte Fowler goes on to say that when word got to Mr. Thompson, through a person named Lee, that Fowler knew that Thompson's son took the watermelons, Thompson confronted and threatened Fowler.*]

Question. What were they talking about?

Answer. . . . Mr. Thompson fetched on so about the watermelons. . . . And then says Mr. Thompson, "Yes, and God damn you, if you had said I had stolen your watermelons, you would not make tracks out of this yard." . . . I ran to the fence and said "Wally, come out of that yard; and if you don't I will call Mr. Jones. If you had threatened Mr. Thompson, as Mr. Thompson has threatened your life, he would have you in Spartanburg jail before sundown."

Question. How long was that before the old man was killed?

Answer. The watermelons were took this summer a year ago, and nobody but him [*Mrs. Fowler presumably refers here to Lee*] and Mr. Thompson had anything against him.

Question. Do you mean by this that Thompson had anything to do with the killing of the old man?

Answer. I am going to tell you my opinion about it. I didn't see Mr. Thompson's face, for he had a mask on; but he was built so. He lives close to us, and I saw him every day and Sunday.

Question. Did these men have masks on?

Answer. Only the one that shot him.

Question. What kind of a mask?

Answer. It was all around the eyes. It was black; and the other part was white and red; and he had horns on his head. He came in the house after he killed the old man and told me about the light, and I made the little girl make a light; he took the light from her and looked over the old man. Another man came out of the gate, and looked down on the old man and dropped a chip of fire on him, and burnt through his shirt – burnt his breast. They had shot him in the head, and every time he breathed his brains would come out.

Question. Do you mean to say that you believe his being killed was caused by the quarrel about watermelons?

Answer. I can tell you my belief. There is a parcel of men who were on the plantation working Mr. Jones's land, and my old man was one of them that tended Mr. Jones's land. Mr. Jones had had a whole parcel of poor white folks on the land, and he turned them off, and put all these blacks on the premises that they had from Mr. Jones, and I don't know what it could be, but for that and the watermelons. That was the cause why my old man is dead, and I am left alone. (Weeping.)

Question. Is that all you can tell about it?

Answer. Yes, sir. That is all that I can tell. I don't want to tell anything more than I know; I don't want to tell a lie on anybody....

By Mr. VAN TRUMP: [*Under Van Trump's questioning, Mrs. Fowler states that four men, one of them the person named Lee, were white tenant farmers dismissed by the plantation owner named Jones.*]

Question. It is your opinion, as given in answer to the question of the chairman: "What was the cause of these men killing Wallace?" that it was either the difficulty growing out of the water-melons, or the fact that these white men were turned off and black men put on that farm?

Answer. Yes, sir.

Question. It was one or the other?

Answer. Yes, sir.

Question. Which is the most probable?

Answer. I will tell you which I think stronger than the other. These men and Mr. Thompson are all kin.

Question. Were all four of these white men his kin?

Answer. Yes, sir; to Mr. Thompson. Mrs. Thompson's mother is Mrs. Millwood's aunt, and they are all kin.

Question. Is Mr. Thompson a respectable man in that county?

Answer. They all said down there that he was a mighty mischievous man.

. . .

Question. Where is he now?

Answer. I don't know. He ran off before I left for some conduct he had done; but his children and wife are there; that is, the old man has run off.

Question. That is since the death of Wallace?

Answer. The old man was gone before Wallace was killed.

Question. Young John Thompson is there yet?

Answer. Yes, sir. Young John Thompson and Frank Thompson and Aaron Thompson and Eliphaz Thompson, all his sons, are there with the old lady.

Question. Was this man who was masked a Thompson?

Answer. I do not know who he was. I tell you the Lord's truth from heaven. . . My old man is gone, but I do not want to take anything from anybody, or do anything to anybody. . . .

By MR. STEVENSON:

Question. What are these men called who go about masked in that way?

Answer. I don't know; they call them Ku-Klux.

Question. How long have they been going about in that neighborhood?

Answer. I don't know how long; they have been going a long time, but they never pestered the plantation until that night. . . .

Question. Did your old man belong to any party?

Answer. Yes, sir.

Question. What party?

Answer. The radicals.

Question. How long had he belonged to them?

Answer. Ever since they started the voting.

Question. Was he a pretty strong radical?

Answer. Yes, sir; a pretty strong radical.

Question. Did he work for that party?

Answer. Yes, sir.

Question. What did he do?

Answer. He held up for it, and said he never would turn against the United States for anybody, as the Democrats wanted him to.

Question. Did he talk to the other colored people about it?

Answer. No, sir; he never said nothing much. He was a man that never said much but just what he was going to do. He never traveled anywhere to visit people only when they had a meeting; then he would go there to the radical meetings, but would come back home again.

Question. Did he make speeches at those meetings?

Answer. No, sir....

By the CHAIRMAN:

Question. Are the colored people afraid of these people that go masked?

Answer. Yes, sir; they are as afraid as death of them. There is now a whole procession of people that have left their houses and are lying out. You see the old man was so old, and he did no harm to anybody; he didn't believe anybody would trouble him.

By Mr. STEVENSON:

Question. Did he vote at the last election?

Answer. Yes, sir.

Document 26

"Plea for Amnesty"
Senator Carl Schurz
January 30, 1872

Reconstruction involved the twin goals of national reconciliation and emancipation for former slaves. As power was returned to restored Southern governments and as the Union army retreated, former rebels tended to rise to power under these restored governments. This threatened the already compromised safety and liberty of the freed slaves. The two goals of reconciliation and emancipation, it seems, could not be pursued to the same extent at the same time. The tension between the two can be seen in the words in and actions surrounding President Ulysses S. Grant's annual address in 1871. On the one hand, Grant bemoaned "the condition of the southern states," where "the old citizens of these states" did not tolerate "freedom of expression and ballot in those entertaining different political convictions." Grant was pointing to his concerns about the Ku Klux Klan, a problem on which Congress had lately legislated (Document 23).

On the other hand, Grant requested that Congress remove prohibitions on office-holding for most former Confederates. Republican and Northern support for a vigorous policy protecting the freed slaves at the expense of reconciliation was waning. A vocal minority of Republicans blamed Grant for too vigorous an exercise of presidential power. These dissident Republicans, who had opposed the Enforcement Acts, eventually constituted their own party called the Liberal Republicans. They ran Horace Greeley as their presidential candidate in 1872 on a platform of conciliation with white Southerners and skepticism toward continued federal intervention to protect blacks. Senator Carl Schurz, who had earlier authored the "Report on the Condition of the South" (Document 10), had, at that time, condemned Johnson's policy of laxity toward restored Southern governments. Now he rose in favor of Liberal Republicanism, limits on federal power, and conciliation. The following excerpt is from a speech delivered by Schurz on the Senate floor, in which he advocates a generous amnesty for all who fought on behalf of the Confederacy.

Source: Speeches, Correspondences, and Political Papers of Carl Schurz, ed. Frederic Bancroft (New York: G. P. Putnam's Sons, 1913), Volume 2: 321–335, 337, 352–53. Available at https://goo.gl/JtnQvk.

... I beg leave to say that I am in favor of general, or as this word is considered more expressive, universal amnesty....

In the course of this debate we have listened to some Senators, as they conjured up before our eyes once more all the horrors of the rebellion ... how terrible its incidents were and how harrowing its consequences. ... I will not combat the correctness of the picture; and yet, if I differ with the gentlemen who drew it, it is because, had the conception of the rebellion been still more wicked, had its incidents been still more terrible, its consequences still more harrowing, I could not permit myself to forget that in dealing with the question now before us we have to deal not alone with the past, but with the present and future interests of this Republic.

What do we want to accomplish as good citizens and patriots? Do we mean only to inflict upon late rebels pain, degradation, mortification, annoyance, for its own sake ... ? Certainly such a spirit could not by any possibility animate high-minded men. I presume, therefore, that those who still favor the continuance of some of the disabilities imposed by the [14th] amendment,[1] do so because they have some higher object of public usefulness in view ... to justify, in their minds at least, the denial of rights to others which we ourselves enjoy.

What can those objects of public usefulness be? Let me assume that, if we differ as to the means to be employed, we are agreed as to the supreme end and aim to be reached. That end and aim of our endeavors can be no other than to secure to all the States the blessings of good and free government and the highest degree of prosperity and well-being they can attain, and to revive in all citizens of this Republic that love for the Union and its institutions, and that inspiring consciousness of a common nationality, which, after all, must bind all Americans together.

What are the best means for the attainment of that end? ... Certainly all will agree that this end is far from having been attained so far. Look at the Southern States as they stand before us today. Some are in a condition bordering upon anarchy, not only on account of the social disorders which are occurring there, or the inefficiency of their local governments in securing the enforcement of the laws; but you will find in many of them fearful corruption pervading the whole political organization; a combination of rascality and ignorance wielding official

---

[1] Schurz refers to Section 3, which excluded those who had broken an oath of office and joined a rebellion against the United States from holding office again. See Document 14.

power; their finances deranged by profligate practices; their credit ruined; bankruptcy staring them in the face; their industries staggering under a fearful load of taxation; their property-holders and capitalists paralyzed by a feeling of insecurity and distrust almost amounting to despair....

What are the causes that have contributed to bring about this distressing condition? I admit that great civil wars resulting in such vast social transformations as the sudden abolition of slavery are calculated to produce similar results; but it might be presumed that a recuperative power such as this country possesses might during the time which has elapsed since the close of the war at least have very materially alleviated many of the consequences of that revulsion, had a wise policy been followed.

Was the policy we followed wise? Was it calculated to promote the great purposes we are endeavoring to serve? Let us see. At the close of the war we had to establish and secure free labor and the rights of the emancipated class. To that end we had to disarm those who could have prevented this, and we had to give the power of self-protection to those who needed it. For this reason temporary restrictions were imposed upon the late rebels, and we gave the right of suffrage to the colored people. Until the latter were enabled to protect themselves, political disabilities even more extensive than those which now exist, rested upon the plea of eminent political necessity. I would be the last man to conceal that I thought so then, and I think now there was very good reason for it.

But, sir, when the enfranchisement of the colored people was secured, when they had obtained the political means to protect themselves, then another problem began to loom up. It was not only to find new guaranties for the rights of the colored people, but it was to secure good and honest government for all. Let us not underestimate the importance of that problem, for in a great measure it includes the solution of the other. Certainly, nothing could have been better calculated to remove the prevailing discontent concerning the changes that had taken place, and to reconcile men's minds to the new order of things, than the tangible proof that that new order of things was practically working well.... And, on the other hand, nothing could have been more calculated to impede a general, hearty and honest acceptance of the new order of things by the late rebel population than just those failures of public administration which involve the people in material embarrassments and so seriously disturb their comfort....

... [W]hat happened in the South? It is a well-known fact that the more intelligent classes of Southern society almost uniformly identified themselves with the rebellion; and by our system of political disabilities just those classes were excluded from the management of political affairs. That they could not be trusted with the business of introducing into living practice the results of the war, to establish true free labor and to protect the rights of the emancipated slaves, is true; I willingly admit it. But when those results and rights were constitutionally secured there were other things to be done.... But just then a large portion of that intelligence and experience was excluded from the management of public affairs by political disabilities, and the controlling power in those States rested in a great measure in the hands of those who had but recently been slaves and just emerged from that condition, and in the hands of others who had sometimes honestly, sometimes by crooked means and for sinister purposes, found a way to their confidence.[2]

This was the state of things as it then existed. Nothing could be farther from my intention than to cast a slur upon the character of the colored people of the South.... Look into the history of the world, and you will find that almost every similar act of emancipation, the abolition of serfdom, for instance, was uniformly accompanied by atrocious outbreaks of a revengeful spirit; by the slaughters of nobles and their families, illumined by the glare of their burning castles. Not so here.... [S]carcely a single act of revenge for injuries suffered or for misery endured has darkened the record of the emancipated bondmen of America. And thus their example stands unrivalled in history, and they as well as the whole American people, may well be proud of it. Certainly, the Southern people should never cease to remember and appreciate it.

But while the colored people of the South thus earned our admiration and gratitude, I ask you in all candor, could they be reasonably expected, when, just after having emerged from a condition of slavery, they were invested with political rights and privileges, to step into the political arena as men armed with the intelligence and experience necessary for the management of public affairs and for the solution of problems made doubly intricate by the disaster which had desolated the Southern country? ... That as a class they were ignorant and inexperienced and lacked a just conception of public interests, was certainly not their fault. ... But the stubborn fact remains that they *were* ignorant and inexperienced; that the public business *was* an unknown world to them, and that in spite of the best intentions they *were* easily misled, not infrequently by the most reckless rascality which had found a way to their confidence. Thus their political rights and privileges were undoubtedly well calculated, and even

---

[2] Schurz seems to refer to carpetbaggers – Northern men who went South to govern and engage in commerce. They had a reputation for corruption, for looking to make a quick dollar, but this reputation is mostly a result of Southern efforts to discredit Northern rule.

necessary, to protect their rights as free laborers and citizens; but they were not well calculated to secure a successful administration of other public interests.

I do not blame the colored people for it; still less do I say that for this reason their political rights and privileges should have been denied them. Nay, sir, I deemed it necessary then, and I now reaffirm that opinion, that they should possess those rights and privileges for the permanent establishment of the logical and legitimate results of the war and the protection of their new position in society. But, while never losing sight of this necessity, I do say that the inevitable consequence of the admission of so large an uneducated and inexperienced class to political power, as to the probable mismanagement of the material interests of the social body, should at least have been mitigated by a counterbalancing policy.... [W]hen universal suffrage was granted to secure the equal rights of all, universal amnesty ought to have been granted to make all the resources of political intelligence and experience available for the promotion of the welfare of all.

But what did we do? To the uneducated and inexperienced classes – uneducated and inexperienced, I repeat, entirely without their fault – we opened the road to power; and, at the same time, we condemned a large proportion of the intelligence of those States, of the property-holding, the industrial, the professional, the tax-paying interest, to a worse than passive attitude. We made it, as it were, easy for rascals who had gone South in quest of profitable adventure to gain the control of masses so easily misled, by permitting them to appear as the exponents and representatives of the National power and of our policy; and at the same time we branded a large number of men of intelligence, and many of them of personal integrity, whose material interests were so largely involved in honest government, and many of whom would have cooperated in managing the public business with care and foresight – we branded them, I say, as outcasts, telling them that they ought not to be suffered to exercise any influence upon the management of the public business, and that it would be unwarrantable presumption in them to attempt it.

I ask you, sir, could such things fail to contribute to the results we read to-day in the political corruption and demoralization, and in the financial ruin of some of the Southern States? These results are now before us. The mistaken policy may have been pardonable when these consequences were still a matter of conjecture and speculation; but what excuse have we now for continuing it when those results are clear before our eyes, beyond the reach of contradiction?

These considerations would seem to apply more particularly to those Southern States in which the colored element constitutes a very large proportion of the voting body. There is another which applies to all....

The introduction of the colored people, the late slaves, into the body-politic as voters pointedly affronted the traditional prejudices prevailing among the Southern whites. What should we care about those prejudices? In war, nothing. After the close of the war, in the settlement of peace, not enough to deter us from doing what was right and necessary; and yet, still enough to take them into account when considering the manner in which right and necessity were to be served. Statesmen will care about popular prejudices as physicians will care about the diseased condition of their patients, which they want to ameliorate. Would it not have been wise for us, looking at those prejudices as a morbid condition of the Southern mind, to mitigate, to assuage, to disarm them by prudent measures and thus to weaken their evil influence? We desired the Southern whites to accept in good faith universal suffrage, to recognize the political rights of the colored man and to protect him in their exercise. Was not that our sincere desire? But if it was, would it not have been wise to remove as much as possible the obstacles that stood in the way of that consummation? But what did we do? When we raised the colored people to the rights of active citizenship and opened to them all the privileges of eligibility, we excluded from those privileges a large and influential class of whites; in other words, we lifted the late slave, uneducated and inexperienced as he was – I repeat, without his fault – not merely to the level of the late master class, but even above it. We asked certain white men to recognize the colored man in a political status not only as high but even higher than their own.... [W]as it wise to do it? If you desired the white man to accept and recognize the political equality of the black, was it wise to embitter and to exasperate his spirit with the stinging stigma of his own inferiority? ... This was not assuaging, disarming prejudice; this was rather inciting, it was exasperating it. American statesmen will understand and appreciate human nature as it has developed itself under the influence of free institutions. We know that if we want any class of people to overcome their prejudices in respecting the political rights and privileges of any other class, the very first thing we have to do is to accord the same rights and privileges to them. No American was ever inclined to recognize in others public rights and privileges from which he himself was excluded; and for aught I know, in this very feeling, although it may take an objectionable form, we find one of the safeguards of popular liberty....

... [T]he existence of disabilities, which put so large and influential a class of whites in point of political privileges below the colored people, could not fail to inflame those prejudices which stood in the way of a general and honest acceptance of the new order of things. They increased instead of diminishing the dangers and difficulties surrounding the emancipated class....

Well, then, what policy does common-sense suggest to us now? If we sincerely desire to give to the Southern States good and honest government, material prosperity and measurable contentment, as far at least as we can contribute to that end; if we really desire to weaken and disarm those prejudices and resentments which still disturb the harmony of society, will it not be wise, will it not be necessary, will it not be our duty to show that we are in no sense the allies and abettors of those who use their political power to plunder their fellow-citizens, and that we do not mean to keep one class of people in unnecessary degradation by withholding from them rights and privileges which all others enjoy? Seeing the mischief which the system of disabilities is accomplishing, is it not time that there should be at least an end of it? Or is there any good it can possibly do to make up for the harm it has already wrought and is still working? ....

We hear the Ku-Klux outrages spoken of as a reason why political disabilities should not be removed. Did not these very same Ku-Klux outrages happen while disabilities were in existence? Is it not clear, then, that the existence of political disabilities did not prevent them? No, sir, if political disabilities have any practical effect, it is, while not in any degree diminishing the power of the evil-disposed for mischief, to incite and sharpen their mischievous inclination by increasing their discontent with the condition they live in.

It must be clear to every impartial observer that, were ever so many of those who are now disqualified, put in office, they never could do with their official power as much mischief as the mere fact of the existence of the system of political disabilities with its inevitable consequences is doing to-day. The scandals of misgovernment in the South which we complain of, I admit, were not the first and original cause of the Ku-Klux outrages. But every candid observer will also have to admit that they did serve to keep the Ku-Klux spirit alive....

We accuse the Southern whites of having missed their chance of gaining the confidence of the emancipated class when, by a fairly demonstrated purpose of recognizing and protecting them in their rights, they might have acquired upon them a salutary influence. That accusation is by no means unjust; but must we not admit, also, that by excluding them from their political rights and privileges we put the damper of most serious discouragement upon the good intentions which might have grown up among them? ... You find nothing, absolutely nothing, in [the] practical effects [of the disabilities] but the aggravation of evils already existing and the prevention of a salutary development....

But I am told that the system of disabilities must be maintained for a certain moral effect. The Senator from Indiana [Mr. Morton[3]] took great pains to inform us that it is absolutely necessary to exclude somebody from office in order to demonstrate our disapprobation of the crime of rebellion. Methinks the American people have signified their disapprobation of the crime of rebellion in a far more pointed manner. They sent against the rebellion a million armed men. We fought and conquered the armies of the rebels; we carried desolation into their land; we swept out of existence that system of slavery which was the soul of their offense and was to be the corner-stone of their new empire. If that was not signifying our disapprobation of the crime of rebellion, then I humbly submit, your system of political disabilities, only excluding some persons from office, will scarcely do it.

I remember, also, to have heard the argument that under all circumstances the law must be vindicated. What law in this case? If any law is meant, it must be the law imposing the penalty of death upon the crime of treason. Well, if at the close of the war we had assumed the stern and bloody virtue of the ancient Roman, and had proclaimed that he who raises his hand against this Republic must surely die, then we might have claimed for ourselves at least the merit of logical consistency. We might have thought that by erecting a row of gallows stretching from the Potomac to the Rio Grande, and by making a terrible example of all those who had proved faithless to their allegiance, we would strike terror into the hearts of this and coming generations, to make them tremble at the mere thought of treasonable undertakings. That we might have done. Why did we not? Because the American people instinctively recoiled from the idea; because every wise man remembered that where insurrections are punished and avenged with the bloodiest hands, there insurrections do most frequently occur . . . .

. . . We instinctively adopted a generous policy, adding fresh luster to the glory of the American name by doing so. . . .

But having once adopted the policy of generosity, the only question for us is how to make that policy most fruitful. The answer is: We shall make the policy of generosity most fruitful by making it most complete. . . .

. . . Whatever may be said of the greatness and the heinous character of the crime of rebellion, a single glance at the history of the world and at the practice of other nations will convince you, that in all civilized countries the measure of punishment to be visited on those guilty of that crime is almost uniformly treated as a question of great policy and almost never as a question of strict

---

[3] Oliver H. P. T. Morton, R (1823–1877)

justice. And why is this? .... Because a broad line of distinction is drawn between a violation of law in which political opinion is the controlling element . . . and those infamous crimes of which moral depravity is the principal ingredient; and because even the most disastrous political conflicts may be composed for the common good by a conciliatory process, while the infamous crime always calls for a strictly penal correction. You may call this just or not, but such is the public opinion of the civilized world, and you find it in every civilized country....

I do not, indeed, indulge in the delusion that this act alone will remedy all the evils which we now deplore. No, it will not; but it will be a powerful appeal to the very best instincts and impulses of human nature; . . . it will give new courage, confidence and inspiration to the well-disposed; it will weaken the power of the mischievous, by stripping of their pretexts and exposing in their nakedness the wicked designs they still may cherish; it will light anew the beneficent glow of fraternal feeling and of National spirit; for, sir, your good sense as well as your heart must tell you that, when this is truly a people of citizens equal in their political rights, it will then be easier to make it also a people of brothers.

Document 27

The Slaughterhouse Cases
The United States Supreme Court
April 14, 1873

President Ulysses S. Grant won reelection in 1872, but it was getting increasingly difficult to protect freed slaves, blacks and loyal union men in the South: "home rule" had returned to most Southern states and, increasingly, ruling majorities hostile to Republican policies formed in these states. These states were "redeemed," the Southerners would say. Minor civil conflicts between white mobs and Republican sympathizers erupted over the South; Southern governments were very little interested in suppressing white violence. Grant swung between moments of conciliation with the former rebels and moments of firmness toward their unwillingness to protect civil rights for all citizens. Grant's firmness was supported by Enforcement Acts passed during his first term (Document 23). Every act of enforcement could be appealed through the national judiciary, so the Enforcement Acts required both executive firmness and judicial support.

Yet, as public support for Reconstruction waned in the North during the mid-1870s, it also waned in the national judiciary. The first sign of the judiciary's lack of support came in a closely divided case that was technically unrelated to Reconstruction. Louisiana granted a monopoly to a corporation for the purposes of butchering in New Orleans. Butchers left out of that monopoly were deprived of a chance to earn a living and they sued in federal court, arguing that the monopoly violated their right to pursue a livelihood. That right, they contended, was guaranteed under the 14th amendment, which precluded states from depriving citizens of the privileges and immunities of citizenship. All noted that this was a crucial case, because if these rights could not be secured through national enforcement, many of the rights promised under the civil rights bills could also not to be secured. The Supreme Court justices considering the case also understood the significance of their decision. The Slaughterhouse Cases became the controlling case for defining national citizenship under the 14th amendment (Document 14) to the United States Constitution, though later courts would provide a broader definition under different constitutional provisions.

Source: The Slaughterhouse Cases, 83 U.S. 36 (1872). Available online from Legal Information Institute, Cornell Law School, https://goo.gl/maHDEQ.

Mr. Justice MILLER[1] ... delivered the opinion of the court.

.... This statute is denounced [*by the plaintiffs*] not only as creating a monopoly and conferring ... exclusive privileges upon a small number of persons at the expense of the great body of the community of New Orleans, but it is asserted that it deprives a large and meritorious class of citizens – the whole of the butchers of the city – of the right to exercise their trade, the business to which they have been trained and on which they depend for the support of themselves and their families....

The power here exercised by the legislature of Louisiana is ... one which has been, up to the present period in the constitutional history of this country, always conceded to belong to the States, however it may *now* be questioned in some of its details....

The proposition is therefore reduced to these terms: can any exclusive privileges be granted to any of its citizens, or to a corporation, by the legislature of a State? ...

The plaintiffs ... allege that the statute is a violation of the Constitution of the United States in these several particulars:

That it creates an involuntary servitude forbidden by the thirteenth article of amendment;[2]

That it abridges the privileges and immunities of citizens of the United States;

That it denies to the plaintiffs the equal protection of the laws; and,

That it deprives them of their property without due process of law, contrary to the provisions of the first section of the fourteenth article of amendment.

This court is thus called upon for the first time to give construction to [the most recent amendments to the Constitution: the 13th, 14th and 15th Amendments].

We do not conceal from ourselves the great responsibility which this duty devolves upon us. No questions so far-reaching and pervading in their consequences, so profoundly interesting to the people of this country, and so important in their bearing upon the relations of the United States, of the several States to each other, and to the citizens of the States and of the United States,

---

[1] Samuel Freeman Miller (1816–1890) served as an Associate Justice of the Supreme Court from 1862 to 1890.

[2] See Document 4.

have been before this court during the official life of any of its present members. ...

... No one can fail to be impressed with the one pervading purpose found in [the 13th, 14th, and 15th Amendments] lying at the foundation of each, and without which none of them would have been even suggested; we mean the freedom of the slave race, the security and firm establishment of that freedom, and the protection of the newly made freeman and citizen from the oppressions of those who had formerly exercised unlimited dominion over him. ...

We do not say that no one else but the Negro can share in this protection. Both the language and spirit of these articles are to have their fair and just weight in any question of construction. ... What we do say, and what we wish to be understood, is that in any fair and just construction of any section or phrase of these amendments, it is necessary to look to the purpose which we have said was the pervading spirit of them all. ...

The first section of the fourteenth article ... opens with a definition of citizenship – not only citizenship of the United States, but citizenship of the States. No such definition was previously found in the Constitution, nor had any attempt been made to define it by act of Congress. ... It had been said by eminent judges that no man was a citizen of the United States except as he was a citizen of one of the States composing the Union. Those, therefore, who had been born and resided always in the District of Columbia or in the Territories, though within the United States, were not citizens. Whether this proposition was sound or not had never been judicially decided. But it had been held by this court, in the celebrated Dred Scott case, only a few years before the outbreak of the civil war, that a man of African descent, whether a slave or not, was not and could not be a citizen of a State or of the United States. ...

To remove this difficulty primarily, and to establish clear and comprehensive definition of citizenship which should declare what should constitute citizenship of the United States and also citizenship of a State, the first clause of the first section was framed.

The first observation we have to make on this clause is that it puts at rest both the questions which we stated to have been the subject of differences of opinion. ... That its main purpose was to establish the citizenship of the Negro can admit of no doubt. ...

The next observation is . . . . that the distinction between citizenship of the United States and citizenship of a State is clearly recognized and established. Not only may a man be a citizen of the United States without being a citizen of a State, but an important element is necessary to convert the former into the latter. He must reside within the State to make him a citizen of it, but it is only necessary that he should be born or naturalized in the United States to be a citizen of the Union.

It is quite clear, then, that there is a citizenship of the United States, and a citizenship of a State, which are distinct from each other, and which depend upon different characteristics or circumstances in the individual.

We think this distinction and its explicit recognition in this amendment of great weight in this argument, because the next paragraph of this same section, which is the one mainly relied on by the plaintiffs ..., speaks only of privileges and immunities of citizens of the United States, and does not speak of those of citizens of the several States. The argument ... in favor of the plaintiffs rests wholly on the assumption that the citizenship is the same, and the privileges and immunities guaranteed by the clause are the same.

The language is, "No State shall make or enforce any law which shall abridge the privileges or immunities of citizens of *the United States.*" It is a little remarkable, if this clause was intended as a protection to the citizen of a State against the legislative power of his own State, that the word citizen of the State should be left out when it is so carefully used, and used in contradistinction to citizens of the United States in the very sentence which precedes it. It is too clear for argument that the change in phraseology was adopted understandingly and with a purpose.

Of the privileges and immunities of the citizen of the United States, and of the privileges and immunities of the citizen of the State, and what they respectively are, we will presently consider; but we wish to state here that it is only the former which are placed by this clause under the protection of the Federal Constitution, and that the latter, whatever they may be, are not intended to have any additional protection by this paragraph of the amendment....

Fortunately, we are not without judicial construction of this clause of the Constitution. The first and the leading case on the subject is that of *Corfield v. Coryell,* decided by Mr. Justice Washington in the Circuit Court for the District of Pennsylvania in 1823.[3]

"The inquiry," he says, "is what are the privileges and immunities of citizens of the several States? We feel no hesitation in confining these expressions to those privileges and immunities which are fundamental; which belong of right to the citizens of all free governments, and which have at all times been enjoyed by citizens of the several States which compose this Union, from the time of their becoming free, independent, and sovereign. What these fundamental

---

[3] Bushrod Washington (1762–1829) was an Associate justice of the Supreme Court (1798–1829). At that time, Associate Justices presided over Circuit Courts.

principles are it would be more tedious than difficult to enumerate. They may all, however, be comprehended under the following general heads: protection by the government, with the right to acquire and possess property of every kind and to pursue and obtain happiness and safety, subject, nevertheless, to such restraints as the government may prescribe for the general good of the whole."[4]

. . .Was it the purpose of the fourteenth amendment, by the simple declaration that no State should make or enforce any law which shall abridge the privileges and immunities of citizens of the United States, to transfer the security and protection of all the civil rights which we have mentioned, from the States to the Federal government? And where it is declared that Congress shall have the power to enforce that article, was it intended to bring within the power of Congress the entire domain of civil rights heretofore belonging exclusively to the States?

All this and more must follow if the proposition of the plaintiffs ... be sound. For not only are these rights subject to the control of Congress whenever, in its discretion, any of them are supposed to be abridged by State legislation, but that body may also pass laws in advance, limiting and restricting the exercise of legislative power by the States, in their most ordinary and usual functions, as in its judgment it may think proper on all such subjects. And still further, such a construction followed by the reversal of the judgments of the Supreme Court of Louisiana in these cases, would constitute this court a perpetual censor upon all legislation of the States, on the civil rights of their own citizens, with authority to nullify such as it did not approve as consistent with those rights, as they existed at the time of the adoption of this amendment.

The argument, we admit, is not always the most conclusive which is drawn from the consequences urged against the adoption of a particular construction of an instrument. But when, as in the case before us, these consequences are so serious, so far-reaching and pervading, so great a departure from the structure and spirit of our institutions; when the effect is to fetter and degrade the State governments by subjecting them to the control of Congress in the exercise of powers heretofore universally conceded to them of the most ordinary and fundamental character; when, in fact, it radically changes the whole theory of the relations of the State and Federal governments to each other and of both these governments to the people, the argument has a force that is irresistible in the absence of language which expresses such a purpose too clearly to admit of doubt.

---

[4] Senator Jacob Howard (R-MI) refers to this opinion in the debates concerning the 14th Amendment, Document 14.

We are convinced that no such results were intended by the Congress which proposed these amendments, nor by the legislatures of the States which ratified them.

Having shown that the privileges and immunities relied on in the argument are those which belong to citizens of the States as such, and that they are left to the State governments for security and protection, and not by this article placed under the special care of the Federal government, we may hold ourselves excused from defining the privileges and immunities of citizens of the United States which no State can abridge until some case involving those privileges may make it necessary to do so.

But lest it should be said that no such privileges and immunities are to be found if those we have been considering are excluded, we venture to suggest some which owe their existence to the Federal government, its national character, its Constitution, or its laws.

[Among] these is . . . the right of the citizen to come to the seat of government to assert any claim he may have upon that government, to transact any business he may have with it, to seek its protection, to share its offices, to engage in administering its functions. . . . the right of free access to its seaports . . . . [the right] to demand the care and protection of the Federal government over his life, liberty, and property when on the high seas or within the jurisdiction of a foreign government. . . . the right to peaceably assemble and petition for redress of grievances . . . . the right to use the navigable waters of the United States . . . .

In the light of the history of these amendments, and the pervading purpose of them, . . . it is not difficult to give a meaning to this clause [*the clause protecting the privileges and immunities of U.S. citizenship*]. The existence of laws in the States where the newly emancipated Negroes resided, which discriminated with gross injustice and hardship against them as a class, was the evil to be remedied by this clause, and by it such laws are forbidden.

If, however, the States did not conform their laws to its requirements, then by the fifth section of the article of amendment Congress was authorized to enforce it by suitable legislation. We doubt very much whether any action of a State not directed by way of discrimination against the Negroes as a class, or on account of their race, will ever be held to come within the purview of this provision. It is so clearly a provision for that race and that emergency that a strong case would be necessary for its application to any other. But as it is a State that is to be dealt with, and not alone the validity of its laws, we may safely leave that matter until Congress shall have exercised its power, or some case of State oppression, by denial of equal justice in its courts, shall have claimed a decision at our hands. We find no such case in the one before us, and do not deem it necessary to go over the argument again, as it may have relation to this particular clause of the amendment....

Mr. Justice FIELD, dissenting.[5]

... The question presented is ... one of the gravest importance not merely to the parties here, but to the whole country. It is nothing less than the question whether the recent amendments to the Federal Constitution protect the citizens of the United States against the deprivation of their common rights by State legislation. In my judgment, the fourteenth amendment does afford such protection, and was so intended by the Congress which framed and the States which adopted it....

The amendment does not attempt to confer any new privileges or immunities upon citizens, or to enumerate or define those already existing. It assumes that there are such privileges and immunities which belong of right to citizens as such, and ordains that they shall not be abridged by State legislation. If this inhibition has no reference to privileges and immunities of this character, but only refers, as held by the majority of the court in their opinion, to such privileges and immunities as were before its adoption specially designated in the Constitution or necessarily implied as belonging to citizens of the United States, it was a vain and idle enactment, which accomplished nothing and most unnecessarily excited Congress and the people on its passage. With privileges and immunities thus designated or implied no State could ever have interfered by its laws, and no new constitutional provision was required to inhibit such interference. The supremacy of the Constitution and the laws of the United States always controlled any State legislation of that character. But if the amendment refers to the natural and inalienable rights which belong to all citizens, the inhibition has a profound significance and consequence.

What, then, are the privileges and immunities which are secured against abridgment by State legislation? ...

... The privileges and immunities designated are those which of right belong to the citizens of all free governments. Clearly among these must be placed the right to pursue a lawful employment in a lawful manner, without other restraint than such as equally affects all persons....

This equality of right, with exemption from all disparaging and partial enactments, in the lawful pursuits of life, throughout the whole country, is the

---

[5] Associate Justice Stephen Johnson Field (1816–1899) served on the Supreme Court from 1863 to 1897.

distinguishing privilege of citizens of the United States. To them, everywhere, all pursuits, all professions, all avocations are open without other restrictions than such as are imposed equally upon all others of the same age, sex, and condition. The State may prescribe such regulations for every pursuit and calling of life as will promote the public health, secure the good order and advance the general prosperity of society, but, when once prescribed, the pursuit or calling must be free to be followed by every citizen who is within the conditions designated, and will conform to the regulations. This is the fundamental idea upon which our institutions rest, and, unless adhered to in the legislation of the country, our government will be a republic only in name....

Document 28

Colfax Massacre Reports
U.S. Senate and the Committee of 70
1874 and 1875

From the point of view of former Confederates, restoring "home rule" meant returning to rule by the old slave owners and rebels. To achieve this end, they used small-scale political violence to intimidate and silence opponents, while counting on Northern exhaustion to eventually quell objections to civil rights violations. The Ku Klux Klan was, as we have seen, a major force behind much of the violence. Federal efforts to stop Klan violence (Documents 23 and 24) were not entirely successful given the unwillingness of Southerners to take action against the Klan. Where Northern arms were present, Republicans and freedmen could achieve political power and live in some security. Where the North's arms were not effective, both were endangered.

No episode better captures the nature of the political violence freedmen and Republicans faced in the South, and the difficulty constitutional government faced in taming the violence, than the Colfax Massacre. Louisiana's 1872 gubernatorial election had pitted a Republican, William Pitt Kellogg (1830-1912), against John McEnery (1833-1921), the candidate of a "Fusion" party (an alliance between Liberal Republicans in favor of home rule and Democrats willing to make limited reforms). Both sides claimed victory. Two slates of officials were appointed for executive offices like sheriff. The conflict over the sheriff's office and control of a courthouse in Colfax, Louisiana led to the Colfax Massacre, in which a force of white Democrats overpowered black Republicans and black State militia, murdering approximately 150, most after they surrendered. It was hardly the first such bloody massacre in Louisiana, but it was the largest.

Below are two documents, one from the U.S. House of Representatives report on political violence in Louisiana generally and at Colfax specifically and the other from a New Orleans based Committee of 70, which wrote a report about the massacre from the perspective of the white desire for home rule. The Committee of 70 Report illustrates the nature of Southern justice under home rule. The Supreme Court case that grew out of the Colfax Massacre (Document 29) resulted in a profound limit on Union efforts to protect freedmen and Republicans in the South, and was part of the impetus for the military withdrawal from the South.

Source: "Condition of the South," *Report Number 261, in* Reports of Committees of the House of Representatives for the Second Session of the Forty-Third Congress *(Washington D.C.: U.S. Printing Office, 1875), pp. 11–14, https://goo.gl/fsC5mu;* Committee of 70, "History of The Riot at Colfax, Grant Parish, Louisiana, April 13th, 1873: With a Brief Sketch of the Trial of The Grant Parish Prisoners In The Circuit Court Of The United States" (New Orleans: Clark & Hofeline, 1874), *1, 4, 5, 6, 7, 8, 10–11, 12, 13.*

House Report on the Condition of the South

In the year 1868, the year of the presidential election, occurred six bloody and terrible massacres....

The testimony shows that over two thousand persons were killed, wounded, and otherwise injured in that state within a few weeks prior to the presidential election; that half the State was overrun by violence; midnight raids, secret murders, and open riot kept the people in constant terror until the Republicans surrendered all claims, and then the election was carried by the democracy.[1] The parish of Orleans contained 29,910 voters, 15,020 black. In the spring of 1868 that parish gave 13,973 Republican votes; in the fall of 1869, it gave Grant 1,178, a falling off of 12,795 votes. Riots prevailed for weeks, sweeping the city of New Orleans, and filling it with scenes of blood, and Ku-Klux notices were scattered through the city, warning the colored men not to vote. In Caddo, there were 2,987 Republicans. In the spring of 1868 [*Republicans*] carried the parish. In the fall, they gave Grant one vote. Here also were bloody riots. But the most remarkable case is that of Saint Landry, a planting parish on the River Teche. Here the Republicans had a registered majority of 1,071 votes. In the spring of 1868 they carried the parish by 678. In the fall they gave Grant no vote – not one, while the Democrats cast 4,787, the full vote of the parish, for Seymour and Blair.

Here occurred one of the bloodiest riots on record, in which the Ku-Klux killed and wounded over two hundred Republicans, hunting and chasing them for two days and nights, through fields and swamps. Thirteen captives were taken from the jail and shot. A pile of twenty-five dead bodies were found half buried in the woods. Having conquered the Republicans, killed and driven off the white leaders, the Ku-Klux captured the masses, marked them with badges

---

[1] The Democratic party

of red flannel, enrolled them in clubs, led them to the polls, made them vote the Democratic ticket, and then gave them certificates of that fact.

In the year 1873 occurred the transaction known as the Colfax massacre, to which the committee directed special attention.... It seems to us there is no doubt as to the truth of the following narrative:

In March, 1873, Nash and Cagaburt claimed to be judge and sheriff of Grant Parish under commissions from Governor Warmouth.[2] After Governor Kellogg[3] succeeded Warmouth, their friends applied to him to renew their commissions. He refused, and commissioned Shaw as sheriff, and Register as judge. They went to the courthouse, which they found locked, and Shaw and the other parish officers entered it through the window. Six days after, hearing rumors of an armed invasion of the town to retake the courthouse, Shaw deputized, in his writing, from fifteen to eighteen men, mostly Negroes, to assist as his posse in holding the courthouse and keeping the peace. The next day, April 1st, a company of from 9 to 15 mounted men, headed by one Hudnot,[4] came into Colfax, some of them armed with guns; and on the same day one or two other small armed squads also came into town. This day no collision occurred.

April 2, a small body of armed white men rode into the town, and were met by a body of armed men, mostly colored, and exchanged shots, but no one was hurt.

These proceedings alarmed the colored people, and many of them, with their women and children, came to Colfax for refuge, perhaps a majority of the men being armed.

April 5, a band of armed whites went to the house of Jesse M. Kinney, a colored man, three miles from Colfax, and found him quietly engaged in making

---

[2] Henry Clay Warmouth (1842–1931), a lawyer and Union officer in the Civil War, was born in Illinois but came to Louisiana when appointed judge of the Department of the Gulf Provost Court. A Republican, he was elected governor in 1868 and allied himself with the pro-conciliation, Liberal Republican branch of the party.

[3] Kellogg – a native of Vermont, lawyer, judge, and Union officer – was collector of the Port of New Orleans from 1865 to 1868. A Radical Republican, he ran against Democrat John McEnery in the gubernatorial election of in 1872. The Warmouth-controlled State Returning Board declared McEnery the winner, while a federal board decided Kellogg had won. Kellogg was seated only after President Grant, in September 1873, issued an executive order declaring him the legal governor.

[4] This was James W. Hadnot, according to a memorial erected by the white citizens of Colfax in 1921 that calls Hadnot and Sidney Harris (mentioned later in the excerpt) "Heroes" who fell in the "Colfax Riot."

a fence. They shot him through the head and killed him. This seems to have been an unprovoked, wanton, and deliberate murder. This aroused the terror of the colored people. Rumors were also spread of threats made by them against the whites. April 7 the court was opened and adjourned. The alarm somewhat subsided and many colored people returned to their homes, the others maintaining an armed organization outside the town. April 12 the colored men threw up a small earthwork near the courthouse. Easter Sunday, April 13, a large body of whites rode into the town, and demanded of the colored men that they should give up their arms and yield possession of the courthouse. This demand not being yielded to, thirty minutes were given them to remove their women and children. The Negroes took refuge behind their earthwork, from which they were driven by an enfilading[5] fire from a cannon which the whites had. Part of them fled for refuge to the courthouse, which was a one-story brick building, which had formerly been a stable. The rest, leaving their arms, fled down the river to a strip of woods, where they were pursued, and many of them were overtaken and shot to death.

About sixty or seventy got into the courthouse. After some ineffectual firing on each side, the roof of the building was set fire to. When the roof was burning over their heads the Negroes held out the sleeve of a shirt and the leaf of a book as flags of truce. They were ordered to drop their arms. A number of them rushed unarmed from the blazing building, but were all captured. The number taken prisoners was about thirty-seven. They were kept till dark, when they were led out two by two, each two with a rank of mounted whites behind them, being told that they were to be taken a short distance and set at liberty. When all the ranks had been formed the word was given, and the Negroes were all shot. A few who were wounded, but not mortally, escaped by feigning death.

The bodies remained unburied till the next Tuesday, when they were buried by a deputy marshal from New Orleans. Fifty-nine dead bodies were found. They showed pistol-shot wounds, the great majority of them in the head, and most of them in the back of the head.

Two white men only were killed in the whole transaction, Hudnot the leader, and one Harris.... [T]his deed was *without palliation or justification*; it was deliberate, barbarous, cold-blooded murder. It must stand, like the *massacre* of Glencoe or St. Bartholomew,[6] a foul blot on the page of history.

---

[5] a sweeping volley

[6] The Massacre of Glencoe was a massacre of Scottish highlanders by British forces in 1692. The Bartholomew Massacre was a massacre of French Huguenots (Protestants) by Catholics in 1572.

Spread over all these years are a large number of murders and other acts of violence done for political ends. In reply to an inquiry of the committee, General Sheridan,[7] who is gathering careful statistics of the number of persons killed and wounded in Louisiana up to February 8, 1875, since 1866, on account of their political opinions, reports the number so far ascertained to be as follows:

Killed 2,141
Wounded 2,115
....

Committee of 70 Report

Grant Parish lies on the North Bank of Red River, some three hundred and fifty miles from New Orleans. It was created by the legislature of 1869; . . . its population is about 5,000; the races are almost equal in numbers; the swamp land, which is a belt of low land that skirts the north bank of the river the entire length of the parish . . . is . . . divided into large plantations. To the north of this belt of low land, the character of the country changes, the land becomes rolling and is covered with pine forests, while the farms are smaller, and not near so productive. The large majority of the Negroes occupy and live in the low lands, upon the great plantation, while in the uplands the white race very largely preponderates.

Colfax – the parish seat – is a small village containing four or five dwelling houses, two or three stores, and perhaps a resident population of 75 or 100 persons. . . .

. . . In November, 1872, a general election was held in the State of Louisiana. The Republican party ran its straight ticket, headed by Wm. Pitt Kellogg. The other party, ran a ticket, at the head of which was John McEnery, and upon which were Democrats, Liberal Republicans and Reformers, and which was known as the "Fusion ticket."[8]

After a spirited contest, remarkable for its peaceful character, the legal returns of the only legal officers of the election showed the triumph of the Fusion ticket by majorities ranging from 9,000 to 16,000 votes.

---

[7] General Phillip Sheridan (1831-1888), Union cavalry general and loyal subordinate to General Grant during the Civil War.

[8] A "Fusion" namely of Democrats and anti-Grant Liberal Republicans (see Document 26).

The order of Judge Durell,[9] the seizure of the State House by Federal soldiers, the assemblage by violence of a legislature at whose doors were armed Federal soldiers... and the inauguration of Wm. Pitt Kellogg, under the shadow of Federal bayonets soon followed.[10] Meanwhile John McEnery had been inaugurated Governor, and the oath of office administered to him in Lafayette Square, in the presence of 30,000 people, and amidst the greatest demonstrations of popular joy. The Fusion legislature was meeting... in regular and constitutional session. The officers elected to fill the various offices in the Districts and Parishes throughout the State had been commissioned by Governor Warmoth [*the former Governor*], on the 4th day of December 1872. Gov. McEnery also, believing himself the rightful Governor of the State, made such appointments throughout the State as were required by existing laws....

Thus it will be seen that there were two Governors, two Legislatures, and two sets of officers throughout the entire State....

Thus it will be seen, that throughout the length and breadth of the State anarchy, confusion and disorder reigned, and the utmost bitterness of feeling between the partisans of the rival governments prevailed.

This state of feeling and disorder had extended also to Grant Parish. At the November election, Alphonse Cazabat and Columbus C. Nash had been the Fusion candidates for the offices of Parish Judge and Sheriff. The election resulted in their success by majorities averaging from two hundred and fifty to three hundred votes, out of a full vote of near one thousand. They were commissioned by Gov. Warmouth on the 4th day of December, 1872, and toward the latter part of that month entered upon their official duties, and discharged them up to the 25th of March, 1873. Upon the same ticket with them, *James W. Hadnot* had been elected to represent Grant Parish in the Legislature, and had been meeting with the McEnery body...

... But Mr. Kellogg had learned that bayonets were stronger than popular will; had learned to look with contempt upon the idea of local self-government, and... [he] commissioned in absolute defiance of popular will, R. C. Register, Parish Judge, and Daniel Shaw as Sheriff. About the 23d of March, Register, [*and Kellogg's other appointees*]... arrived at Colfax.

---

[9] Edward Henry Durell (1810 – 1887) was a New Orleans lawyer and Unionist who had opposed secession. He was appointed US District Judge for Louisiana in 1863.
[10] Union law-enforcement and military forces judged the Fusion victory had been won more through corruption and intimidation than through legitimate means, so the legal and military arms supported the Republican candidate as the winner.

It will be borne in mind that Judge Cazabat and Sheriff Nash, up to that time, had been in full and complete possession of their offices, and were still exercising their functions. On that day, however, Register and Shaw took forcible and violent possession of the court-house.... There was no one to resist them. That same night, for reasons best known to themselves, they began to summon armed Negroes into Colfax. At first Shaw, acting under the order of Register, pretended to summon these Negroes as a sheriff's posse. But within five or six days Shaw's authority was set at naught and no longer regarded, and he himself detained in Colfax, watched and guarded, virtually a prisoner; and when he attempted to escape, was pursued and brought back under guard....

Thereafter the assemblage increased in Colfax, and from the 24th of March to April 13th the crowd of Negroes in Colfax was variously estimated at from 150 to 400 men. After the deposition of Sheriff Shaw's authority, the assemblage assumed a semi-military character. Three Captains were elected, and lieutenants, sergeants and corporals were appointed; men were regularly enrolled.... The Negroes were armed with shot-guns and Enfield rifles, and seizing upon an old steam pipe they cut it up, and by plugging one end of each piece and drilling vents, they improvised and mounted three cannon. They constructed a line of earth-works, some 300 yards in length and from 2 ½ to 4 feet high. Drilling was regularly kept up by Ward, Flowers and Levi Allen, all of whom had been soldiers of the United States Army. Guards were mounted and pickets posted, while mounted squads scouted the neighboring country. No white citizens were permitted to pass into Colfax.

In the meantime the white citizens of the Parish were filled with apprehension and alarm. A mass meeting was called for April 1st. It was proposed by Hadnot ... and others that a meeting be held at Colfax; that the colored people be invited, and an attempt made to compromise the existing difficulties. ...

In the meanwhile, affairs grew more alarming – Rapine, riot and outrage held high sway in Colfax....

Judge Rutland and family had left the town early in the beginning of the troubles, having been obliged to leave his house and effects unguarded.

On the night of the 4th of April, Flowers, a little sleek, black negro – a school master – at the head of a band of Negroes, broke open the house, plundered it, broke open and threw on the gallery of the house the coffin, containing the body of Judge Rutlaud's child, rifled trunks, armoirs and bureaus, carried away all articles of value, and then ... spent the night in riot and debauch....

Over forty families of white people left their homes, and taking their household goods, fled twenty or thirty miles into the interior. It is worth note that of the nine men recently tried in the U. S. Circuit Court, four of them with their families were among these refugees, and the day of the fight were over twenty miles away from Colfax. This fact was shown by 12 or 14 witnesses, and yet the three embittered and prejudiced Negroes on the jury, persisted in declaring for their guilt. . . .

The most terrible and alarming threats of murder and rapine were made by the Negroes, and borne to the ears of the whites and terror, uncertainty and lawlessness prevailed from one end of the Parish to the other. . . .

During the week prior to April 13th, C. C. Nash, the duly elected, commissioned and acting sheriff of Grant parish was busy summoning a posse of men to retake the court-house and put down the lawlessness that had filled the parish with terror and alarm.

On Sunday, April 13th, he found himself at the head of about 150 armed men, four miles northwest of Colfax. . . . Besides his posse of mounted men, he had a small piece of artillery mounted on wagon wheels, and to fit which he had obtained some oblong slugs of iron. Halting his men, he advanced . . ., under a flag of truce, and asked a colored man – John Miles – whom he there met, who commanded in Colfax. He was told "Lev Allen is in command." He then said, "Go and tell Lev to come here, that I want to see him." Miles obeyed, and soon Lev Allen and a few other Negroes came out to where Nash was. From Miles's testimony we learn that Allen acknowledged he was in command; that Nash told him he had come to retake the Court House; that he had force enough to accomplish it, and advised him that he had better disperse his men, and assured him that none of them would be molested. Allen peremptorily refused to disperse his men, and informed Nash that he and his men intended to fight to the last.

Nash then told him to remove all the women and children, and that half an hour would be granted for that purpose; and he and Allen separated, the former returning to his men, and the latter issuing orders for the women and children to leave the quarters and town of Colfax.

Up to this hour every effort at pacification had been made, and each time the advance had been made by the whites. . . .

About 12 o'clock, . . . the Negroes opened fire upon his force from the two pieces of improvised cannon which had been posted there. The whites returned the fire with small arms, and the Negroes retired to within their line of works near the Court House, and, lying down behind them, kept up a brisk fire with their shot-guns, rifles and pistols. The whites fired several shots from their cannon, which seemed to have done no harm whatever. Affairs continued thus for two hours, when about 2 P.M., the force under Nash, having secured a position for their cannon which commanded the inside of the line of works, opened fire upon the Negroes, who, finding their position untenable, retreated in all directions. Perhaps one hundred and fifty retreated into the woods and fields, and about one hundred took refuge in the Court House. Nash then opened fire upon that building, and one or two shots seemed to have struck its walls, without material damage. Up to this time no blood had been shed.

At this juncture the Court House was set on fire. It is doubtful as to how the fire originated. Some of the Negro witnesses testify that it was fired by combustible matter projected from the cannon, while others assert that it was fired by a Negro prisoner, sent on purpose by the whites. At all events, the building was in flames when two white flags were displayed from the windows.

Instantly, the firing ceased. Mr. James W. Hadnot and Mr. Harris – unarmed, and with hands raised to show that they were unarmed – approached the Court House, calling upon the negroes to throw down their arms, and that they would not be troubled. Approaching to within ten or fifteen feet of the Court House, these gentlemen were met by a volley from the negroes, who by this time were coming out of the burning building, and both fell, mortally wounded. The whites – exasperated beyond endurance at the cowardly and treacherous murder of their comrades, thus lured to their death by the false flag of truce held out by the Negroes – closed upon them and slaughtered a large majority of them. The Court House was entirely destroyed, together with its books and records. Sixty-four negroes were killed and wounded, the loss of the whites being four wounded and three killed....

That excesses were committed by the outraged and exasperated whites, there can be no doubt. But let it be remembered that they had appealed for aid, and none came; that they tried four times to avoid bloodshed, and without avail; that civil government in the State seemed wholly subverted; that their families were fleeing in terror from their homes; that rapine, and pillage and lawlessness held high revel, and made their lives, their property, and all they held dear, totally insecure. And finally, let it be remembered that, in the heat of the fight, they saw two prominent citizens, their comrades, go upon an errand of peace, summoned by flags of truce displayed by the negroes, unarmed, and with words of peace upon their lips, shot down, killed by the very persons they wished to save, and by the very hands that held the white flags of peace!...

In October, 1873, E. J. Cruikshank, A. C. Lewis, W. D. Irwin, John P. Hadnot, Denis Lemoine, Prudhomme Lemoine, A. P. Gibbons and Clement Penn were arrested and brought to New Orleans, and lodged in the Parish prison....

We deplore in common with all good citizens, the bloody affair at Colfax. We can view it in no other light than affording another evidence of the results of the misrule and oppression of the Southern States at the hands of the Federal power.

It has its lesson to the Negro and to the white.

It teaches the former what he may expect, if in obedience to the devilish teachings of the Radical emissary,[11] he arrays himself in hostility to the whites of the South.

It teaches the latter that acts of violence, no matter what the provocation, are construed into hostility and hatred of the National Government, and retards the day of conservative triumph.

It should teach both that their interests, their homes and destiny being identical, they should cultivate assiduously amicable relations the one with the other, and be co-laborers in the noble work of regenerating and restoring our once happy State to its pristine position of power and prosperity.

---

[11] Republicans from the North or carpetbaggers, as they came to be called.

Document 29

United States v. Cruikshank
The United States Supreme Court
March 27, 1876

The United States arrested nine men for the murders at Colfax. Prosecution for the Colfax massacre became a test of national resolve to continue protecting civil rights in the reconstructed South under the Enforcement Acts (Document 23). The Slaughterhouse Cases (Document 27), which was decided just after the Colfax Massacre (Document 28), offered a narrow reading of federal power under the new constitutional amendments. President Ulysses S. Grant's Attorney General, Amos T. Akerman (1821-1880), had, prior to the Slaughterhouse Cases, been increasing the number of prosecutions throughout the South under the Enforcement Acts—from 879 in 1871 to 1,960 in 1873. Soon after the Slaughterhouse decision he became leery of using his authority. The extraordinary violence of the Colfax case, however, called for a federal response. Some conspirators were identified and legal proceedings began, with a heavy federal military presence to protect attorneys, judges, jury members and witnesses for the prosecution from mob violence. The federal prosecutor indicted William Cruikshank and his co-conspirators on more than a dozen charges of violating the rights of those killed at Colfax. The defendants appealed on the grounds that the federal prosecutor had no jurisdiction over this case since, according to the Slaughterhouse Cases, prosecuting such crimes was a state matter. The circuit court agreed with the defendants, but the federal prosecutor appealed the case to the United States Supreme Court. A 5 - 4 majority of the Supreme Court agreed that the 14th Amendment had not vested Congress with sufficient powers to conduct such prosecutions.

Source: United States v. Cruikshank, 92 U.S. 542 (1876). Available online from Legal Information Institute, Cornell Law School. https://goo.gl/JMfYBc.

MR. CHIEF JUSTICE WAITE delivered the opinion of the court.

. . .

We have in our political system a government of the United States and a government of each of the several States. Each one of these governments is distinct from the others, and each has citizens of its own who owe it allegiance, and whose rights, within its jurisdiction, it must protect. The same person may be at the same time a citizen of the United States and a citizen of a State, but his rights of citizenship under one of these governments will be different from those he has under the other. [*Chief Justice Waite cited the Slaughterhouse cases as precedent for this opinion.*] ...

Experience made the fact known to the people of the United States that they required a national government for national purposes. The separate governments of the separate States, bound together by the Articles of Confederation alone, were not sufficient for the promotion of the general welfare of the people in respect to foreign nations, or for their complete protection as citizens of the confederated States. For this reason, the people of the United States, "in order to form a more perfect union, establish justice, insure domestic tranquility, provide for the common defense, promote the general welfare, and secure the blessings of liberty" to themselves and their posterity [preamble to the Constitution], ordained and established the government of the United States, and defined its powers by a constitution, which they adopted as its fundamental law, and made its rule of action.

The government thus established and defined is to some extent a government of the States in their political capacity. It is also, for certain purposes, a government of the people. Its powers are limited in number, but not in degree. Within the scope of its powers, as enumerated and defined, it is supreme and above the States; but beyond, it has no existence....

The people of the United States resident within any State are subject to two governments: one State, and the other National; but there need be no conflict between the two. The powers which one possesses, the other does not.... True, it may sometimes happen that a person is amenable to both jurisdictions for one and the same act. Thus, if a marshal of the United States is unlawfully resisted while executing the process of the courts within a State, and the resistance is accompanied by an assault on the officer, the sovereignty of the United States is violated by the resistance, and that of the State by the breach of peace, in the assault. ... This does not, however, imply that the two governments possess powers in common, or bring them into conflict with each other. It is the natural consequence of a citizenship which owes allegiance to two sovereignties, and claims protection from both....

The government of the United States is one of delegated powers alone. Its authority is defined and limited by the Constitution. All powers not granted to it by that instrument are reserved to the States or the people. No rights can be acquired under the Constitution or laws of the United States, except such as the government of the United States has the authority to grant or secure. All that cannot be so granted or secured are left under the protection of the States.

We now proceed to an examination of the indictment, to ascertain whether the several rights, which it is alleged the defendants intended to interfere with, are such as had been in law and in fact granted or secured by the Constitution or laws of the United States.

The first and ninth counts state the intent of the defendants to have been to hinder and prevent the citizens named in the free exercise and enjoyment of their "lawful right and privilege to peaceably assemble together with each other and with other citizens of the United States for a peaceful and lawful purpose." The right of the people peaceably to assemble for lawful purposes existed long before the adoption of the Constitution of the United States. . . . It was not, therefore, a right granted to the people by the Constitution. The government of the United States when established found it in existence, with the obligation on the part of the States to afford it protection. As no direct power over it was granted to Congress, it remains . . . subject to State jurisdiction. . . .

The first amendment to the Constitution prohibits Congress from abridging "the right of the people to assemble and to petition the government for a redress of grievances." This, like the other amendments proposed and adopted at the same time, was not intended to limit the powers of the State governments in respect to their own citizens, but to operate upon the National government alone . . . .

The particular amendment now under consideration assumes the existence of the right of the people to assemble for lawful purposes, and protects it against encroachment by Congress. The right was not created by the amendment; neither was its continuance guaranteed, except as against congressional interference. For their protection in its enjoyment . . . the people must look to the States. . . .

The second and tenth counts are equally defective. The right there specified is that of "bearing arms for a lawful purpose." This is not a right granted by the Constitution. Neither is it in any manner dependent upon that instrument for its existence. The second amendment declares that it shall not be infringed; but this, as has been seen, means no more than that it shall not be infringed by Congress. . . .

The third and eleventh counts are even more objectionable. They charge the intent to have been to deprive the citizens named, they being in Louisiana, "of their respective several lives and liberty of person without due process of law." This is nothing else than alleging a conspiracy to falsely imprison or murder citizens of the United States, being within the territorial jurisdiction of the State of Louisiana. The rights of life and personal liberty are natural rights of man. "To secure these rights," says the Declaration of Independence, "governments are instituted among men, deriving their just powers from the consent of the governed." The very highest duty of the States, when they entered into the Union under the Constitution, was to protect all persons within their boundaries in the enjoyment of these "unalienable rights with which they were endowed by their Creator." Sovereignty, for this purpose, rests alone with the States. It is no more the duty or within the power of the United States to punish for a conspiracy to falsely imprison or murder within a State, than it would be to punish for false imprisonment or murder itself.

The fourteenth amendment prohibits a State from depriving any person of life, liberty, or property, without due process of law; but this adds nothing to the rights of one citizen as against another. It simply furnishes an additional guaranty against any encroachment by the States upon the fundamental rights which belong to every citizen as a member of society. . . . These counts in the indictment do not call for the exercise of any of the powers conferred by this provision in the amendment.

The fourth and twelfth counts charge the intent to have been to prevent and hinder the citizens named, who were of African descent and persons of color, in "the free exercise and enjoyment of their several rights and privileges to the full and equal benefit of all laws and proceedings . . . ." There is no allegation that this was done because of the race or color of the persons conspired against. When stripped of its verbiage, the case as presented amounts to nothing more than that the defendants conspired to prevent certain citizens of the United States, being within the State of Louisiana, from enjoying the equal protection of the laws of the State and of the United States.

The fourteenth amendment prohibits a State from denying to any person within its jurisdiction the equal protection of the laws; but this provision does not, any more than the one which precedes it, and which we have just considered, add anything to the rights which one citizen has under the Constitution against another. The equality of the rights of citizens is a principle of republicanism. Every republican government is in duty bound to protect all its citizens in the enjoyment of this principle, if within its power. That duty was originally assumed by the States; and it still remains there. The only obligation resting upon the United States is to see that the States do not deny the right. . . .

The sixth and fourteenth counts state the intent of the defendants to have been to hinder and prevent the citizens named, being of African descent, and colored, "in the free exercise and enjoyment of their several and respective rights and privileges to vote at any election to be thereafter by law had and held by the people in and of the said State of Louisiana".... [W]e hold that the fifteenth amendment has invested the citizens of the United States with a new constitutional right, which is, exemption from discrimination in the exercise of the elective franchise on account of race, color, or previous condition of servitude. From this it appears that the right of suffrage is not a necessary attribute of national citizenship; but that exemption from discrimination in the exercise of that right on account of race, &c., is. The right to vote in the States comes from the States; but the right of exemption from the prohibited discrimination comes from the United States. The first has not been granted or secured by the Constitution of the United States; but the last has been.

Inasmuch, therefore, as it does not appear in these counts that the intent of the defendants was to prevent these parties from exercising their right to vote on account of their race, &c., it does not appear that it was their intent to interfere with any right granted or secured by the Constitution or laws of the United States. We may suspect that race was the cause of the hostility; but it is not so averred....

We are, therefore, of the opinion that the [indictments] do not contain charges of a criminal nature made indictable under the laws of the United States. .. They do not show that it was the intent of the defendants, by their conspiracy, to hinder or prevent the enjoyment of any right granted or secured by the Constitution....

The order of the Circuit Court arresting the judgment upon the verdict is . . . affirmed; and the cause remanded, with instructions to discharge the defendants.

Document 30

Inaugural Address
Rutherford B. Hayes
March 5, 1877

Rutherford B. Hayes (1822–1893) had been a Union general early in the Civil War. Elected to Congress in 1864, he voted consistently in favor of measures such as the Civil Rights Act of 1866 (Document 13), the 14th Amendment (Document 14), and the Reconstruction Acts (Document 17). Hayes then served two terms as Ohio governor. He was responsible for shepherding the 15th Amendment (Document 22) through the ratification process in his state. Hayes won the Republican nomination for president and faced the Democratic nominee, New York Governor Samuel Tilden (1814-1886) in the presidential election. It was among the most hotly contested presidential elections in American history. Three states – Louisiana, South Carolina, and Florida – had disputed elections. It was up to the Congress to decide which electoral outcome to accept. Through an unusual mechanism (Congress passed a law establishing an electoral commission to decide the disputed elections), Hayes was deemed to have won all the disputed state elections and their electoral college votes (Hayes lost the popular vote nationally). This gave Hayes a one vote victory in the electoral college; he won the Presidency. Hayes became president as a Democratic House and a Republican Senate were returned to Congress. In the House, where money bills originate, there was no will to continue appropriating funds for military supervision of civil rights in the South. There would no longer be available monies to sustain military supervision of civil rights in the South pursuant to the Enforcement Acts (Document 23). In any event, that approach had been declared unconstitutional by the Supreme Court (Document 29). Realizing the old ways could not be sustained, Hayes announced another somewhat new approach to Reconstruction. His approach would be based on "home rule" in the South with national supervision through legal channels (as opposed to military channels). The election of 1876 is often linked, in historical accounts, to the compromise of 1877, a putative bargain between Democrats and Republicans: Hayes, the Republican, became president, while military rule in the South came to an end. His inaugural address marks the general principles that would guide Republican Party policies for the next generation.

Source: Rutherford B. Hayes: Inaugural Address, March 5, 1877. Online by Gerhard Peters and John T. Woolley, The American Presidency Project. https://goo.gl/REsidc.

We have assembled to repeat the public ceremonial, begun by Washington, observed by all my predecessors, and now a time-honored custom, which marks the commencement of a new term of the Presidential office. Called to the duties of this great trust, I proceed in compliance with usage to announce some of the leading principles, on the subjects that now chiefly engage the public attention, by which it is my desire to be guided in the discharge of those duties. I shall ... undertake ... to speak of the motives which should animate us, and to suggest certain important ends to be attained in accordance with our institutions and essential to the welfare of our country....

The permanent pacification of the country upon such principles and by such measures as will secure the complete protection of all its citizens in the free enjoyment of all their constitutional rights is now the one subject in our public affairs which all thoughtful and patriotic citizens regard as of supreme importance.

Many of the calamitous efforts of the tremendous revolution which has passed over the Southern States still remain. The immeasurable benefits which will surely follow, sooner or later, the hearty and generous acceptance of the legitimate results of that revolution have not yet been realized. Difficult and embarrassing questions meet us at the threshold of this subject. The people of those States are still impoverished, and the inestimable blessing of wise, honest, and peaceful local self-government is not fully enjoyed. Whatever difference of opinion may exist as to the cause of this condition of things, the fact is clear that in the progress of events the time has come when such government is the imperative necessity required by all the varied interests, public and private, of those States. But it must not be forgotten that only a local government which recognizes and maintains inviolate the rights of all is a true self-government.

With respect to the two distinct races whose peculiar relations to each other have brought upon us the deplorable complications and perplexities which exist in those States, it must be a government which guards the interests of both races carefully and equally. It must be a government which submits loyally and heartily to the Constitution and the laws – the laws of the nation and the laws of the States themselves – accepting and obeying faithfully the whole Constitution as it is.

Resting upon this sure and substantial foundation, the superstructure of beneficent local governments can be built up, and not otherwise. In furtherance of such obedience to the letter and the spirit of the Constitution, and in behalf of all that its attainment implies, all so-called party interests lose their apparent importance, and party lines may well be permitted to fade into insignificance. The question we have to consider for the immediate welfare of those States of the Union is the question of government or no government; of social order and all the peaceful industries and the happiness that belongs to it, or a return to barbarism. It is a question in which every citizen of the nation is deeply interested, and with respect to which we ought not to be, in a partisan sense, either Republicans or Democrats, but fellow-citizens and fellowmen, to whom the interests of a common country and a common humanity are dear.

The sweeping revolution of the entire labor system of a large portion of our country and the advance of 4,000,000 people from a condition of servitude to that of citizenship, upon an equal footing with their former masters, could not occur without presenting problems of the gravest moment, to be dealt with by the emancipated race, by their former masters, and by the General Government, the author of the act of emancipation. That it was a wise, just, and providential act, fraught with good for all concerned, is not [now][1] generally conceded throughout the country. That a moral obligation rests upon the National Government to employ its constitutional power and influence to establish the rights of the people it has emancipated, and to protect them in the enjoyment of those rights when they are infringed or assailed, is also generally admitted.

The evils which afflict the Southern States can only be removed or remedied by the united and harmonious efforts of both races, actuated by motives of mutual sympathy and regard; and while in duty bound and fully determined to protect the rights of all by every constitutional means at the disposal of my Administration, I am sincerely anxious to use every legitimate influence in favor of honest and efficient local "self"-government as the true resource of those States for the promotion of the contentment and prosperity of their citizens. In the effort I shall make to accomplish this purpose I ask the cordial cooperation of all who cherish an interest in the welfare of the country, trusting that party ties and the prejudice of race will be freely surrendered in behalf of the great purpose to be accomplished. In the important work of

---

[1] Some manuscripts suggest that this word is "now," which is consistent with the tenor of Hayes' speech, which aimed to suggest a national consensus on fundamental matters such as the goodness of emancipation and the duty of the national government to protect it.

restoring the South it is not the political situation alone that merits attention. The material development of that section of the country has been arrested by the social and political revolution through which it has passed, and now needs and deserves the considerate care of the National Government within the just limits prescribed by the Constitution and wise public economy.

But at the basis of all prosperity, for that as well as for every other part of the country, lies the improvement of the intellectual and moral condition of the people. Universal suffrage should rest upon universal education. To this end, liberal and permanent provision should be made for the support of free schools by the State governments, and, if need be, supplemented by legitimate aid from national authority.

Let me assure my countrymen of the Southern States that it is my earnest desire to regard and promote their truest interest – the interests of the white and of the colored people both and equally – and to put forth my best efforts in behalf of a civil policy which will forever wipe out in our political affairs the color line and the distinction between North and South, to the end that we may have not merely a united North or a united South, but a united country. . . .

Document 31

"The United States Cannot Remain Half-Slave and Half-Free"
July 26, 1945

Frederick Douglass (1818–1895), a former slave, was the premier figure in abolitionist circles before the Civil War and a leading advocate for racial equality after it. His career in writing and oratory began in 1841, only two years after he escaped from slavery in Maryland, and lasted more than fifty years. During the years before the Civil War, Douglass advocated for an anti-slavery interpretation of the Constitution. After the Civil War, he saw any doubts about the Constitution's position on slavery resolved through the 13th, 14th, and 15th amendments. Yet he saw clearly that changes in law, important as they are, were not enough to win genuine emancipation for freedmen. By the time Douglass helped to celebrate the twenty-first anniversary of emancipation in Washington D.C., many of the hard-won fruits of the war were in jeopardy. Black Codes had been passed (Document 8) and national efforts to roll them back met with limited success (Documents 13 and 23). The Ku Klux Klan had arisen as a threat to the lives, property, and liberty of freedmen (Documents 10, 25, 28). The Supreme Court had given the Civil War amendments increasingly narrow interpretations (Documents 27 and 29) that inhibited the national government's ability to secure freedmen's rights and safety. Northern troops had pulled out of the South with the election of Rutherford B. Hayes (Document 30). A new segregation of the races, enforced through law and opinion, arose across the South.

The title of Douglass's speech lamenting the new segregation pointedly alludes to Abraham Lincoln's "House Divided" speech in 1858, in which Lincoln predicted that the government of the United States could not endure "half slave and half free." That Douglass could entertain the same thought 35 years after Lincoln's speech and 21 years after the emancipation of slaves in Washington D.C. is testimony to how far America still had to go if it was to live up to its promise of equal liberty for all.

Source: Frederick Douglass, Address by Hon. Frederick Douglass, Delivered in the Congregational Church, Washington, D.C., on the Twenty-first Anniversary of Emancipation in the District of Columbia, 1883, Library of Congress, Manuscript/Mixed Material, https://goo.gl/1D9vLq.

...At the outset, as an old watchman on the walls of liberty, eagerly scanning the social and political horizon, you naturally ask me, What of the night? It is easy to break forth in joy and thanksgiving for Emancipation in the District of Columbia. It is easy to call up the noble sentiments and the startling events which made that measure possible. It is easy to trace the footsteps of the negro in the past, marked as they are all the way along with blood. But the present occasion calls for something more. How stands the Negro today? What are the relations subsisting between him and the powerful people among whom he lives, moves, and has his being? What is the outlook, and what is his probable future?

You will readily perceive that I have raised more questions than I shall be able for the present to answer. My general response to these inquiries is a mixed one. The sky of the American Negro is dark, but not rayless; it is stormy, but not cheerless. The grand old party of liberty, union, and progress, which has been his reliance and refuge so long, though less cohesive and strong than it once was, is still a power and has a future.... Peace with the old master class has been war to the Negro. As the one has risen, the other has fallen. The reaction has been sudden, marked, and violent. It has swept the Negro from all the legislative halls of the Southern States, and from those of the Congress of the United States. It has, in many cases, driven him from the ballot box and the jury box. The situation has much in it for serious thought, but nothing to cause despair....

...Time and events which have done so much for us in the past, will, I trust, not do less for us in the future. The moral government of the universe is on our side, and cooperates, with all honest efforts, to lift up the downtrodden and oppressed in all lands, whether the oppressed be white or black. In whatever else the Negro may have been a failure, he has, in one respect, been a marked and brilliant success. He has managed by one means or another to make himself one of the most prominent and interesting figures that now attract and hold the attention of the world...

Men of all lands and languages make him a subject of profound thought and study. To the statesman and philosopher he is an object of intense curiosity. Men want to know more of his character, his qualities, his attainments, his mental possibilities, and his probable destiny....

Great, however, as is his advantage at this point, he is not altogether fortunate after all, as to the manner in which his claims are canvassed. His misfortune is that few men are qualified to discuss him candidly and impartially. ...

It was so in time of slavery, and it is so now. Then, the cause was interest, now, the cause is pride and prejudice. Then, the cause was property. He was then worth twenty hundred millions to his owner. He is now worth uncounted millions to himself. While a slave there was a mountain of gold on his breast to keep him down – now that he is free there is a mountain of prejudice to hold him down.

Let any man now claim for the Negro, or worse still, let the Negro now claim for himself, any right, privilege or immunity which has hitherto been denied him by law or custom, and he will at once open a fountain of bitterness, and call forth overwhelming wrath.

It is his sad lot to live in a land where all presumptions are arrayed against him, unless we except the presumption of inferiority and worthlessness. If his course is downward, he meets very little resistance, but if upward, his way is disputed at every turn of the road. If he comes in rags and in wretchedness, he answers the public demand for a Negro, and provokes no anger, though he may provoke derision, but if he presumes to be a gentleman and a scholar, he is then entirely out of his place.... If he offers himself to a builder as a mechanic, to a client as a lawyer, to a patient as a physician, to a university as a professor, or to a department as a clerk, no matter what may be his ability or his attainment, there is a presumption based upon his color or his previous condition, of incompetency, and if he succeeds at all, he has to do so against this most discouraging presumption.

It is a real calamity, in this country, for any man, guilty or not guilty, to be accused of crime, but it is an incomparably greater calamity for any colored man to be so accused. Justice is often painted with bandaged eyes. She is described in forensic eloquence, as utterly blind to wealth or poverty, high or low, white or black, but a mask of iron, however thick, could never blind American justice, when a black man happens to be on trial. Here, even more than elsewhere, he will find all presumptions of law and evidence against him....

... In many parts of our common country, the action of courts and juries is entirely too slow for the impetuosity of the people's justice. When the black man is accused, the mob takes the law into its own hands, and whips, shoots, stabs, hangs or burns the accused, simply upon the allegation or suspicion of crime. Of such proceedings Southern papers are full. A crime almost unknown [*on the part of*] the colored man in the time of slavery seems now, from report, the most common. I do not believe these reports [*of black crimes*]. There are too many reasons for trumping up such charges.

Another feature of the situation is, that this mob violence is seldom rebuked by the press and the pulpit, in its immediate neighborhood, because the public opinion, which sustains and makes possible such outrages, intimidates both press and pulpit. Besides, nobody expects that those who participate in such mob violence will ever be held answerable to the law, and punished.... The situation, my colored fellow citizens, is discouraging, but with all its hardships, and horrors, I am neither desperate nor despairing as to the future.

One ground of hope is found in the fact referred to in the beginning, and that is, the discussion concerning the Negro still goes on.

The country in which we live is happily governed by ideas as well as by laws, and no black man need despair while there is an audible and earnest assertion of justice and right on his behalf. He may be riddled with bullets, or roasted over a slow fire by the mob, but his cause cannot be shot or burned or otherwise destroyed. Like the impalpable ghost of the murdered Hamlet, it is immortal. All talk of its being a dead issue is a mistake. It may for a time be buried, but it is not dead. Tariffs, free trade, civil service, and river and harbor bills, may for a time cover it, but it will rise again, and again, and again, with increased life and vigor. Every year adds to the black man's numbers. Every year adds to his wealth and to his intelligence. These will speak for him....

... Without putting my head to the ground, I can even now hear the anxious inquiry as to when this discussion of the Negro will cease. When will he cease to be a bone of contention between the two great parties? Speaking for myself... I long to see the Negro utterly out of the whirlpool of angry political debate.... I want the whole American people to unite with the sentiment of their greatest captain, U.S. Grant, and say with him on this subject "Let us have peace."[1] ... But it is idle, utterly idle to dream of peace anywhere in this world, while any part of the human family are the victims of marked injustice and oppression....

Fellow citizens, the present hour is full of admonition and warning....

No matter what the Democratic party may say; no matter what the old master class of the South may say; no matter what the Supreme Court of the United States may say, the fact is beyond question that the loyal American people, in view of the services of the Negro in the national hour of peril, meant to make him, in good faith and according to the letter and spirit of the Constitution of the United States, a full and complete American citizen.

The amendments to the Constitution of the United States mean this, or they are a cruel, scandalous and colossal sham, and deserve to be so branded before the civilized world. What Abraham Lincoln said in respect of the United States is as true of the colored people as of the relations of those States. They

---

[1] Grant made this remark in his speech accepting the Republican Party's nomination for the Presidency in 1868. See the introduction to Document 23.

cannot remain half slave and half free. You must give them all or take from them all. Until this half-and-half condition is ended, there will be just ground of complaint. You will have an aggrieved class, and this discussion will go on. Until the public schools shall cease to be caste schools in every part of our country, this discussion will go on. Until the colored man's pathway to the American ballot box, North and South, shall be as smooth and as safe as the same is for the white citizen, this discussion will go on. Until the colored man's right to practice at the bar of our courts, and sit upon juries, shall be the universal law and practice of land, this discussion will go on. Until the courts of the country shall grant the colored man a fair trial and a just verdict, this discussion will go on. Until color shall cease to be a bar to equal participation in the offices and honors of the country, this discussion will go on. Until the trades-unions and the workshops of the country shall cease to proscribe the colored man and prevent his children from learning useful trades, this discussion will go on. Until the American people shall make character, and not color, the criterion of respectability, this discussion will go on....

...The rights of the Negro, as a man and a brother, began to be asserted with the earliest American Colonial history, and I derive hope from the fact, that the discussion still goes on, and the claims of the Negro rise higher and higher as the years roll by. Two hundred years of discussion has abated no jot of its power or its vitality. Behind it we have a great cloud of witnesses, going back to the beginning of our country and to the very foundation of our government. Our best men have given their voices and their votes on the right side of it, through all our generations....

The first publication in assertion and vindication of any right of the Negro, of which I have any knowledge, was written more than two hundred years ago, by Rev. Morgan Godwin, a missionary of Virginia and Jamaica.[2] This was only a plea for the right of the Negro to baptism and church membership. The last publication of any considerable note, of which I have any knowledge, is a recent article in the *Popular Science Monthly*, by Professor Gilliam.[3] The distance and difference between these two publications, in point of time, gives us a gauge by which we may in good degree measure the progress of the Negro. The book of

---

[2] Morgan Godwin (1640 circa – 1690) was an Anglican missionary and author of *The Negro's and Indians Advocate, Suing For Their Admission into the Church*, published in 1680.

[3] Prof. E.W. Gilliam penned an article entitled "The African in the United States," (22 February 1883) expressing worries that America was yielding to a black supremacy based on the natural birth rates among freedmen.

Godwin was published in 1680, and the article of Gilliam was published in 1883. The space in time between the two is not greater than the space in morals and enlightenment. The ground taken in respect to the Negro, in the one, is low. The ground taken in respect to the possibilities of the Negro, in the other, is so high as to be somewhat startling, not only to the white man, but also to the black man himself.

The book of Morgan Godwin is a literary curiosity and an ethical wonder. I deem myself fortunate in being the owner of a copy of it.... [Dr. Godwin] very evidently was not a Negro worshiper, nor what in our day would be called an abolitionist. He proposed no disturbance of the relation of master and slave. On the contrary, he conceded the right of the master to own and control the body of the Negro, but insisted that the soul of the Negro belonged to the Lord. ... [T]he ground taken in this book by Dr. Godwin was immensely important. It was, in fact, the starting point, the foundation of all the grand concession yet made to the claims, the character, the manhood and the dignity of the Negro. In the light of his present acknowledged position among men, here and elsewhere, a book to prove the Negro's right to baptism seems ridiculous, but so it did not seem two hundred years ago. Baptism was then a vital and commanding question, one with which the moral and intellectual giants of that day were required to grapple.

The opposition to baptizing and admitting the Negro to membership in the Christian church, was serious, determined, and bitter. That ceremony was, in his case, opposed on many grounds, but especially upon three. First, the Negro's unfitness for baptism; secondly, the nature of the ordinance itself; and thirdly, because it would disturb the relation of master and slave. The wily slaveholders of that day were sharp-eyed and keen scented, and snuffed danger from afar....

They contended that this holy ordinance could only be properly administered to free and responsible agents, men, who, in all matters of moral conduct, could exercise the sacred right of choice; and this proposition was very easily defended. For, plainly enough, the Negro did not answer that description. The law of the land did not even know him as a person. He was simply a piece of property, an article of merchandise, marked and branded as such, and no more fitted to be admitted to the fellowship of the saints than horse, sheep or swine....

... To thrust baptism and the church between the slave and his master was a dangerous interference with the absolute authority of the master. The slaveholders were always logical. When they assumed that slavery was right, they easily saw that everything inconsistent with slavery was wrong.... There was a more controlling motive for opposing baptism. Baptism had a legal as well as a religious significance. By the common law at that time, baptism was made a sufficient basis for a legal claim for emancipation....

For in that day of Christian simplicity, honest rules of Biblical interpretation were applied. The Bible was thought to mean just what it said. When a heathen ceased to be a heathen and became a Christian, he could no longer be held as a slave. Within the meaning of the accepted word of God it was the heathen, not the Christian, who was to be bought and sold, and held as bondman forever.

This fact stood like a roaring lion ready to tear and devour any Negro who sought the ordinance of baptism.

In the eyes of the wise and prudent of his times, Dr. Godwin was a dangerous man, a disturber of the peace of the church....

In fact, when viewed relatively, low as was the ground assumed by this good man two hundred years ago, he was as far in advance of his times then as Charles Sumner was when he first took his seat in the United States Senate. What baptism and church membership were for the Negro in the days of Godwin, the ballot and civil rights were for the Negro in the days of Sumner....

... Friends and fellow-citizens, in conclusion I return to the point from which I started, namely: What is to be the future of the colored people of this country? Some change in their condition seems to be looked for by thoughtful men everywhere; but what that change will be, no one yet has been able with certainty to predict.

Three different solutions to this difficult problem have been given and adopted by different classes of the American people. 1. Colonization in Africa; 2. Extinction through poverty, disease and death; 3. Assimilation and unification with the great body of the American people....

... We neither know the evil nor the good which may be in store for us. Twenty-five years ago the system of slavery seemed impregnable. Cotton was king and the civilized world acknowledged his sway. Twenty-five years ago, no man could have foreseen that in less than ten years from that time no master would wield a lash and no slave would clank a chain in the United States. Who at that time dreamed that Negroes would ever be seen as we have seen them today marching through the streets of this superb city, the Capital of this great Nation with eagles on their buttons, muskets on their shoulders and swords by their sides, timing their high footsteps to the Star Spangled Banner and the Red, White and Blue? Who at that time dreamed that colored men would ever sit in the House of Representatives and in the Senate of the United States?

With a knowledge of the events of the last score of years, with a knowledge of the sudden and startling changes which have already come to pass, I am not prepared to say what the future will be.

But I will say that I do not look for colonization either in or out of the United States. Africa is too far off, even if we desired to go there, which we do not. The navy of all the world would not be sufficient to remove our natural increase to that far off country. Removal to any of the territories is out of question.

We have no business to put ourselves before the bayonet of the white race. We have seen the fate of the Indian. As to extinction, the prospect in that direction has been greatly clouded by the census just taken, in which it is seen that our increase is ten per cent greater than that of the white people of the South.

There is but one destiny, it seems to me, left for us, and that is to make ourselves and be made by others a part of the American people in every sense of the word. Assimilation and not isolation is our true policy and our natural destiny. Unification for us is life: separation is death. We cannot afford to set up for ourselves a separate political party, or adopt for ourselves a political creed apart from the rest of our fellow citizens. Our own interests will be subserved by a generous care for the interests of the Nation at large. All the political, social and literary forces around us tend to unification.

I am the more inclined to accept this solution because I have seen the steps already taken in that direction. The American people have their prejudices, but they have other qualities as well. They easily adapt themselves to inevitable conditions, and all their tendency is to progress, enlightenment and to the universal.

> It's comin' yet for a' that,
> That man to man the world o'er
> Shall brothers be for a' that.[4]

---

[4] From Robert Burns, "A Man's a Man for A' That" (1795). See https://goo.gl/UYLYUT

Appendices

Appendix A:
Declaration of Independence

In CONGRESS, July 4, 1776

The unanimous Declaration of the thirteen united States of America,

When in the Course of human events, it becomes necessary for one people to dissolve the political bands which have connected them with another, and to assume among the powers of the earth, the separate and equal station to which the Laws of Nature and of Nature's God entitle them, a decent respect to the opinions of mankind requires that they should declare the causes which impel them to the separation.

We hold these truths to be self-evident, that all men are created equal, that they are endowed by their Creator with certain unalienable Rights, that among these are Life, Liberty and the pursuit of Happiness. — That to secure these rights, Governments are instituted among Men, deriving their just powers from the consent of the governed, — that whenever any Form of Government becomes destructive of these ends, it is the Right of the People to alter or to abolish it, and to institute new Government, laying its foundation on such principles and organizing its powers in such form, as to them shall seem most likely to effect their Safety and Happiness. Prudence, indeed, will dictate that Governments long established should not be changed for light and transient causes; and accordingly all experience hath shewn, that mankind are more disposed to suffer, while evils are sufferable, than to right themselves by abolishing the forms to which they are accustomed. But when a long train of abuses and usurpations, pursuing invariably the same Object evinces a design to reduce them under absolute Despotism, it is their right, it is their duty, to throw off such Government, and to provide new Guards for their future security. — Such has been the patient sufferance of these Colonies; and such is now the necessity which constrains them to alter their former Systems of Government. The history of the present King of Great Britain is a history of repeated injuries and usurpations, all having in direct object the establishment of an absolute Tyranny over these States. To prove this, let Facts be submitted to a candid world.

He has refused his Assent to Laws, the most wholesome and necessary for the public good.

He has forbidden his Governors to pass Laws of immediate and pressing importance, unless suspended in their operation till his Assent should be obtained; and when so suspended, he has utterly neglected to attend to them.

He has refused to pass other Laws for the accommodation of large districts of people, unless those people would relinquish the right of Representation in the Legislature, a right inestimable to them and formidable to tyrants only.

He has called together legislative bodies at places unusual, uncomfortable, and distant from the depository of their public Records, for the sole purpose of fatiguing them into compliance with his measures.

He has dissolved Representative Houses repeatedly, for opposing with manly firmness his invasions on the rights of the people.

He has refused for a long time, after such dissolutions, to cause others to be elected; whereby the Legislative powers, incapable of Annihilation, have returned to the People at large for their exercise; the State remaining in the mean time exposed to all the dangers of invasion from without, and convulsions within.

He has endeavoured to prevent the population of these States; for that purpose obstructing the Laws for Naturalization of Foreigners; refusing to pass others to encourage their migrations hither, and raising the conditions of new Appropriations of Lands.

He has obstructed the Administration of Justice, by refusing his Assent to Laws for establishing Judiciary powers.

He has made Judges dependent on his Will alone, for the tenure of their offices, and the amount and payment of their salaries.

He has erected a multitude of New Offices, and sent hither swarms of Officers to harrass our people, and eat out their substance.

He has kept among us, in times of peace, Standing Armies without the Consent of our legislatures.

He has affected to render the Military independent of and superior to the Civil power.

He has combined with others to subject us to a jurisdiction foreign to our constitution, and unacknowledged by our laws; giving his Assent to their Acts of pretended Legislation:

For Quartering large bodies of armed troops among us:

For protecting them, by a mock Trial, from punishment for any Murders which they should commit on the Inhabitants of these States:

For cutting off our Trade with all parts of the world:

For imposing Taxes on us without our Consent:

For depriving us in many cases, of the benefits of Trial by Jury:

For transporting us beyond Seas to be tried for pretended offences:

For abolishing the free System of English Laws in a neighbouring Province, establishing therein an Arbitrary government, and enlarging its Boundaries so as to render it at once an example and fit instrument for introducing the same absolute rule into these Colonies:

For taking away our Charters, abolishing our most valuable Laws, and altering fundamentally the Forms of our Governments:

For suspending our own Legislatures, and declaring themselves invested with power to legislate for us in all cases whatsoever.

He has abdicated Government here, by declaring us out of his Protection and waging War against us.

He has plundered our seas, ravaged our Coasts, burnt our towns, and destroyed the lives of our people.

He is at this time transporting large Armies of foreign Mercenaries to compleat the works of death, desolation and tyranny, already begun with circumstances of Cruelty & perfidy scarcely paralleled in the most barbarous ages, and totally unworthy the Head of a civilized nation.

He has constrained our fellow Citizens taken Captive on the high Seas to bear Arms against their Country, to become the executioners of their friends and Brethren, or to fall themselves by their Hands.

He has excited domestic insurrections amongst us, and has endeavoured to bring on the inhabitants of our frontiers, the merciless Indian Savages, whose known rule of warfare, is an undistinguished destruction of all ages, sexes and conditions.

In every stage of these Oppressions We have Petitioned for Redress in the most humble terms: Our repeated Petitions have been answered only by repeated injury. A Prince whose character is thus marked by every act which may define a Tyrant, is unfit to be the ruler of a free people.

Nor have We been wanting in attentions to our British brethren. We have warned them from time to time of attempts by their legislature to extend an unwarrantable jurisdiction over us. We have reminded them of the circumstances of our emigration and settlement here. We have appealed to their native justice and magnanimity, and we have conjured them by the ties of our common kindred to disavow these usurpations, which, would inevitably interrupt our connections and correspondence. They too have been deaf to the voice of justice and of consanguinity. We must, therefore, acquiesce in the necessity, which denounces our Separation, and hold them, as we hold the rest of mankind, Enemies in War, in Peace Friends.

We, THEREFORE, the Representatives of the UNITED STATES OF AMERICA, in General Congress, Assembled, appealing to the Supreme Judge of the world for the rectitude of our intentions, do, in the Name, and by Authority of the good People of these Colonies, solemnly publish and declare, That these United Colonies are, and of Right ought to be FREE AND INDEPENDENT STATES; that they are Absolved from all Allegiance to the British Crown, and that all political connection between them and the State of Great Britain, is and ought to be totally dissolved; and that as Free and Independent States, they have full Power to levy War, conclude Peace, contract Alliances, establish Commerce, and to do all other Acts and Things which Independent States may of right do. And for the support of this Declaration, with a firm reliance on the protection of divine Providence, we mutually pledge to each other our Lives, our Fortunes and our sacred Honor.

Declaration of Independence

[Georgia:]
Button Gwinnett
Lyman Hall
George Walton

[North Carolina:]
William Hooper
Joseph Hewes
John Penn

[South Carolina:]
Edward Rutledge
Thomas Heyward, Jr.
Thomas Lynch, Jr.
Arthur Middleton

[Maryland:]
Samuel Chase
William Paca
Thomas Stone
Charles Carroll of Carrollton

[Virginia:]
George Wythe
Richard Henry Lee
Thomas Jefferson
Benjamin Harrison

Thomas Nelson, Jr.
Francis Lightfoot Lee
Carter Braxton

[Pennsylvania:]
Robert Morris
Benjamin Rush
Benjamin Franklin
John Morton
George Clymer
James Smith
George Taylor
James Wilson
George Ross

[Delaware:]
Caesar Rodney
George Read
Thomas McKean

[New York:]
William Floyd
Philip Livingston
Francis Lewis
Lewis Morris

[New Jersey:]
Richard Stockton

John Witherspoon
Francis Hopkinson
John Hart
Abraham Clark

[New Hampshire:]
Josiah Bartlett
William Whipple
Matthew Thornton

[Massachusetts:]
John Hancock
Samuel Adams
John Adams
Robert Treat Paine
Elbridge Gerry

[Rhode Island:]
Stephen Hopkins
William Ellery

[Connecticut:]
Roger Sherman
Samuel Huntington
William Williams
Oliver Wolcott

Appendix B:
Constitution of the United States of America
September 17, 1787

[Editors' note: Bracketed sections in the text of the Constitution have been superceded or modified by Constitutional amendments.]

We the People of the United States, in Order to form a more perfect Union, establish Justice, insure domestic Tranquility, provide for the common defence, promote the general Welfare, and secure the Blessings of Liberty to ourselves and our Posterity, do ordain and establish this Constitution for the United States of America.

Article. I.

Section. 1. All legislative Powers herein granted shall be vested in a Congress of the United States, which shall consist of a Senate and House of Representatives.

Section. 2. The House of Representatives shall be composed of Members chosen every second Year by the People of the several States, and the Electors in each State shall have the Qualifications requisite for Electors of the most numerous Branch of the State Legislature.

No Person shall be a Representative who shall not have attained to the Age of twenty five Years, and been seven Years a Citizen of the United States, and who shall not, when elected, be an Inhabitant of that State in which he shall be chosen.

[Representatives and direct Taxes shall be apportioned among the several States which may be included within this Union, according to their respective Numbers, which shall be determined by adding to the whole Number of free Persons, including those bound to Service for a Term of Years, and excluding Indians not taxed, three fifths of all other Persons.][1] The actual Enumeration shall be made within three Years after the first Meeting of the Congress of the United States, and within every subsequent Term of ten Years, in such Manner as they shall by Law direct. The Number of Representatives shall not exceed one for every thirty Thousand, but each State shall have at Least one Representative;

---

[1] modified by Section 2 of the Fourteenth Amendment

and until such enumeration shall be made, the State of New Hampshire shall be entitled to chuse three, Massachusetts eight, Rhode-Island and Providence Plantations one, Connecticut five, New-York six, New Jersey four, Pennsylvania eight, Delaware one, Maryland six, Virginia ten, North Carolina five, South Carolina five, and Georgia three.

When vacancies happen in the Representation from any State, the Executive Authority thereof shall issue Writs of Election to fill such Vacancies.

The House of Representatives shall chuse their Speaker and other Officers; and shall have the sole Power of Impeachment.

Section. 3. The Senate of the United States shall be composed of two Senators from each State, [chosen by the Legislature thereof,][2] for six Years; and each Senator shall have one Vote.

Immediately after they shall be assembled in Consequence of the first Election, they shall be divided as equally as may be into three Classes. The Seats of the Senators of the first Class shall be vacated at the Expiration of the second Year, of the second Class at the Expiration of the fourth Year, and of the third Class at the Expiration of the sixth Year, so that one third may be chosen every second Year; [and if Vacancies happen by Resignation, or otherwise, during the Recess of the Legislature of any State, the Executive thereof may make temporary Appointments until the next Meeting of the Legislature, which shall then fill such Vacancies.][3]

No Person shall be a Senator who shall not have attained to the Age of thirty Years, and been nine Years a Citizen of the United States, and who shall not, when elected, be an Inhabitant of that State for which he shall be chosen.

The Vice President of the United States shall be President of the Senate, but shall have no Vote, unless they be equally divided.

The Senate shall chuse their other Officers, and also a President pro tempore, in the Absence of the Vice President, or when he shall exercise the Office of President of the United States.

The Senate shall have the sole Power to try all Impeachments. When sitting for that Purpose, they shall be on Oath or Affirmation. When the President of the United States is tried, the Chief Justice shall preside: And no Person shall be convicted without the Concurrence of two thirds of the Members present.

Judgment in Cases of Impeachment shall not extend further than to removal from Office, and disqualification to hold and enjoy any Office of honor, Trust or Profit under the United States: but the Party convicted shall

---

[2] superseded by the Seventeenth Amendment
[3] modified by the Seventeenth Amendment

nevertheless be liable and subject to Indictment, Trial, Judgment and Punishment, according to Law.

Section. 4. The Times, Places and Manner of holding Elections for Senators and Representatives, shall be prescribed in each State by the Legislature thereof; but the Congress may at any time by Law make or alter such Regulations, except as to the Places of chusing Senators.

The Congress shall assemble at least once in every Year, and such Meeting shall be [on the first Monday in December,][4] unless they shall by Law appoint a different Day.

Section. 5. Each House shall be the Judge of the Elections, Returns and Qualifications of its own Members, and a Majority of each shall constitute a Quorum to do Business; but a smaller Number may adjourn from day to day, and may be authorized to compel the Attendance of absent Members, in such Manner, and under such Penalties as each House may provide.

Each House may determine the Rules of its Proceedings, punish its Members for disorderly Behaviour, and, with the Concurrence of two thirds, expel a Member.

Each House shall keep a Journal of its Proceedings, and from time to time publish the same, excepting such Parts as may in their Judgment require Secrecy; and the Yeas and Nays of the Members of either House on any question shall, at the Desire of one fifth of those Present, be entered on the Journal.

Neither House, during the Session of Congress, shall, without the Consent of the other, adjourn for more than three days, nor to any other Place than that in which the two Houses shall be sitting.

Section. 6. The Senators and Representatives shall receive a Compensation for their Services, to be ascertained by Law, and paid out of the Treasury of the United States. They shall in all Cases, except Treason, Felony and Breach of the Peace, be privileged from Arrest during their Attendance at the Session of their respective Houses, and in going to and returning from the same; and for any Speech or Debate in either House, they shall not be questioned in any other Place.

No Senator or Representative shall, during the Time for which he was elected, be appointed to any civil Office under the Authority of the United States, which shall have been created, or the Emoluments whereof shall have been encreased during such time; and no Person holding any Office under the United States, shall be a Member of either House during his Continuance in Office.

---

[4] modified by Section 2 of the Twentieth Amendment

Section. 7. All Bills for raising Revenue shall originate in the House of Representatives; but the Senate may propose or concur with Amendments as on other Bills.

Every Bill which shall have passed the House of Representatives and the Senate, shall, before it become a Law, be presented to the President of the United States; If he approve he shall sign it, but if not he shall return it, with his Objections to that House in which it shall have originated, who shall enter the Objections at large on their Journal, and proceed to reconsider it. If after such Reconsideration two thirds of that House shall agree to pass the Bill, it shall be sent, together with the Objections, to the other House, by which it shall likewise be reconsidered, and if approved by two thirds of that House, it shall become a Law. But in all such Cases the Votes of both Houses shall be determined by yeas and Nays, and the Names of the Persons voting for and against the Bill shall be entered on the Journal of each House respectively. If any Bill shall not be returned by the President within ten Days (Sundays excepted) after it shall have been presented to him, the Same shall be a Law, in like Manner as if he had signed it, unless the Congress by their Adjournment prevent its Return, in which Case it shall not be a Law.

Every Order, Resolution, or Vote to which the Concurrence of the Senate and House of Representatives may be necessary (except on a question of Adjournment) shall be presented to the President of the United States; and before the Same shall take Effect, shall be approved by him, or being disapproved by him, shall be repassed by two thirds of the Senate and House of Representatives, according to the Rules and Limitations prescribed in the Case of a Bill.

Section. 8. The Congress shall have Power To lay and collect Taxes, Duties, Imposts and Excises, to pay the Debts and provide for the common Defence and general Welfare of the United States; but all Duties, Imposts and Excises shall be uniform throughout the United States;

To borrow Money on the credit of the United States;

To regulate Commerce with foreign Nations, and among the several States, and with the Indian Tribes;

To establish an uniform Rule of Naturalization, and uniform Laws on the subject of Bankruptcies throughout the United States;

To coin Money, regulate the Value thereof, and of foreign Coin, and fix the Standard of Weights and Measures;

To provide for the Punishment of counterfeiting the Securities and current Coin of the United States;

To establish Post Offices and post Roads;

To promote the Progress of Science and useful Arts, by securing for limited Times to Authors and Inventors the exclusive Right to their respective Writings and Discoveries;

To constitute Tribunals inferior to the supreme Court;

To define and punish Piracies and Felonies committed on the high Seas, and Offenses against the Law of Nations;

To declare War, grant Letters of Marque and Reprisal, and make Rules concerning Captures on Land and Water;

To raise and support Armies, but no Appropriation of Money to that Use shall be for a longer Term than two Years;

To provide and maintain a Navy;

To make Rules for the Government and Regulation of the land and naval Forces;

To provide for calling forth the Militia to execute the Laws of the Union, suppress Insurrections and repel Invasions;

To provide for organizing, arming, and disciplining, the Militia, and for governing such Part of them as may be employed in the Service of the United States, reserving to the States respectively, the Appointment of the Officers, and the Authority of training the Militia according to the discipline prescribed by Congress;

To exercise exclusive Legislation in all Cases whatsoever, over such District (not exceeding ten Miles square) as may, by Cession of particular States, and the Acceptance of Congress, become the Seat of the Government of the United States, and to exercise like Authority over all Places purchased by the Consent of the Legislature of the State in which the Same shall be, for the Erection of Forts, Magazines, Arsenals, dock-Yards, and other needful Buildings; —And

To make all Laws which shall be necessary and proper for carrying into Execution the foregoing Powers, and all other Powers vested by this Constitution in the Government of the United States, or in any Department or Officer thereof.

Section. 9. The Migration or Importation of such Persons as any of the States now existing shall think proper to admit, shall not be prohibited by the Congress prior to the Year one thousand eight hundred and eight, but a Tax or duty may be imposed on such Importation, not exceeding ten dollars for each Person.

The Privilege of the Writ of Habeas Corpus shall not be suspended, unless when in Cases of Rebellion or Invasion the public Safety may require it.

No Bill of Attainder or ex post facto Law shall be passed.

No Capitation, or other direct, Tax shall be laid, unless in Proportion to the Census or Enumeration herein before directed to be taken.[5]

No Tax or Duty shall be laid on Articles exported from any State.

No Preference shall be given by any Regulation of Commerce or Revenue to the Ports of one State over those of another: nor shall Vessels bound to, or from, one State, be obliged to enter, clear, or pay Duties in another.

No Money shall be drawn from the Treasury, but in Consequence of Appropriations made by Law; and a regular Statement and Account of the Receipts and Expenditures of all public Money shall be published from time to time.

No Title of Nobility shall be granted by the United States: And no Person holding any Office of Profit or Trust under them, shall, without the Consent of the Congress, accept of any present, Emolument, Office, or Title, of any kind whatever, from any King, Prince, or foreign State.

Section. 10. No State shall enter into any Treaty, Alliance, or Confederation; grant Letters of Marque and Reprisal; coin Money; emit Bills of Credit; make any Thing but gold and silver Coin a Tender in Payment of Debts; pass any Bill of Attainder, ex post facto Law, or Law impairing the Obligation of Contracts, or grant any Title of Nobility.

No State shall, without the Consent of the Congress, lay any Imposts or Duties on Imports or Exports, except what may be absolutely necessary for executing it's inspection Laws: and the net Produce of all Duties and Imposts, laid by any State on Imports or Exports, shall be for the Use of the Treasury of the United States; and all such Laws shall be subject to the Revision and Controul of the Congress.

No State shall, without the Consent of Congress, lay any Duty of Tonnage, keep Troops, or Ships of War in time of Peace, enter into any Agreement or Compact with another State, or with a foreign Power, or engage in War, unless actually invaded, or in such imminent Danger as will not admit of delay.

Article. II.

Section. 1. The executive Power shall be vested in a President of the United States of America. He shall hold his Office during the Term of four Years, and, together with the Vice President, chosen for the same Term, be elected, as follows:

Each State shall appoint, in such Manner as the Legislature thereof may direct, a Number of Electors, equal to the whole Number of Senators and

---

[5] modified by the Sixteenth Amendment

Representatives to which the State may be entitled in the Congress: but no Senator or Representative, or Person holding an Office of Trust or Profit under the United States, shall be appointed an Elector.

[The Electors shall meet in their respective States, and vote by Ballot for two Persons, of whom one at least shall not be an Inhabitant of the same State with themselves. And they shall make a List of all the Persons voted for, and of the Number of Votes for each; which List they shall sign and certify, and transmit sealed to the Seat of the Government of the United States, directed to the President of the Senate. The President of the Senate shall, in the Presence of the Senate and House of Representatives, open all the Certificates, and the Votes shall then be counted. The Person having the greatest Number of Votes shall be the President, if such Number be a Majority of the whole Number of Electors appointed; and if there be more than one who have such Majority, and have an equal Number of Votes, then the House of Representatives shall immediately chuse by Ballot one of them for President; and if no Person have a Majority, then from the five highest on the List the said House shall in like Manner chuse the President. But in chusing the President, the Votes shall be taken by States, the Representation from each State having one Vote; A quorum for this purpose shall consist of a Member or Members from two thirds of the States, and a Majority of all the States shall be necessary to a Choice. In every Case, after the Choice of the President, the Person having the greatest Number of Votes of the Electors shall be the Vice President. But if there should remain two or more who have equal Votes, the Senate shall chuse from them by Ballot the Vice President.][6]

The Congress may determine the Time of chusing the Electors, and the Day on which they shall give their Votes; which Day shall be the same throughout the United States.

No Persons except a natural born Citizen, or a Citizen of the United States, at the time of the Adoption of this Constitution, shall be eligible to the Office of President; neither shall any Person be eligible to that Office who shall not have attained to the Age of thirty five Years, and been fourteen Years a Resident within the United States.

[In Case of the Removal of the President from Office, or of his Death, Resignation, or Inability to discharge the Powers and Duties of the said Office, the Same shall devolve on the Vice President, and the Congress may by Law provide for the Case of Removal, Death, Resignation or Inability, both of the President and Vice President, declaring what Officer shall then act as President,

---

[6] modifed by the Twelfth Amendment

and such Officer shall act accordingly, until the Disability be removed, or a President shall be elected.][7]

The President shall, at stated Times, receive for his Services, a Compensation, which shall neither be increased nor diminished during the Period for which he shall have been elected, and he shall not receive within that Period any other Emolument from the United States, or any of them.

Before he enter on the Execution of his Office, he shall take the following Oath or Affirmation:— "I do solemnly swear (or affirm) that I will faithfully execute the Office of President of the United States, and will to the best of my Ability, preserve, protect and defend the Constitution of the United States."

Section. 2. The President shall be Commander in Chief of the Army and Navy of the United States, and of the Militia of the several States, when called into the actual Service of the United States; he may require the Opinion, in writing, of the principal Officer in each of the executive Departments, upon any Subject relating to the Duties of their respective Offices, and he shall have Power to grant Reprieves and Pardons for Offences against the United States, except in Cases of Impeachment.

He shall have Power, by and with the Advice and Consent of the Senate, to make Treaties, provided two thirds of the Senators present concur; and he shall nominate, and by and with the Advice and Consent of the Senate, shall appoint Ambassadors, other public Ministers and Consuls, Judges of the supreme Court, and all other Officers of the United States, whose Appointments are not herein otherwise provided for, and which shall be established by Law: but the Congress may by Law vest the Appointment of such inferior Officers, as they think proper, in the President alone, in the Courts of Law, or in the Heads of Departments.

The President shall have Power to fill up all Vacancies that may happen during the Recess of the Senate, by granting Commissions which shall expire at the End of their next Session.

Section. 3. He shall from time to time give to the Congress Information of the State of the Union, and recommend to their Consideration such Measures as he shall judge necessary and expedient; he may, on extraordinary Occasions, convene both Houses, or either of them, and in Case of Disagreement between them, with Respect to the Time of Adjournment, he may adjourn them to such Time as he shall think proper; he shall receive Ambassadors and other public Ministers; he shall take Care that the Laws be faithfully executed, and shall Commission all the Officers of the United States.

---

[7] modified by the Twenty-Fifth Amendment

Section. 4. The President, Vice President and all civil Officers of the United States, shall be removed from Office on Impeachment for, and Conviction of, Treason, Bribery, or other high Crimes and Misdemeanors.

Article. III.

Section. 1. The judicial Power of the United States, shall be vested in one supreme Court, and in such inferior Courts as the Congress may from time to time ordain and establish. The Judges, both of the supreme and inferior Courts, shall hold their Offices during good Behaviour, and shall, at stated Times, receive for their Services, a Compensation, which shall not be diminished during their Continuance in Office.

Section. 2. The judicial Power shall extend to all Cases, in Law and Equity, arising under this Constitution, the Laws of the United States, and Treaties made, or which shall be made, under their Authority;—to all Cases affecting Ambassadors, other public Ministers and Consuls;—to all Cases of admiralty and maritime Jurisdiction;—to Controversies to which the United States shall be a Party;—to Controversies between two or more States;—[between a State and Citizens of another State;—][8] between Citizens of different States;—between Citizens of the same State claiming Lands under Grants of different States, [and between a State, or the Citizens thereof, and foreign States, Citizens or Subjects.][9]

In all Cases affecting Ambassadors, other public Ministers and Consuls, and those in which a State shall be Party, the supreme Court shall have original Jurisdiction. In all the other Cases before mentioned, the supreme Court shall have appellate Jurisdiction, both as to Law and Fact, with such Exceptions, and under such Regulations as the Congress shall make.

The Trial of all Crimes, except in Cases of Impeachment, shall be by Jury; and such Trial shall be held in the State where the said Crimes shall have been committed; but when not committed within any State, the Trial shall be at such Place or Places as the Congress may by Law have directed.

Section. 3. Treason against the United States, shall consist only in levying War against them, or in adhering to their Enemies, giving them Aid and Comfort. No Person shall be convicted of Treason unless on the Testimony of two Witnesses to the same overt Act, or on Confession in open Court.

---

[8] superseded by the Eleventh Amendment
[9] superseded by the Eleventh Amendment

The Congress shall have Power to declare the Punishment of Treason, but no Attainder of Treason shall work Corruption of Blood, or Forfeiture except during the Life of the Person attained.

Article. IV.

Section. 1. Full Faith and Credit shall be given in each State to the public Acts, Records, and judicial Proceedings of every other State. And the Congress may by general Laws prescribe the Manner in which such Acts, Records and Proceedings shall be proved, and the Effect thereof.

Section. 2. The Citizens of each State shall be entitled to all Privileges and Immunities of Citizens in the several States.

A Person charged in any State with Treason, Felony, or other Crime, who shall flee from Justice, and be found in another State, shall on Demand of the executive Authority of the State from which he fled, be delivered up, to be removed to the State having Jurisdiction of the Crime.

[No Person held to Service or Labour in one State, under the Laws thereof, escaping into another, shall, in Consequence of any Law or Regulation therein, be discharged from such Service or Labour, but shall be delivered up on Claim of the Party to whom such Service or Labour may be due.][10]

Section. 3. New States may be admitted by the Congress into this Union; but no new State shall be formed or erected within the Jurisdiction of any other State; nor any State be formed by the Junction of two or more States, or Parts of States, without the Consent of the Legislatures of the States concerned as well as of the Congress.

The Congress shall have Power to dispose of and make all needful Rules and Regulations respecting the Territory or other Property belonging to the United States; and nothing in this Constitution shall be so construed as to Prejudice any Claims of the United States, or of any particular State.

Section. 4. The United States shall guarantee to every State in this Union a Republican Form of Government, and shall protect each of them against Invasion; and on Application of the Legislature, or of the Executive (when the Legislature cannot be convened) against domestic Violence.

Article. V.

The Congress, whenever two thirds of both Houses shall deem it necessary, shall propose Amendments to this Constitution, or, on the Application of the Legislatures of two thirds of the several States, shall call a Convention for

---

[10] superseded by the Thirteenth Amendment

proposing Amendments, which, in either Case, shall be valid to all Intents and Purposes, as Part of this Constitution, when ratified by the Legislatures of three fourths of the several States, or by Conventions in three fourths thereof, as the one or the other Mode of Ratification may be proposed by the Congress; Provided that no Amendment which may be made prior to the Year One thousand eight hundred and eight shall in any Manner affect the first and fourth Clauses in the Ninth Section of the first Article; and that no State, without its Consent, shall be deprived of its equal Suffrage in the Senate.

Article. VI.

All Debts contracted and Engagements entered into, before the Adoption of this Constitution, shall be as valid against the United States under this Constitution, as under the Confederation.

This Constitution, and the Laws of the United States which shall be made in Pursuance thereof; and all Treaties made, or which shall be made, under the Authority of the United States, shall be the supreme Law of the Land; and the Judges in every State shall be bound thereby, any Thing in the Constitution or Laws of any State to the Contrary notwithstanding.

The Senators and Representatives before mentioned, and the Members of the several State Legislatures, and all executive and judicial Officers, both of the United States and of the several States, shall be bound by Oath or Affirmation, to support this Constitution; but no religious Test shall ever be required as a Qualification to any Office or public Trust under the United States.

Article. VII.

The Ratification of the Conventions of nine States, shall be sufficient for the Establishment of this Constitution between the States so ratifying the Same.

Done in Convention by the Unanimous Consent of the States present the Seventeenth Day of September in the Year of our Lord one thousand seven hundred and Eighty seven and of the Independence of the United States of America the Twelfth In Witness whereof We have hereunto subscribed our Names,

Go. Washington—
Presidt. and deputy from Virginia

New Hampshire
John Langdon
Nicholas Gilman

Massachusetts
Nathaniel Gorham
Rufus King

Connecticut
Wm. Saml. Johnson
Roger Sherman

New York
Alexander Hamilton

New Jersey
Wil: Livingston
David Brearley
Wm. Paterson
Jona: Dayton

Pennsylvania
B Franklin
Thomas Mifflin
Robt. Morris
Geo. Clymer
Thos. FitzSimons
Jared Ingersoll
James Wilson
Gouv Morris

Delaware
Geo: Read
Gunning Bedford jun
John Dickinson
Richard Bassett
Jaco: Broom

Maryland
James McHenry
Dan of St Thos. Jenifer
Danl. Carroll

Virginia
John Blair—
James Madison Jr.

North Carolina
Wm. Blount
Richd. Dobbs Spaight
Hu Williamson

South Carolina
J. Rutledge
Charles Cotesworth Pinckney
Charles Pinckney
Pierce Butler

Georgia
William Few
Abr Baldwin

Attest William Jackson Secretary

AMENDMENTS TO THE CONSTITUTION OF THE UNITED STATES OF AMERICA

Amendment I.
Ratified December 15, 1791

Congress shall make no law respecting an establishment of religion, or prohibiting the free exercise thereof; or abridging the freedom of speech, or of the press; or the right of the people peaceably to assemble, and to petition the Government for a redress of grievances.

Amendment II.
Ratified December 15, 1791

A well regulated Militia, being necessary to the security of a free State, the right of the people to keep and bear Arms, shall not be infringed.

Amendment III.
Ratified December 15, 1791

No Soldier shall, in time of peace be quartered in any house, without the consent of the Owner, nor in time of war, but in a manner to be prescribed by law.

Amendment IV.
Ratified December 15, 1791

The right of the people to be secure in their persons, houses, papers, and effects, against unreasonable searches and seizures, shall not be violated, and no Warrants shall issue, but upon probable cause, supported by Oath or affirmation, and particularly describing the place to be searched, and the persons or things to be seized.

Amendment V.
Ratified December 15, 1791

No person shall be held to answer for a capital, or otherwise infamous crime, unless on a presentment or indictment of a Grand Jury, except in cases arising in the land or naval forces, or in the Militia, when in actual service in time of War or public danger; nor shall any person be subject for the same offence to be twice put in jeopardy of life or limb, nor shall be compelled in any criminal case to be a witness against himself, nor be deprived of life, liberty, or property, without due process of law; nor shall private property be taken for public use, without just compensation.

Amendment VI.
Ratified December 15, 1791

In all criminal prosecutions, the accused shall enjoy the right to a speedy and public trial, by an impartial jury of the State and district wherein the crime shall have been committed, which district shall have been previously ascertained by law, and to be informed of the nature and cause of the accusation; to be confronted with the witnesses against him; to have compulsory process for obtaining witnesses in his favor, and to have the assistance of counsel for his defence.

Amendment VII.
Ratified December 15, 1791

In Suits at common law, where the value in controversy shall exceed twenty dollars, the right of trial by jury shall be preserved, and no fact tried by a jury, shall be otherwise reexamined in any Court of the United States, than according to the rules of the common law.

Amendment VIII.
Ratified December 15, 1791

Excessive bail shall not be required, nor excessive fines imposed, nor cruel and unusual punishments inflicted.

Amendment IX.
Ratified December 15, 1791

The enumeration in the Constitution, of certain rights, shall not be construed to deny or disparage others retained by the people.

Amendment X.
Ratified December 15, 1791

The powers not delegated to the United States by the Constitution, nor prohibited by it to the States, are reserved to the States respectively, or to the people.

Appendix C:
Thematic Table of Contents

Presidential Proclamations

2. President Abraham Lincoln, Proclamation on Amnesty and Reconstruction, December 8, 1863

3. Wade-Davis Bill and President Abraham Lincoln's Pocket Veto Proclamation, July 2 and 8, 1864

6. President Andrew Johnson, Proclamation on Reorganizing Constitutional Government in Mississippi, June 13, 1865

24. President Ulysses S. Grant, Proclamation on Enforcement of the 14th Amendment, May 3, 1871

Constitutional Amendments

3. Wade-Davis Bill and President Abraham Lincoln's Pocket Veto Proclamation, July 2 and 8, 1864

14. Congressional Debate on the 14th Amendment, February – May, 1866

22. The 15th Amendment, February 2, 1870

National Laws on Reconstruction

4. The 13th Amendment to the Constitution, December 18, 1865

13. An Act to protect all Persons in the United States in their Civil Rights, and furnish the Means of their Vindication, April 9, 1866

17. Reconstruction Acts, March 2 and 23, and July 19, 1867

23. The Enforcement Acts, 1870, 1871

Supreme Court Cases

27. Associate Justices Samuel Miller and Stephen Field, The Slaughterhouse Cases, The United States Supreme Court, April 14, 1873

29. Chief Justice Morrison Waite, *United States v. Cruikshank*, The United States Supreme Court, March 27, 1876

Reports on Conditions in the South

8. Black Codes of Mississippi, October – December, 1865

10. Carl Schurz, Report on the Condition of South, December 19, 1865

Thematic Table of Contents 189

11. Frederick Douglass, Reply of the Colored Delegation to the President, February 7, 1866

21. Executive Documents on State of the Freedmen, November 20, 1868

25. Charlotte Fowler's Testimony to Sub-Committee on Reconstruction in Spartanburg, South Carolina, July 6, 1871

28. Colfax Massacre Reports, U.S. Senate and the Committee of 70, 1874 and 1875

Amnesty

1. President Abraham Lincoln to General Nathaniel Banks, August 5, 1863

2. President Abraham Lincoln, Proclamation on Amnesty and Reconstruction, December 8, 1863

3. Wade-Davis Bill and President Abraham Lincoln's Pocket Veto Proclamation, July 2 and 8, 1864

7. Richard Henry Dana, "Grasp of War," June 21, 1865

9. President Andrew Johnson, First Annual Message, December 4, 1865

12. Alexander Stephens, Address before the General Assembly of the State of Georgia, February 22, 1866

15. Charles Sumner, "The One Man Power vs. Congress!" October 2, 1866

16. Thaddeus Stevens, Speech on Reconstruction, January 3, 1867

19. Thaddeus Stevens, "Damages to Loyal Men," March 19, 1867

26. Senator Carl Schurz, "Plea for Amnesty," January 30, 1872

30. President Rutherford B. Hayes, Inaugural Address, March 5, 1877

Reconstruction and Readmittance of Southern Governments

2. President Abraham Lincoln, Proclamation on Amnesty and Reconstruction, December 8, 1863

3. Wade-Davis Bill and President Abraham Lincoln's Pocket Veto Proclamation, July 2 and 8, 1864

5. President Abraham Lincoln's Last Public Address, April 11, 1865

6. President Andrew Johnson, Proclamation on Reorganizing Constitutional Government in Mississippi, June 13, 1865

9. President Andrew Johnson, First Annual Message, December 4, 1865

10. Carl Schurz, Report on the Condition of South, December 19, 1865

12. Alexander Stephens, Address before the General Assembly of the State of Georgia, February 22, 1866

15. Charles Sumner, "The One Man Power vs. Congress!" October 2, 1866

16. Thaddeus Stevens, Speech on Reconstruction, January 3, 1867

17. Reconstruction Acts, March 2 and 23, and July 19, 1867

18. President Andrew Johnson, Veto of the First Reconstruction Act, March 2, 1867

23. The Enforcement Acts, May 31, 1870 and April 20, 1871

Civil Rights and Protection of Freedmen and Loyalists

10. Carl Schurz, Report on the Condition of the South, December 19, 1865

11. Frederick Douglass, Reply of the Colored Delegation to the President, February 7, 1866

12. Alexander Stephens, Address before the General Assembly of the State of Georgia, February 22, 1866

13. An Act to protect all Persons in the United States in their Civil Rights, and furnish the Means of their Vindication, April 9, 1866

15. Charles Sumner, "The One Man Power vs. Congress!" October 2, 1866

16. Thaddeus Stevens, Speech on Reconstruction, January 3, 1867

19. Thaddeus Stevens, "Damages to Loyal Men," March 19, 1867

23. The Enforcement Acts, May 31, 1870 and April 20, 1871

24. President Ulysses S. Grant, Proclamation on Enforcement of the 14th Amendment, May 3, 1871

27. Associate Justices Samuel Miller and Stephen Field, The Slaughterhouse Cases, The United States Supreme Court, April 14, 1873

29. Chief Justice Morrison Waite, *United States v. Cruikshank*, The United States Supreme Court, March 27, 1876

31. Frederick Douglass, "The United States Cannot Remain Half-Slave and Half-Free," April 16, 1883

Speeches

9. President Andrew Johnson, First Annual Message, December 4, 1865

12. Alexander Stephens, Address before the General Assembly of the State of Georgia, February 22, 1866

15. Charles Sumner, "The One Man Power vs. Congress!" October 2, 1866

16. Thaddeus Stevens, Speech on Reconstruction, January 3, 1867

19. Thaddeus Stevens, "Damages to Loyal Men," March 19, 1867

26. Senator Carl Schurz, Plea for Amnesty, January 30, 1872

31. Frederick Douglas, "The United States Cannot Remain Half-Slave and Half-Free," April 16, 1883

Appendix D:
Study Questions

For each of the Documents in this collection, we suggest below in section A questions relevant for that document alone and in Section B questions that require comparison between documents.

1. President Abraham Lincoln to General Nathaniel Banks (August 1863)

A. What policies does President Lincoln want the new constitution of Louisiana to embody? What powers does President Lincoln think he has? On what kinds of issues does he merely suggest what should be done? Why does President Lincoln think himself empowered only to suggest, not to order, that Louisiana adopt certain constitutional provisions?

B. Compare the tone and orders of President Lincoln in this letter to General Nathaniel Banks with the tone and orders found in Documents 3 and 17 where variations of Radical Republican policies are pursued and Document 18 where President Andrew Johnson vetoes Radical bills.

2. President Abraham Lincoln, Proclamation of Amnesty and Reconstruction (December 8, 1863)

A. How can people receive amnesty under President Lincoln's Proclamation? Who could in good conscience take the oath that President Lincoln suggests? Who must ask for special pardon under the Proclamation? Does this seem to be a large group of people? Describe the process whereby states will come back into the union under the Proclamation.

B. Compare the people allowed to vote for the states' new constitutional convention under President Lincoln's Proclamation with those able to participate under the Wade-Davis Bill (Document 3). Compare the process of restoration under President Lincoln's Proclamation with the process of restoration under the Wade-Davis Bill (Document 3) and the Reconstruction Acts (Document 17). What accounts for the differences? What different visions of Reconstruction are in each of the proposals? What would be the result of each process?

3. Wade-Davis Bill and President Lincoln's Pocket Veto Proclamation (July 1864)

A. What is the process for reconstruction under the Wade-Davis Bill? Describe it step-by-step from the creation of the provisional government to the seating of the states' congressional delegations. What standards must state constitutional conventions adhere to in order to win approval? What threats does the Wade-Davis Bill imagine will continue to plague the Southern states? How does it propose to deal with the threat? How will states be governed until they are fully reconstructed and allowed back into the Union? Why does President Lincoln veto the Bill? What is his chief complaint against it?

B. Compare the people allowed to vote for the states' new constitutional convention under President Lincoln's Proclamation (Document 2) with those able to participate under the Wade-Davis Bill. Compare the process of restoration under the Wade-Davis Bill with the process under President Lincoln's Proclamation (Document 2) and the process under the Reconstruction Acts (Document 17). What accounts for the differences? How do the differences reflect different ideas about the American Union and the goals of the Civil War? How might history have been different had President Lincoln signed the Wade-Davis Bill?

4. The 13th Amendment to the Constitution (January 31, 1865 [passed] and December 18, 1865 [ratified])

A. How does the 13th Amendment change relations between the state and national governments? Imagine how the 13th Amendment would be enforced if a state tried to institute slavery within its borders.

B. Compare the restructuring of national and state relations under the 13th Amendment with the restructuring under the 14th Amendment (Document 14) and the 15th Amendment (Document 22).

5. President Abraham Lincoln's Last Public Address (April 11, 1865)

A. What defects does President Lincoln identify in the Louisiana constitution? What does he suggest be done about those defects? What is the broader theory of reconstruction within his statement?

Study Questions 193

B. How does President Lincoln's policy as stated in his "Last Public Address" differ from the Radical policies as found in the Reconstruction Acts (Document 17)? How does it compare with the theory implicit in the speeches of Representative Thaddeus Stevens (Documents 16 and 19)? What are the pitfalls of each policy?

6. President Andrew Johnson, "Proclamation on Reorganizing Constitutional Government in Mississippi" (June 13, 1865)

A. What standards would President Johnson hold new Southern states to? What process does he lay out for the restoration of Southern government to the union?

B. Compare the process of restoration under President Johnson's Proclamation with the Wade-Davis Bill (Document 3), with the process under President Lincoln's Proclamation (Document 2) and with the process under the Reconstruction Acts (Document 17). What accounts for the differences? How do the differences reflect different ideas about the American Union and the goals of the Civil War? Rank the processes from the easiest to satisfy to the most difficult to satisfy.

7. Richard Henry Dana, "Grasp of War" (June 21, 1865)

A. What kind of power does Dana think the Union has over the defeated South? What should it use its power to accomplish? What is secession in Dana's view? What are the limits, if any, of the Union's power in Dana's view? How would Reconstruction end in his view?

B. How does Dana's view of the war compare with President Andrew Johnson's view (Document 9 and 18) and President Lincoln's view (Document 5)?

8. Black Codes of Mississippi (October – December, 1865)

A. Describe the various ways that freedom for freed slaves is compromised under the black codes of Mississippi. How is life under the black codes different from slavery?

B. Would the 13th Amendment (Document 4) help to limit the powers of the state to pass black codes? Under what reading of the 13th Amendment would it be of help to freed slaves? What vision of federal power would be necessary to prevent states from passing and enforcing Black Codes (consider Documents 13, 14, and 23)? What might explain why black codes arose in these states (consider Document 26)?

9. President Andrew Johnson, First Annual Address (December 4, 1865)

A. Why did President Johnson think that it was wrong and imprudent to impose military governments on the South? Why does President Johnson think that all acts of secession are "null and void"? What is the significance of that idea? In what ways has the national authority come to be operating in the South? What is the national government doing? By what authority? What is President Johnson's reconstruction policy? What are the risks associated with President Johnson's policy? What policy to promote the welfare of freedmen does President Johnson offer? What standards would he hold the new Southern governments to? What, in President Johnson's view, was wrong with slavery?

B. How does President Johnson's understanding of secession differ from Richard Henry Dana's vision of secession (as articulated in Document 7)? What is the significance of this difference? How does the report of Carl Schurz (Document 10) account for the risks associated with President Johnson's policy? How might those risks be mitigated?

10. Carl Schurz, Report on the Condition of the South (December 19, 1865)

A. According to Schurz, what are the attitudes of Southerners toward Union men, the Union, and freedmen? What kind of evidence would convince you that Schurz had accurately described Southern opinion on these matters?

B. If you were a member of the U.S. Congress and had just heard President Johnson's First Annual Address (Document 9), how would you compare and contrast Johnson's view of the South to Schurz's? If you believed Schurz, what actions would you consider taking? How does Schurz's description of the South compare to the descriptions in Documents 8, 21, 25, and 28?

11. Frederick Douglass, Reply of the Colored Delegation to the President (February 7, 1866)

A. Why did President Johnson think that a party uniting poor white Southerners and freedmen would be impossible? What does Frederick Douglass think the foundation for a permanent peace among whites and blacks in the South must be? How did Douglass respond to President Johnson's views? Why does Douglass oppose colonization? What ultimately is Douglass's vision for a multi-racial American South? What are the obstacles to that vision?

B. Does this document show President Johnson's actual Reconstruction policy to correspond to or differ from the policy he presented in this first annual address to Congress (Document 9)? Does the argument Douglass makes about the foundations for a permanent peace support a position of general amnesty for the Southerners as put forward later by Carl Schurz (Document 26)? How does Douglass's position compare with the position of President Lincoln in his letter to General Nathaniel Banks (Document 1)?

12. Alexander H. Stephens, Address before the General Assembly of the State of Georgia (February 22, 1866)

A. What moral virtues are necessary for all Americans to adopt, in Stephens's view? Why? Why does Stephens think that President Johnson's policy of restoration offers the best hope for peace within the Union? What policies does Stephens recommend Georgia adopt for freedmen? What ultimately is Stephens's vision for a multi-racial American South? What are the obstacles to that vision?

B. How do Stephens's recommendations compare with the recommendations of President Lincoln (Documents 1 and 2) and President Johnson (Document 9)? What in Stephens's view was the status of secession – were the states out of the Union or not? What implications do Stephens's views have for his recommended national and state policies?

13. An Act to Protect All Persons in the United States in Their Civil Rights, and Furnish the Means of their Vindication (April 9, 1866)

A. What rights does the Civil Rights Act seek to protect? What actions does the Civil Rights Act make illegal? What actions of state governments in particular does it make illegal? What is the process whereby the national government will seek to protect these rights? If someone's rights are violated, what happens? What institutions will be involved in protecting these rights? What kinds of conspiracies is the Civil Rights Act aimed to ferret out and prosecute? How will the act accomplish this?

B. In what ways does the Civil Rights Act embody or contradict President Johnson's vision of the Union (as found in Document 9)? In what ways does it embody or contradict the vision of Union announced in Dana's speech (Document 7), the ideas of Senator Charles Sumner (Document 15) or the speech of Representative Thaddeus Stevens (Document 16)? What difficulties can you imagine confronted those enforcing the Civil Rights Act, given the situation as described by Carl Schurz in his Report on the Condition of the South (Document 10) or the testimony later gathered about the activities of the Ku Klux Klan (Documents 25 and 28)? Did the Civil Rights Act have a solid constitutional justification before the 14th Amendment (Document 14)? How are the Enforcement Acts (Document 23) related to the Civil Rights Bill?

14. Congressional Debate on the 14th Amendment, (February – May, 1866)

A. What standards does the 14th Amendment hold states to? What incentives does Section 2 of the 14th Amendment put in place for encouraging states to grant the vote to the freedmen and others? Who does the 14th Amendment seek to prohibit from holding national office? Why? In what ways can Congress enforce the 14th Amendment? What were the prominent arguments in favor of the 14th Amendment? Why was debate about the 14th Amendment postponed at the end of February 1866? What changes to the amendment were made before its passage? What is the significance of those changes? How is the vision of federalism different in the first draft of the amendment compared to the second draft?

B. How might states violate the 14th Amendment? Consider in this light the evidence from Documents 10, 25 and 28. How might the courts be involved in enforcing the 14th Amendment, especially given the role assigned to the courts by the Civil Rights Bill (Document 13)? If you are a citizen of a state and the state does not investigate a crime against you because you are black, while it does investigate the same crime when it is committed against whites, would you be able to take the state to federal court even without other enabling legislation (such as the Civil Rights Act (Document 13) or the Enforcement Acts (Document 23)?

Study Questions 197

15. Charles Sumner, "The One Man Power vs. Congress!" (January 3, 1867)

A. What is Senator Sumner's critique of President Johnson? What extensions of federal policy does Senator Sumner envision? What would he like to do, and what would he like to undo? What are his reasons for departing from what has been done? What role of the national government does he envision during Reconstruction? Why does he think Congress should take the lead in Reconstruction?

B. How does Senator Sumner go beyond the Civil Rights Act of 1866 and the 14th Amendment (Documents 13 and 14)? How does Senator Sumner's treatment of the political situation in 1867 compare with Representative Thaddeus Stevens's treatment (Documents 16 and 19)?

16. Thaddeus Stevens, Speech on Reconstruction (January 3, 1867)

A. What extensions of federal policy does Representative Stevens envision? What would he like to do? What would he like to undo? What are his reasons for departing from what had been done? What role of the national government does he envision in Reconstruction?

B. How does Stevens's vision of the national government compare to Schurz's in his "Plea for Amnesty" (Document 26)? What does Stevens think the 14th Amendment empowers the national government to do (Document 14)? Does he think that the 14th Amendment is enough? Why? Why not? Would, in your view, Stevens have made the same speech after The Slaughterhouse Cases (Document 27) and *United States v. Cruikshank* (Document 29)?

17. Reconstruction Acts (March 2, 1867, March 23, 1867, and July 19, 1867)

A. What role would the military play under these acts? How would laws be made and how would violations of the law be judged? What does the Reconstruction Act have to say about the legality of the governments created under President Johnson's restoration policy? Describe the process by which states would make new constitutions under the Reconstruction Acts. What standards would states be held to in making these constitutions? How would Congress and the President be involved in acknowledging the reconstructed states? How can the states so affected get the military to leave their states? Under what circumstances might Section 5 of the March 23, 1867 act be used to deny the legality of a state's convention and vote?

B. How does the oath of the March 23, 1867 act compare to the oath that President Lincoln penned in his Proclamation of Amnesty and Reconstruction (Document 2)? Generally speaking, how does the process of readmitting states in the Reconstruction Acts compare with the process President Lincoln imagines (Document 2), with the Wade-Davis Bill (Document 3), and with President Johnson's approach (Documents 6 and 9)?

18. President Andrew Johnson, Veto of the First Reconstruction Act (March 2, 1867)

A. What arguments does President Johnson make against military rule in the South? How well are the Southerners re-integrated into the Union at this point, according to President Johnson? What according to President Johnson is the purpose of the Reconstruction Act? Why does he think that purpose is outside the power of the Constitution? Why, in his view, might it be outside the Declaration and its principles as well?

B. How do you think that the Republicans who passed the Reconstruction Acts (Document 17) would respond to the arguments made by President Johnson in his veto message? How might President Lincoln respond to them in light of his last public address (Document 5)?

19. Thaddeus Stevens, "Damages to Loyal Men" (March 19, 1867)

A. Who are the loyal men, according to Representative Stevens? What damages have been done to them? How can those loyal men be rewarded for their loyalty? What must the national government do to so reward them? How might the redistribution of land assist in the restructuring of the South? How far would Representative Stevens be willing to go in redistributing land? What obstacles might there have been to Stevens' approach as outlined in this speech? What national support would have been necessary to make the Stevens' plan work?

B. Placing Representative Stevens' speech in context, how does his approach differ from the approach of The Reconstruction Acts (Document 17) and the approach of President Johnson (Document 18)? How does his

Study Questions 199

approach to land redistribution compare with the civil rights approach initiated in 1866 (Document 13 and 14) and the voting approach initiated in 1870 (Document 22 and 23)? Do you think that his approach would have worked better than the other two approaches? What benefits and costs might this approach have had over the others?

20. Democratic and Republican Party Platforms of 1868 (May 20, 1868 and July 4, 1868)

A. What goals do the Republicans embrace for Reconstruction? How do their goals compare to the Democrats' goals? What things are present in the Republicans' goals that are absent in the Democrats' goals? What things are absent in the Republicans' goals but present in the Democrats' goals? How do the two parties judge President Johnson's tenure in office? What picture do the respective parties paint of the South as eventually reconstructed? What is the role of blacks in that new order each party envisions?

B. To what extent is the Republican Party platform a continuation of the Reconstruction Acts (Document 17)? To what extent is it an extension of Lincoln's policy of Amnesty and Reconstruction (Document 2)? To what extent is the Democratic Party's platform a continuation of President Johnson's approach (Documents 6, 9, and 18)? How would each platform deal with problems that might arise from violent private organizations, operating without interference from the state, such as the Ku Klux Klan?

21. Executive Documents on the State of the Freedmen (November 20, 1868)

A. What does the Secretary of War report as happening in the sections of Texas under investigation? Are the goals of Reconstruction policy being achieved? Why or why not?

B. Have the Civil Rights and Reconstruction Acts (Documents 13 and 17) been successful up to this point? If not, what would be necessary to make them successful? How does Carl Schurz's description of the South compare to the descriptions in Documents 8, 10, 25 and 28? What has changed in the South since Schurz made his report (Document 10)? How does the reality described here compare with the reality that gave rise to the Enforcement Acts (Document 23)?

22. The 15th Amendment (February 26, 1869 [passed] and February 2, 1870 [ratified])

A. How does the 15th Amendment change relations between the national and state governments? How might Congress use its law-making powers to enforce the provisions of the 15th Amendment? How is the approach in the 15th Amendment different from granting the national government the power to insist upon uniform voting requirements in the states? How might states circumvent the 15th Amendment in an attempt to prevent bs from voting?

B. How does the 15th Amendment compare to the 14th Amendment (Document 14) on the issue of protecting rights? In what ways does the 15th Amendment enforce itself? In what ways does it require Congressional action for its enforcement (Document 23)? What hopes did Republicans hang on granting the vote to blacks nationwide (Documents 15 and 16)? Why did President Johnson want to keep the question of the vote at the state level (Document 9)? Who had the stronger argument – the Republicans, or President Johnson? Why? What long-term implications would the 15th Amendment have for the nature of the national government?

23. The Enforcement Acts (March 30, 1870 and April 20, 1871)

A. What actions are made illegal under the Acts? What powers are given to the national government to enforce the acts? What kinds of actions would prompt the national government into action under these acts?

B. What kinds of threats do states and state actions and inaction pose to the execution of the 15th Amendment (Document 22)? How does this Enforcement Act compare to the Civil Rights Act (Document 13)? Which rights does each focus on, and what processes does each set up to protect these rights? Which act is more extensive in its attempt to protect freedmen? Which abridges state power the most? How might the different emphases and mechanisms for enforcement be explained by events that happened between the passage of the Civil Rights Bill of 1866 and the Enforcement Acts of 1870 and 1871 (Document 23)?

24. President Ulysses S. Grant, Proclamation on Enforcement of the 14th Amendment (May 3, 1871)

A. What is the substance of President Grant's Proclamation concerning the Enforcement Acts? Why do you think that President Grant issued this Proclamation?

B. In what ways does President Grant's Proclamation amplify the First and Second Enforcement Acts (Document 23)?

25. Charlotte Fowler's Testimony to Sub-Committee on Reconstruction in Spartanburg, South Carolina (July 6, 1871)

A. What do we learn about Southern society after the war from Charlotte Fowler's testimony? Who would be threatened by the Ku Klux Klan? What purposes did their violence serve? Why was Wallace Fowler killed?

B. How does the portrait of Southern society presented in the testimony compare with that in Carl Schurz's Report on the Condition of the South (Document 10) and in the Executive Documents on the State of the Freedmen (Document 21)? What kinds of laws would be necessary to protect people such as Wallace and Charlotte Fowler? Had such laws been passed by Congress? What does this tell us about Reconstruction?

26. Senator Carl Schurz, "Plea for Amnesty" (January 30, 1872)

A. What are Senator Schurz's arguments for amnesty? How far should that amnesty extend? What benefits does he expect to flow from granting amnesty? What in his view are the reasons white Southerners perpetrate violence against Southern blacks?

B. How do Schurz's views in his "Plea for Amnesty" compare and contrast with his views in his Report on the Condition of the South (Document 10)? What has changed? What other speeches and views present arguments similar to Schurz's? Do you think his "Plea" or Representative Thaddeus Stevens's "Damages" (Document 19) presents a surer basis for peace? Should the Southerners be treated like vanquished foes or fellow citizens? Is there any tenable ground *between* these two positions?

27. Associate Justices Samuel Miller and Stephen Field, The Slaughterhouse Cases, The United States Supreme Court (April 14, 1873)

A. What, according to the Court, were the purposes of the Civil War Amendments (Documents 4, 14, and 22)? What are the "privileges and immunities" of United States citizenship? What rights come with U.S. citizenship? What argument does the Court make for this understanding of U.S. citizenship? Would you characterize it as a broad or a narrow understanding of U.S. citizenship? How does Justice Field's dissenting opinion differ from the Court's opinion? What rights does Justice Field think come with U.S. citizenship? What is his reading of these amendments?

B. Would the Supreme Court's reasoning in the Slaughterhouse Cases support the Civil Rights Bill of 1866 (Document 13)? Do the deliberations on the 14th Amendment (Document 14) support the Court's reading of the 14th Amendment or that of Justice Field?

28. Colfax Massacre Reports, U.S. Senate and the Committee of 70, 1874 and 1875

A. What happened at Colfax? How does the account offered by Congress differ from the account offered by the Committee of Seventy? What explains the difference? What do the two accounts of the Colfax Massacre tell us about white Southerners' views of the freedmen?

B. What does this massacre tell us about the need for the Enforcement Acts (Document 23) and the Civil Rights Bill (Document 13)? How does it complement or contradict the Executive Documents on the State of the Freedmen from December 1868 (Document 21)? What could the national government do to prevent such massacres? What obstacles existed to effective national action on such matters?

29. Chief Justice Morrison Waite, *United States v. Cruikshank,* The United State Supreme Court (March 27, 1876)

A. What powers reside with the states and what powers with the national government according to *United States v. Cruikshank*? How would that division of power between the levels of government foster the investigation of crimes such as the Colfax Massacre? What does *United States v. Cruikshank* do to the Enforcement Acts (Document 23)?

B. Does the vision of national and state power in *United States v. Cruikshank* resemble or contradict the arguments made for the 14th Amendment (Document 14)? Would the Civil Rights Act of 1866 (Document 13) survive the analysis of *United States v. Cruikshank* and the Slaughterhouse Cases (Document 27)? What reconstruction powers are left in the national government after *United States v. Cruikshank*?

30. President Rutherford B. Hayes, Inaugural Address (March 5, 1877)

A. What federal obligations does President Hayes emphasize? What promises does he extend for the protection of freedmen? What measures will he pursue to reconcile Southerners to the new Union? What problems might arise from his approach?

B. How do the Slaughterhouse Cases (Document 27) and *United States v. Cruikshank* (Document 29) shape President Hayes's policy? Which President does Hayes most seem to resemble (compare Documents 5, 9, 18, and 24)? Why do you think he adopts the policy he adopts?

31. Frederick Douglass, "The United States Cannot Remain Half-Slave and Half-Free" (April 16, 1883)

A. What are the grounds for pessimism about race relations, according to Douglass? Why are the grounds for optimism more compelling in his view?

B. How does Douglass's account of what has been accomplished in Reconstruction compare with Hayes's treatment his Inaugural Address (Document 30)? What specific events from the Reconstruction Era support Douglass's optimism? Which support his pessimism?

Appendix E:
Suggestions For Further Reading

Belz, Herman. *A New Birth of Freedom: The Republican Party and the Freedmen's Rights, 1861 to 1866.* Westport, Connecticut: Greenwood Press, 1976.

Donald, David Herbert. *Liberty and Union.* Lexington, MA: D.C Heath and Company, 1978.

Curtis, Michael K. *No State Shall Abridge: The Fourteenth Amendment and the Bill of Rights.* Durham, North Carolina: Duke University Press, 1986.

Foner, Eric. *Reconstruction: America's Unfinished Revolution, 1863-1877.* New York: Harper and Row Publishers, 1988.

Guelzo, Allen C. *Reconstruction: A Concise History.* New York: Oxford University Press, 2018.

Jaffa, Harry V. *A New Birth of Freedom: Abraham Lincoln and the Coming of the Civil War.* New York, Rowman & Littlefield Publishers, 2000.

Keith, LeeAnna. *The Colfax Massacre: The Untold Story of Black Power, White Terror, and the Death of Reconstruction.* New York: Oxford University Press, 2008.

Krug, Mark M. *Lyman Trumbull: Conservative Radical.* New York: A. S Barnes, 1965.

Lyons, Philip B. *Statesmanship and Reconstruction: Moderate versus Radical Republicans on Restoring the Union after the Civil War.* Lanham, MD: Lexington Books, 2014.

Magliocca, Gerard N. *American Founding Son: John Bingham and the Invention of the Fourteenth Amendment.* New York: New York University Press, 2013.

McPherson, James M. *The Struggle for Equality: Abolitionists and the Negro in the Civil War and Reconstruction.* Princeton: Princeton University Press, 1964.

Millard, Candice. *Destiny of the Republic: A Tale of Madness, Medicine, and the Murder of a President.* New York: Doubleday, 2011.

Nabors, Forrest A. *From Oligarchy to Republicanism: The Great Task of Reconstruction.* Columbia, Missouri: University of Missouri Press, 2017.

Oakes, James. *Freedom National: The Destruction of Slavery in the United States, 1861- 1865.* New York: W. W. Norton & Company, 2012.

Perman, Michael. *Reunion Without Compromise: The South and Reconstruction, 1865-1868.* New York: Cambridge University Press, 1973.

Perman, Michael. *The Road to Redemption: Southern Politics, 1869-1879.* Chapel Hill: The University of North Carolina Press, 1984.

Schurz, Carl. *The Autobiography of Carl Schurz.* New York: Charles Scribner's Sons, 1908.

Stampp, Kenneth M. *The Era of Reconstruction, 1865-1877.* New York: Alfred A. Knopf, 1965.

Simpson, Brooks D. *The Reconstruction Presidents.* Lawrence: University Press of Kansas, 1998.

Sands, Eric C. *American Public Philosophy and the Mystery of Lincolnism.* Columbia: University of Missouri Press, 2009.

Valelly, Richard M. *The Two Reconstructions: The Struggle for Black Enfranchisement.* Chicago: The University of Chicago Press, 2004.

White, Ronald C. *American Ulysses: A Life of Ulysses S. Grant.* New York: Random House, 2016.